People, Passions, and Power: Social Movements, Interest Organizations, and the Political Process
John C. Green, Series Editor

RAGE ON THE RIGHT

The American Militia Movement from Ruby Ridge to Homeland Security

LANE CROTHERS

ROWMAN & LITTLEFIELD PUBLISHERS, INC.
Lanham • Boulder • New York • Oxford

ROWMAN & LITTLEFIELD PUBLISHERS, INC.

Published in the United States of America
by Rowman & Littlefield Publishers, Inc.
A Member of the Rowman & Littlefield Publishing Group
4501 Forbes Boulevard, Suite 200, Lanham, Maryland 20706
www.rowmanlittlefield.com

PO Box 317
Oxford
OX2 9RU, UK

British Library Cataloguing in Publication Information Available

Library of Congress Cataloging-in-Publication Data

Crothers, Lane.
    Rage on the right : the American militia movement from Ruby Ridge to homeland security / Lane Crothers.
        p. cm. — (People, passions, and power)
    Includes bibliographical references and index.
        ISBN 0-7425-2546-5 (cloth : alk. paper) — ISBN 0-7425-2547-3 (pbk. : alk. paper)
    1. Militia movement—United States. 2. Right-wing extremists—United States. I. Title. II. Series.
    HN90.R3 C77 2003
    322.4'2'0973--dc21

                                                    2002014892

Printed in the United States of America

♾™ The paper used in this publication meets the minimum requirements of American National Standard for Information Sciences—Permanence of Paper for Printed Library Materials, ANSI/NISO Z39.48-1992.

Contents

Acknowledgments

Every book is the result of hard work on the part not only of the author but also of the many people authors rely on to help them stay focused and critical during a project that can last for years. This is certainly the case with this book. I want to take a few lines to thank the people who have helped me finish this project. The work benefited from their assistance; its flaws are entirely mine.

Special thanks need to be offered to Manfred B. Steger of the Department of Politics and Government at Illinois State University. His careful reading of this work and thoughtful suggestions added to the book's final form in innumerable ways. Julie Webber, too, of Illinois State University's Department of Politics and Government, deserves great thanks for her assistance and serious review of the entire work. Their insights are embedded everywhere in the text.

In addition, I discussed pieces of the project with many colleagues over the years. Jamal Nassar, Carlos Parodi, and Tom Eimermann, all of Illinois State University, made insightful comments that sent my research in new and important directions. I also need to thank S. W., who otherwise wishes to remain anonymous, for stimulating the original interest that eventually evolved into this work. Finally, I wish to thank Richard Pride, of Vanderbilt University, for sending a disillusioned first-year graduate student down an intellectual path that led to the linkage of culture and politics—to this book, although I did not know it at the time.

I also received support from a number of excellent graduate students whose work tracking down references, articles, and other materials greatly aided the project. Of special note is Zachary Callen of Illinois State University, although Rob Miller and Susan

Megy, also of Illinois State, deserve my thanks.

The research that culminated in this book began in August 1992 when I moved to Spokane, Washington, just as Randy Weaver and the FBI began their fateful confrontation. I have discussed this project with so many people in the ensuing decade that it is impossible for me to remember or name them all. Let this work stand as my thanks, and know that you all made a difference.

Introduction:
Approaching the Militia Movement

Rage is a powerful, angry emotion. It is a passionate, intense expression of frustration and aggression. It is almost always triggered by some event that may or may not be related to the root causes of the explosion and so is an unfocused, frighteningly irrational experience—both for the person feeling rage and for those who suffer its effects.

"Rage" is also a very powerful word. To say that someone is in a rage is to imply that he is feeling and expressing an emotion that is exceptional, out of control. It is to say that his actions are in a unique category; that however justified the person in the rage state feels in his behavior, to an outside observer it is clear that he is in fact behaving inappropriately, even dangerously. Accordingly, the word rage should not be used lightly.

As will be explored throughout this book, rage is a central principle of the modern American militia movement. This movement, which is also sometimes known as the Patriot movement, swept across the rural areas of western, midwestern, and southern states in the 1990s. It became an important dimension of American political life. Indeed, at its most extreme, members of the movement engaged in acts of intimidation and terrorism across the country, most notably epitomized in Timothy McVeigh's destruction of the Alfred P. Murrah Federal Building in Oklahoma City, Oklahoma, on April 19, 1995.

Motivated by values core to American democracy, the movement's members hold a set of beliefs that encourage violence and other extreme forms of political behavior. While the rest of this

1

work addresses the cultural, ideological, and behavioral dimensions of the American militia movement in detail, a brief introduction to the argument that follows will set the stage for the analysis to follow.

In short, the character of American political culture informs militia ideology, activities, and potential influence in American political life. The contemporary militia is not "alien" or "exceptional." Instead, militia members invoke core principles that are commonly recognized as central to American political life. They then interpret these values in a way that ultimately justifies their actions and attitudes. Members believe they are struggling to protect America as they think it ought to be, and no price, including violence, is too high. In particular, militiamen and -women argue that the federal government has been corrupted. Its activities, controlled by some conspiracy of bankers, international agencies like the United Nations and the International Monetary Fund, American political elites that members of the militia movement refer to as the "Shadow Government" or the "New World Order," and others, are aimed at the destruction of American liberties and freedoms. Members claim that the federal government has passed a series of laws that improperly limit the rights of Americans to, for example, own guns, associate with (and discriminate against) anyone they wish, or use their land as they please. Resistance, including violent resistance, against these corrupt laws is believed to be appropriate and moral.

As the rest of this book makes clear, the ideas and values that shape militia activity tend to encourage and legitimate the use of violence for political ends. Moreover, these ideas, while informed by principles, myths, and historical events that are common in the United States, are actually well outside the political mainstream. By closely examining the contemporary militia movement, this book seeks to understand the threat the militia poses in both the near and the long term. It also explores the ideas and attitudes that shape the militia movement and link it to broader traditions in American political history.

Social Movements and the Militia

This book takes the position that the modern militia movement can best be understood as a culturally embedded social movement. In order to clarify this point, some attention to the nature and content of social movement theory is necessary. However, since this is a book not about social movement theory but about a particular social movement, and since the literature in this field is so extensive, the following brief discussion of the field will serve to frame this work.

Social movements involve challenges to established political and social institutions and practices. Groups form to oppose the "normal" way society works. In addition, movements often use tactics that fall outside the political mainstream in order to achieve their goals.[1] For example, the civil rights movement used mass rallies, economic boycotts, and civil disobedience, rather than voting, to challenge established patterns of racial discrimination in the United States. Such tactics were necessary because the racism that was central to U.S. society guaranteed that activities like voting would not lead to the changes the civil rights movement sought. Movements, then, link individuals into groups that work to change society through nontraditional means.

So why do social movements form? Why do some people break established patterns and norms of behavior in order to challenge the status quo? First, as might be expected, it is generally the case that those who form and participate in social movements are motivated by ideas and values. In particular, as della Porta and Diani put it, "social action is driven largely by the fundamental principles with which the actor identifies. Values influence the ways in which the actor defines specific goals and identifies behavioral strategies which are both efficient and morally acceptable."[2] In times of social stability, then, individual values correspond, at least in general, with the individual's perception of the general goals of the broader community. But when social and individual goals begin to diverge, the individual may be motivated to try to change society so that its actions correspond with the individual's beliefs.[3] This is particularly likely to occur when individuals perceive injustices, suffered either by themselves or by others with whom the actor is sympathetic.[4] In other words, individuals who perceive that injustices have been committed against the values and ideals through which they define the purpose of their lives, the nature of right and wrong, and the purposes and ends of the community's shared life are likely to react and push for social change.

Second, the literature on social movements often emphasizes the role(s) the mobilization of resources plays in group formation, action, and outcomes. For example, external forces, sometimes known as structural conditions, can also shape movement formation.[5] A social crisis like economic chaos, losing a war, or the mass migration of populations into or out of a particular country can make it difficult for the government or other groups to provide services to a people. Under such conditions, individuals may rise up to demand changes intended to fix the problems they believe society is facing. Thus, when structural conditions are tense, when established patterns of social norms and behaviors are under stress, social movements rise to remake the social order in light of new—or resurrected—ideas about what rules, behaviors, and values ought to organize society.

Similarly, changes in the existing political system can serve as resources that can be mobilized by emerging social movements. New leaders capable of mobilizing previously latent groups can arrive on the scene. The wealth embedded in societies or groups experiencing significant levels of economic growth may provide previously inactive groups with the means to organize and struggle for change. Shifts in patterns of support for the dominant regime may provide formerly weak groups with potential alliances that may advantage their group's interests, thereby encouraging group formation and activity. Thus, when examining a social movement, it is important to consider the resources that were available to it and how group members and leaders used these resources to attempt to achieve their goals.

From a resource mobilization perspective, the late 1980s and early 1990s were a time of remarkable economic and social transition in the United States. Globalization and economies of scale increasingly led to the transformation of the American farming industry from family- to corporate-owned enterprises. This, in turn, caused many family farmers to search for explanations of their loss; militias and similar groups provided answers.[6] Similarly, a shift in political power to the suburbs, with the attendant values-shift to postmodern attitudes regarding appropriate lifestyles,[7] led to the assertion of new rules for land use, restrictions on hunting, and other examples of nonrural people shaping policies for rural land usage that undermined the traditional patterns of local life.[8] Thus, at the same moment the social-political order was remaking itself (the power shift to the suburbs combined with the rise of the globalist economy), it stimulated policies that caused feelings of injustice to rise among many who saw their way of life undermined and attacked.

In addition, as is developed in chapter 3, the existence of previous movements played a crucial role in militia formation. Longstanding right-wing groups like the Ku Klux Klan and the John Birch Society established a pattern of antigovernment activity and rhetoric. Groups like the Order, the Aryan Nations, and other hate groups that emerged in the 1970s and 1980s but were substantially eliminated prior to the militias' rise in the 1990s nonetheless provided a template of paranoia and anger from which the militias drew their ideas and organizational structure.[9] And, of course, the original militias of the Revolutionary War stood as a model for militia formation and action: whatever the reality of the Revolutionary militia, the modern militias constructed an idealized image of citizen-farmers arming themselves, leaving their homes, and defeating the occupying British Army. These historical foundations, when linked to the events described in detail in chapters 4, 5, and 6, provided significant resources for the development of the militia movement.

Another important consideration when engaging in social movement analysis is why movements take the organizational forms they do. Two factors, previous movements and the response of the political system, can be seen as particularly important in the construction of particular movement organizations.

Like individuals, movements are embedded in cultural, historical, and ideological contexts. New movements inevitably are inspired by, draw on the language of, and develop the successes of earlier movements and social challenges through mechanisms like cultural frames and long-standing activist subcultures.[10] Thus, rather than forming entirely new modes of organization and operation, movements develop systems of action and goals that mimic previous movements.

In addition to previous movements, newer movements are also shaped by the reaction of the established authorities to the group's challenge. Thus, if the state responds to social challenges with violence—arrests, coercion, or other means of isolating the deviant actors—there is a tendency for the movement to react with violence or to go underground, hiding its operations. If the state fails to respond in any way, the movement's members may be emboldened, pressing their challenges publicly and actively. Or if the state acts to co-opt the movement, addressing some of its concerns while ignoring others, the result may encourage group members to use established means of political participation, such as voting, lobbying, and the like.[11]

In the case of militias, organizational forms have varied over time. In their formative period, the "typical" militia group consisted of a central leader, often referred to as a colonel regardless of former rank, if any, in the armed forces of the United States. Such a group purchased or used the land of a member as a training compound in which its members practiced guerrilla warfare tactics against agents of the federal government. Members came to the site at some predetermined period to train. In addition to weapons training, the group also engaged in education of members and sympathizers. Finally, all groups maintained an active Internet presence—some more sophisticated than others—to recruit new members and raise funds for their operations. These organizations formed the nucleus of an armed resistance to the evil intrusions of the corrupted government—the Shadow Government.

In its early days, there were few, if any, connections among different parts of the militia movement. It was less a unified movement than clusters of individuals who shared values and attitudes. Two groups, the Militia of Montana (MOM) and the Michigan Militia, were the early progenitors of the militia model: isolation, guns, and ideology. These groups then provided a template that hundreds of other groups and individuals followed.[12] However, these groups did share a common reliance on the Internet to advance their ideology: its existence has provided members and leaders the opportunity to spread their messages quickly, easily, and cheaply around the world. This common ideological front tended to give a greater appearance of movement unity than was really the case; there were limited, if any, institutional structures linking different groups.

In recent years, particularly after the Oklahoma City bombing, the shape of the movement has changed in two significant ways. First, as the number of groups and overt members has declined, group activities have gone underground. (These events are described in detail in chapter 7.) Indeed, like the French Resistance in World War II, some groups have moved to the model of leaderless resistance, with cell members knowing the names and personal information of only a few others in the movement. Thus, in theory, if one is captured (a real fear in terms of their ideology), that person cannot betray more than a few other members of the group. Second, many militia groups and sympathizers have reopened an ideological and political dialogue with the reemergent components of the racist right. Thus, the militia movement is transforming itself into a more explicitly racist movement that is organized, ominously, for violent resistance to the operations of the federal government.

Finally, some sense of how and why movements succeed—and how and why they fail—is important if the way(s) the modern militia movement is likely to affect the United States is to be understood. Several key factors, like the breadth of the movement's goals and the relations between the movement and the dominant culture, are relevant here. For example, specific social movements can lead to the development of "master protest frames."[13] These are ideologies of legitimate protest activity that come to be shared by a variety of social movements. These frames can promote movement success over time as new modes of life are recognized as legitimate and appropriate by large segments of the community. Alternatively, social movements can lead to the foundation of new identities within a community. Thus, as more and more people identify themselves with the movement's ideals, the movement becomes embedded in a given society. Successful social movements can also serve as examples of techniques that future social movements can use to advance their own protests and political activities. Thus, while a specific movement may or may not achieve its goals, the legacy of ideas and strategies it leaves behind can inform other, potentially more successful, movements. Finally, when a group has broad goals it is more likely to be a powerful influence in society; such goals provide a platform on which large segments of society can stand for shared political action, thus enhancing the movement's chances of success.[14] The successes and failures of the militia movement are discussed in chapter 7.

Social movements, then, involve collective action by individuals and groups dissatisfied with current conditions to reshape the political and/or social order. This transformative enterprise is inevitably shaped and informed by the institutional, political, and cultural contexts in which it operates. The broader environment similarly contextualizes its successes and failures. In order to understand any social movement, then, it is necessary to engage the

goals it pursues (and why these goals are chosen), the organizational form it takes (and why this is the case), and the cultural and
political context in which it exists.

A note on methods. This project involves an ethnographic, inter-
pretive examination of the militia movement in the broader context
of American culture. In particular, it focuses on several related
questions: (1) How do militia groups explain their ideas, ideals,
and programs? (2) How do militia members define their enemies?
(3) What is the relationship between the ideas, ideals, and values
militia members espouse and the values contained in American political culture? The purpose of focusing on these questions is to expose the interaction between militias' self-presentations and American political culture. In explaining their ideas and programs,
militia groups can draw on values inherent in American political
culture. In defining their enemies, such groups articulate a particular version of "the good life" that contrasts with some "wrong" alternative. Combined, these questions provide insight into the cultural values that shape militia group formation, values, and,
ultimately, action.

Ethnography is an approach aimed at understanding how individuals perceive the world. Its focus is on how individuals explain
events to themselves and how they justify their actions in terms of
their own values and ideals. As a consequence, the analytic purpose is to recognize the systems of meaning by which individuals
live. Questions like "What do people say they believe?" and "How
do individuals legitimize their actions and behaviors in their own
lives?" are the analytic lenses through which individuals and
groups are studied.[15]

To do ethnographic research, it is necessary to gain access to information about individuals' beliefs and values. The primary
source of information gathered for this project was the Internet.
Militia groups have a substantial presence on the World Wide Web.
Their sites typically explain what the militia group believes and
what activities its members think are justified and why and offer
commentaries on government and other mainstream groups' actions that the militia group finds troublesome. They are, in short,
exactly the kinds of self-presentational material that make it possible to carry forward ethnographic analysis. As such, militia websites provide a treasure trove of information waiting to be mined.

In addition to Internet sources, this project relied on media and other accounts of militia group activities. Journalistic approaches provide a good day-to-day record of what group members do. They also provide an up-to-the-minute record of what members say about why they undertake the actions they do. Accordingly, a survey of major newspapers—for example, the *New York Times*, the *Los Angeles Times*, and the *Chicago Tribune*—was conducted for the dates of major militia events like Randy Weaver's mountaintop stand and Timothy McVeigh's destruction of the Murrah Federal Office Building. The focus was not on the commentary such sources provide on the events; rather, it was on gathering first-person statements from group members and self-identified supporters about why they undertook such actions and how they justified these behaviors to themselves. Newsmagazines like *Time* and *Newsweek* were also covered for similar information.

Plan of the Book

The remainder of this book is organized into seven chapters and an epilogue. The first chapter examines three core components of the work's analysis: culture, ideology, and myth. It explores the nature and content of American political culture and builds a framework of ideas, values, and ideals that shape political action in the United States.

Chapter 2 relates this foundation to the organization and actions of the contemporary militia movement. It examines the myth of the militia in the American Revolution as the foundation of the contemporary militia movement, finding that the actual events of the Revolution do not conform to the elements of the myth. It then critiques the process by which the myth was constructed over time, providing a means to understand the way current believers use the myth to justify and frame their actions and ideas.

Chapter 3 provides a detailed analysis of militia ideology. The ideas that militia members bring with them to the political system profoundly shape their actions, goals, and political plans. To study militia ideology is to focus on the heart of the modern militia movement.

Chapter 4 examines the actions surrounding, and the political impact of, the standoff at Ruby Ridge, Idaho, in 1992. Arguably, the siege of Randy Weaver's mountaintop cabin by the Federal Bureau of Investigation and the Bureau of Alcohol, Tobacco, and Firearms lit the match that ignited the militia movement. This event requires careful attention if the militia movement is to be properly understood.

Chapter 5 focuses on the next significant event that shaped the movement: the conflagration at the Branch Davidian compound in Waco, Texas. This incident spread antigovernment fervor throughout the nation and was the "final straw" that drove many antigovernment sympathizers into the militia movement. Moreover, it made right-wing ideology seem credible in the eyes of many Americans. It is a central source of the modern militia movement.

Chapter 6 considers what might be seen as the logical culmination of antigovernment extremism: the destruction of the Alfred P. Murrah Federal Building in Oklahoma City. While Timothy McVeigh and his coconspirators were not militia members, their actions symbolized the level of hatred and paranoia that some elements of militia beliefs engendered. Additionally, the nationwide shock that accompanied this attack undermined and transformed the movement, and so must be addressed.

Chapter 7 discusses the decline of the movement after Oklahoma City. Neither the militia movement nor right-wing extremist groups have disappeared; however, the way they organize and act has changed. Four factors are shown to have encouraged the movement's downward turn: the extremism of militia actions alienated many potential supporters; state action undermined militia ideology and activities; militia groups were successful in promoting core ideas in the political system, particularly their opposition to gun control; and parts of the movement were co-opted by established political forces, particularly the conservative wing of the Republican Party.

The epilogue assesses the prospects for resurgence of militia groups in the future, particularly in light of the terrorist attacks in New York City, Washington, D.C., and Pennsylvania on September 11, 2001. While many might assume that an antigovernment movement cannot survive in an era of high patriotism, this is not necessarily the case. Given the nature of American political culture, such groups can be expected to survive and influence American politics for a long time to come. Where things go from here is, quite literally, a matter of the choices we make as a society.

1

Fuel:
The Cultural Foundations
of the Militia Movement

When Timothy McVeigh lit the fuse that fired the bomb that destroyed the Alfred P. Murrah Federal Building in Oklahoma City, Oklahoma, on April 19, 1995, most Americans asked, "Why?" "Why," people wondered, "would anyone do such a thing?"

This book sets out to answer the question Timothy McVeigh's horrible act inspired. While the details of the answers it provides will be developed in the next six chapters, an outline of the answer can be sketched here as an introduction and a prologue.

The Oklahoma City bombing and a host of other, less destructive but similarly violent events are linked not by people but by ideology and culture. There is today a new social movement in the United States, a movement grounded in the context of American political culture and motivated by an ideology of fear and hate. Thus, many individuals—both activists and sympathizers, some open and others latent—believe the government of the United States has been completely corrupted. They believe that the goals and purposes of the American experiment—meaning, from their perspective, rights and freedom for the individual, the sacredness of property rights, and the nonintrusion of the federal government on the private lives of ordinary citizens, among other things—have been literally stolen by agents of what they call, adopting President George H. W. Bush's phrase, the "New World Order." Alternatively, members of this new social movement refer to the source of the corruption affecting American life as the "Shadow Government."

This shadow government is believed to serve the interests of some "other"—the United Nations, the international banking community (and thus, according to some militia rhetoric, the Zionist conspiracy of Nazi ideology), or the preferences of some other international elite. The rulers of this shadow government have hired the agents of the U.S. government to enforce their will. Bent only on gaining power for its own sake, this conspiracy uses the language and institutions of American government to legitimize what are, for the members of this new social movement, corrupt and evil policies such as gun control, the abandonment of the gold standard, and the assertion of women's and minority rights through programs like affirmative action. Each of these programs, and many more, is seen to violate the sacred intent of the Founders to, in the mind of the militia, create a political system that promotes individual rights and autonomy above all else.

There are obviously many dimensions to this outline. Two in particular deserve brief introduction here. First, as will be explored in more detail in this chapter and the next, it should be admitted that at least some of what the new right argues about the nature of the American founding is true. The American colonies were, to some degree, settled by people who were trying to assert their individual rights and escape apparent tyranny. Moreover, the settlers' story has become a central theme in American political culture. Thus, the new right's complaint that contemporary American policies have tended to concentrate power in the hands of governing officials rather than individuals has "traction": it expresses values, ideals, and perceptions that, however much they may be distorted and misremembered by contemporary actors, make sense in American political life. Accordingly, the contemporary militia movement, and for that matter the new right in general, has the potential to have significant influence in the American political system by drawing supporters and encouraging action.

Second, the new right is virtually unique in contemporary American politics because its ideology justifies and encourages violence—the use of force to promote and defend its adherents' point of view. As will be seen, this, too, is informed by their interpretation of American political culture and history. Thus, not only do militia members and other right-wing-group adherents tell a story that has meaning in the context of American political culture, but also they tell it in a way that promotes extremism. Their actions, then, may encompass more than conventional political activity like voting, interest-group membership, and media relations. They may also be deadly.

The rest of this chapter lays out the theoretical foundations on which this study rests. It focuses on three concepts that are central to the work's approach: culture, ideology, and myth. Interacting as a system, culture provides the vessel in which are held all *possible* ideas, attitudes, values, and actions that make sense in a given community; ideologies shape cultural raw materials into specific forms; and myths imbue these particular ideological constructions with a sacred, enduring significance. This chapter explores key dimensions of American political culture that are relevant for understanding the modern militia movement and highlights certain aspects of American political culture that have been mythologized and from which militia groups draw inspiration.

Political Culture, Ideology, and Myth in Political Life

This work rests on the interaction of political culture, ideology, and mythology. Each of these elements plays an important role in shaping the nature of the militia, the dimensions of support the movement enjoys in American political life, and the prospects for its continued significance in the future. Accordingly, some discussion of these concepts—and their interrelationships—is necessary before moving the study forward.

The Power of Political Culture

Political culture can be conceived of as a set (or, for that matter, sets) of relatively shared ideas, ideals, concepts, stories, and myths that orient citizens within their political systems, that explain how and why people act as they do within a given polity.[1] In other words, political culture constitutes the broad array of options, questions, and attitudes that groups of people in specific societies accept as politically relevant and meaningful.

Embedded in this definition is a set of assumptions about the nature of human conduct and thought that deserves brief attention. First among these assumptions is: *Nothing is given.* Nothing has an obvious meaning and significance in and of itself. It is only through association and interaction with others that terms, concepts, or actions become meaningful.

By way of illustration, take the ubiquitous handshake. Upon meeting another person, most Americans will extend their right hand in an attempt to shake the other person's right hand. This action is so common that it is remarkable only if it is not immediately reciprocated. That is, handshakes are so expected in normal conduct that it is only their absence that really draws attention to the artificiality and yet profound significance of this symbolic gesture. After all, what is there in the grasping of two hands that makes it a valuable act? And why the right hand? Is there any reason that humans might not use some mechanism other than the handshake to exchange greetings? The answer to all of these questions, of course, is that nothing makes the handshake meaningful except that people who believe it to be significant find it to be important. A handshake is a symbol of friendliness, respect, and trust because that is what people who shake each other's hands believe it to mean. Conversely, the failure to shake hands when another expects it is an insult only because either the recipient, the community, or even the person who refuses to shake hands believes it to be an insult.

It is important to note that, despite the artificiality of the symbolic insult of not shaking hands when a handshake is expected, it is an insult nonetheless. Humans do not, as a practical matter, intellectualize gestures and decide that, since the handshake is a social construct, its absence has no inherent meaning. Instead, symbols, ideas, stories, myths, and concepts have meanings that orient understanding and motivate action. Thus, a second assumption embedded in the definition of culture offered above is: *Human beings make sense of their world in symbolic, referential terms.* Just as nothing is given, it is only through understanding the contextual meanings of gestures, words, concepts, and symbols that humans can make sense of the world with which they interact.

Returning again to the handshake, once a human understands that an extended right hand is an invitation/expectation to extend his or her own right hand, that person has both a guide to personal action *and* a baseline from which to anticipate the actions of others: once I extend my right hand, the understanding is that the other person will extend his or her right hand. If the person extends his or her hand, I can then assume the person holds a particular set of attitudes and values, at least to the degree that I can assume the person understand the rituals of polite greeting in my culture. By contrast, if he or she fails to extend a hand, I can just as easily make a different set of assumptions about that person's ignorance, rudeness, or both. The contextual meanings and patterns of action associated with gestures, symbols, concepts, and ideas thus provide tools through which humans can understand what is going on *and* can orient themselves for action and interaction.

Third, *the symbolic, referential terms through which human beings understand life and orient action contain embedded evaluative criteria by which appropriate action can be judged.* Actions, statements, attitudes, and even concepts are inevitably associated with evaluations of their appropriateness or inappropriateness. The refusal to shake hands, for example, is likely to be considered inappropriate because it is a behavioral signal of attitudes and ideas that people who believe in the importance of shaking hands find objectionable. More broadly, any socially constructed term, concept, act, or symbol is embedded in complex patterns of evaluation. For those who share similar understandings of what certain behaviors and attitudes mean, then, there will also be a shared interpretation of whether given acts or statements are appropriate or not.

The point that contextually constructed terms and symbols are bound up in concepts of evaluation leads to a fourth dimension of the definition of culture offered above: *Sanctions are associated with particular understandings of appropriate and inappropriate conduct and attitudes.* Humans do not simply evaluate behaviors or ideas as right or wrong and then move on with their lives. Rather, as part of the general process of socialization, human beings sanction those who deviate from what is normal, expected, and generally held to be appropriate. Such sanctions can range from verbal challenges, to possibly ostracism of someone who is believed to inappropriately refuse to shake another's hand, to the execution of someone who has transgressed shared understandings of appropriate conduct. To violate local norms, then, is to face the wrath of the community.

Fifth, *there is a virtually infinite variety of meanings, behavioral assumptions, and evaluative standards that can be associated with specific gestures, concepts, terms, symbols, ideas, or acts.* It does not follow that, because one community views extending the right hand to be a symbol of openness and friendship, all communities will do so.

Instead, particular groups and communities may share relatively similar understandings of the meaning and appropriateness of a range of ideas, attitudes, behaviors, concepts, symbols, and gestures. Such groups can be said to share a culture. Groups that ascribe different meanings and evaluative standards to the range of human activities constitute different cultures. The potential variation, at least theoretically, is infinite.

This possible endless variety of cultures is perhaps best demonstrated by discussing basic human needs that would seem to transcend culture. Everyone, for example, needs to eat. Thus, all living people have the potential to get hungry. Yet whatever the biological basis of hunger is, different groups and communities have wildly divergent ideas about how it is appropriate to satisfy that need. Some groups think nothing of eating meat; others find such behavior to be disgusting. Adherents of some cultures fry and eat maggots as the norm; adherents of other cultures cannot conceive the circumstance that would lead a person to eat bugs. Accordingly, the sixth dimension of the definition of culture offered above is: *Cultures shape what is admitted as an appropriate question, choice, or act in a particular group and so shape the kinds of issues that concern the group and motivate it to action.*

To return to the example of food, human experience demonstrates that people will go hungry rather than eat a convenient product considered appropriate for consumption in some cultures but excluded in their own. Even starving persons may reject meat in a vegetarian culture, for example, and cannibalism is taboo almost everywhere. This is true because the culture defines what is and is not a food product as such. A product not on the cultural checklist of appropriate foods is, essentially, inedible because it is conceived to be edible.

By extension, in the political sphere, a political culture delimits what are political issues and what are not, establishes what kinds of actions are appropriate and what kinds are not, and shapes the universe of the possible in a given polity. Moreover, despite the artificiality of specific cultural constructions, individual political cultures contain evaluative criteria through which its members interpret right and wrong. They also embody and define sanctions through which these conceptualizations are enforced within the group. Thus, within their limits, specific cultures provide clues for appropriate action and establish standards by which individuals can justify and legitimate their actions and ideas—including the imposition of sanctions on social deviants.

The Role of Ideology

Ideology can be defined as "a value system or belief system accepted as fact or truth by some group. It is composed of sets of attitudes towards the various institutions and processes of society. An ideology provides the believer with a picture of the world both as it is and as it should be, and, in doing so, organizes the tremendous complexity of the world into something fairly simple and understandable."[2] Put another way, ideology is "an agenda of things to discuss, questions to ask, hypotheses to make. We should be able to use it when considering the interaction between ideas and politics, especially systems of ideas that make claims, whether justificatory or hortatory."[3] Whereas political culture is the vessel of all possible political goals, ideals, and values, ideologies take the raw material of political culture and construct it into specific forms that define what concepts *mean,* what actions *ought to be* taken, and how individuals *ought* to behave.

In addition, ideology simplifies reality. It links the abstract to the concrete. For example, "liberty" is a broad concept. A specific ideology, however, may define liberty as "freedom from government interference in all areas of life," whereas a separate ideology may define it as "freedom of the individual from fears of hunger, cold, and other human needs." Within a specific ideology, the concept means what the ideology holds, thus linking the ideational to the concrete.

Ideology further embodies power relationships. It establishes certain patterns of policies, programs, ideas, and interests as appropriate and proper while denigrating others. To study ideology, then, is to assess which power interests are being promoted by the ideology's concepts and which are being limited.

Ideology performs these roles through three processes that Paul Ricoeur has labeled distortion, legitimation, and integration. Distortion means that the particular ways ideas, beliefs, values, and attitudes combine in specific ideologies inevitably distort reality. No ideology describes truth; rather, ideologies link condensed, composed, and simplified versions of experience into coherent wholes available for humans to use to organize their lives. Thus, all political understanding is distorted, untrue at some fundamental level—which, as will be seen throughout this book, provides fodder for endless debates, challenges, and vitality in political life.[4]

Further, Ricoeur argues that ideology performs the function of legitimation. Legitimation in this context means one's acceptance—or rejection—of another's power and authority. Ideology constructs terms in which the appropriateness of obedience and opposition are made clear to both leader and led.[5] Thus, ideology may enhance authority or may undermine it in favor of some countervailing force or position. Importantly, it is the ideology, not some objective or structural force, that establishes the legitimacy of particular political relationships.

Finally, according to Ricoeur, ideology performs the function of integration. Integration in this sense means that it provides a means by which individuals and groups establish, protect, and preserve their social identities.[6] "We" believe this, an ideology establishes; "they" believe something else. Thus, the particular distortions of specific ideologies are linked to legitimation values of right and wrong to construct "our" group as right and decent and "their" group as wrong in an integrated whole.[7]

It is important to note that in the definitions offered above, the concept of ideology is stripped of the negative connotations with which it is often associated. Ideology is not a term used to denigrate an opponent's point of view as "false"; instead, it is used to describe particular relationships of terms, concepts, attitudes, and beliefs. Ideologies thus can differ; but everyone has one, and everyone interprets the political world through the particular constructions of ideas and meanings that are incorporated in the ideologies he accepts. Indeed, everyone requires an ideology: it is precisely because ideologies take complex terms and concepts like freedom and equality and imbue them with an empirical content—for example, equality of opportunity and not equality of outcome; freedom from government pressure and not freedom in the form of government provision of the basic needs of life—that political life becomes manageable. Ideologies make it possible to make assumptions about others' attitudes, beliefs, and likely behaviors even as they provide evaluative criteria through which individuals can quickly decide to support or oppose specific political programs and policies. They provide guides for action by defining what kinds of steps can and should be taken (or not) in specific contexts.

And, perhaps most important, ideologies provide standards by which one can legitimate one's own political preferences.

Accordingly, it is crucial to understand any group's or individual's ideology if the goal is to recognize what motivates the group to act or what shape any political action is likely to take. Further, it is important to recognize that the terms and values of any group's ideology are meaningful to its members no matter how absurd they may seem to outsiders—whether outsiders believe and are likely to act on the terms of the group's ideology is not the point. Members of the group take it seriously. Adherents will use it to evaluate the politics they experience and establish the kinds of actions they will or will not take. And members of the group will legitimate their choices in terms of their ideologies.

The Construction of Myth

Myths are often conceptualized as fictional stories with some moral lesson. This perception, however, misses the depth of importance myths play in human life. Extending the images of culture as a vessel and ideologies as particular forms into which selected cultural values are shaped, myths serve to imbue ideologies with meanings that have broad social effect. Myths promote the extension of one's private point of view to the community at large as a moral duty.

As Henry Tudor has noted, myths are stories that may or may not be grounded on factual events. A myth is an interpretation of reality, whether fictionalized or not, that the mythmaker (and believer) takes to be fact. Myths, then, are true not because they are factual but because they are believed to be true by their adherents.[8]

Moreover, myths have structure: they have protagonists who experience beginnings, middles, and ends. Political myths focus on how the politics of a society ought to be configured and how participants in that society ought to act. Thus, by extension, mythic protagonists serve as models of ideal public action, at least for the members of the group who believe in the myth and its teaching. Myths and their heroes place a particular community in an ongoing dramatic struggle that, the lesson explains, the community can win if it follows the model of the hero. They also provide a common way members of communities can recognize themselves as neighbors and friends, as "us" versus whatever "them" is challenging "our" way of life. Myths, then, take the stuff of culture and the logic of ideology and make them the foundation of a public, communal, proper way of life for an entire society.[9]

One particularly important myth for understanding the militia movement, as was implied above, is the myth of the hero. The hero's journey, as Joseph Campbell has explained, is inevitably a struggle against multiple challenges, enemies, and even self-doubts. Yet, through will, action, and the timely intervention of others (including gods), the hero is able to achieve his—almost always his—goals and "save" the community. This occurs despite the daunting odds facing the hero, and indeed the difficulty of the challenge is itself the cause and measure of the hero's greatness.[10]

The interaction of myth, ideology, and culture can be seen to frame and profoundly influence the formation, actions, and future course of the militia movement. American political culture will be shown to contain raw materials from which the movement could be constructed. Militia ideology takes these resources and shapes them into a form that establishes meaning for movement members. Then, specific myths of American political life, particularly the Revolutionary myth of the militia, imbues the movement with a model for action that inspires confidence in its ultimate success and an understanding of what the "right" structure of society ought to be.

American Political Culture

To undertake any foray into the question of a nation's "culture" is to enter dangerous territory. Challenges to specific arguments can be raised from a host of perspectives. One can claim, for example, that a particular interpretation is empirically inaccurate, that it is ahistorical, that it is insensitive to the dynamics of gender, race, ethnicity, region, and other subcultural factors, or all of the above in any combination. This problem is particularly acute in the case of the United States, given the complexity of its political, economic, and social systems.

Describing the nature, complexity, and meaning of all the values, ideas, myths, and stories extant in American political culture is beyond the scope of this book, of course, and indeed is well beyond the scope of any single book. The number of key concepts within U.S. political culture—democracy, liberty, freedom, antiauthoritarianism, political tolerance, and the like—are in and of themselves

too numerous to allow for easy identification and are often in sufficient tension with each other to make the discovery of an axiomatic relationship between some value and some political action
problematic at best.[11] Moreover, each of the concepts, stories,
myths, and values embedded in American political culture is itself
vague enough in language and expression to support multiple interpretations and attitudes within the American polity.[12] As a consequence, different actors can draw on different dimensions of political culture to support their agendas or can provide different
interpretations for terms and concepts that competitors use in common. A simple correlation between beliefs and outcomes cannot be
expected in such circumstances.

One possible path through the minefield of "national culture"
studies is to distinguish between public and private culture. Rather
than extrapolating from survey data to determine modal private
characters within different polities and claiming that this mode
represents the national culture, as was done in the early cross-cul-
ture studies, public culture refers to the common terms of reference, symbols, and ideologies within which different groups and
individuals press their claims for power, policy and identity.[13] Such
terms are not a matter of private conscience; instead, they can be
found, among other places, in public documents, speeches and
campaigns, and political symbols referred to by others as they promote their agendas. Such public cultural symbols can constitute a
shareable language through which different groups and individuals can press for their goals in intersubjectively recognizable—and
supportable—terms.[14] Importantly, this sharing can go on regardless of the private values, attitudes, and motives of the actors ref-
erencing the public culture. As a practical matter, the public culture
sets the terms in which political debate and struggle can occur.

While the specific dimensions of any public culture can and
ought to be the subject of serious debate and attention, some factors can, with little debate, be seen as significant in the American
case. For understanding the militia movement, two values seem
particularly important. The first of these is the liberal character of
American public life. As many analysts of American politics have
found, liberalism is at the core of the American experience.[15] In specific, the American version of liberalism is characterized by the assertion of individual rights versus the state, representative and limited government, political universalism, political equality among

all citizens (egalitarianism), political tolerance, and capitalism. American public culture contains an array of symbols, rituals, practices, and policies that tend to favor the rights of individuals to act with few constraints on their behavior whether the arena of action is political, economic, or social. Moreover, the public culture valorizes these rights as universally applicable to all persons everywhere. Accordingly, American public culture tends to favor those policies, proposals, or ideas that are understood to advance individual liberty in whatever context people find themselves acting.

This favoring of a certain type of plan or program does not translate into an axiomatic linkage of culture and policy, however. It does not follow that, because American public culture insists that capitalism is the "best" way for individuals to maximize their liberty, all Americans will decide that any government regulation of the economy is inappropriate. Instead, the specific policies, programs, and decisions that can be seen to derive from liberal principles are many. Thus, American "liberals" today insist that the best way to achieve political equality is through government programs like affirmative action, while American "conservatives" assert that affirmative action makes it impossible to achieve real political equality. Similarly, eighteenth-century Americans argued that slavery and the oppression of Native Americans were acceptable since such people were not "persons" capable of self-government, while twentieth-century reformers artfully recast liberal language to accommodate the rights of African and Native Americans.[16] In *both* cases, the core principles were liberal: the debate was over how best to achieve the liberal ideal, not whether liberalism was an appropriate approach to social and political life in the first place.

Public culture thus provides tools and approaches to political life that adherents can recognize even when they disagree about the specific policies and programs that ought to derive from shared principles. In its liberalism, then, American public culture valorizes those plans and ideas that *can be* seen, by the actors of the time, to advance individual rights—however those rights are defined in context. Liberalism is a broad, interpretable, shareable concept even among those who may derive dramatically different plans and programs from its principles.

In addition to its liberalism, American public political culture is also remarkable for its exceptionalism. American liberal public culture is exceptionalist in the sense that its universalism is linked to a religious, proselytizing urge. Rather than believing that everyone, regardless of race, religion, creed, or national origin has "unalienable Rights" and that political systems ought to recognize and encourage this fact and then going home, American public culture manifests the ideal that Americans have a mission—in the religious sense of the word—to spread the fruits of liberty around the world. It is not enough to believe in liberty in American public culture. Instead, one must achieve it, both for oneself and for the rest of the world.

The source of this missionary zeal is complex but can be outlined briefly. The religious founding of many of the early European colonies on the North American continent encouraged many Protestant sects to view themselves as working in a "New World" to make whatever kind of society they wished free from the limitations of the old, corrupted order. America would be a "shining city on a hill"—the new Eden. These sects established the language through which many generations of succeeding immigrants came to press their interests. Then, once the religious sects lost much of their influence in New England, the mission to create a new Jerusalem was updated: with the mission to tame a continent while "civilizing" Native American populations (Manifest Destiny); to remake nature and order it as desired (the scientific and technological revolutions); and ultimately, by the twentieth century, to "save" the world for democracy (World Wars I and II, as well as the Cold War). Hence the significance of the frontier in American political culture: its existence meant that it was always possible to make things better for yourself if you were willing to move—it was possible to complete the mission of creating real liberty in political life, if only elsewhere. Cumulatively, such factors created a language that gives political actions in America a religious tone, meaning that one was either sinner or saved, good or evil, punished or punishing.[17]

Together, liberalism and exceptionalism create a language through which Americans, in making public appeals for public support for public policies, can find the kinds of intersubjective understandings that make political life possible. While specific appeals may shade the terms of reference differently, casting them in different lights and illuminating different features, the underlying structure of the appeals, if they are to be successful, must be framed in terms of the common, public culture.

Moreover, these pillars of American political culture tend to promote a politics of self-reliance, action, and responsibility. They are not neutral, available to adherents of any political ideology for equal use. Rather, liberalism and exceptionalism have been constructed to favor conservative models of individual responsibility, personal morality, and the potential for individual actions to change social structures as the foundation of "proper" political action. For example, Americans are generally more opposed to taxes, even in return for substantial welfare and other social benefits, than are most Europeans. Similarly, Americans impose much harsher penalties for individuals' illegal drug use than do most European nations. Both of these policies can be seen as manifestations of the underlying American cultural predisposition to emphasize personal responsibility for one's own well-being, including poor individual choice-making as a source of drug use. Thus, as will be seen throughout this work, the militia movement had fertile ground in which to grow in the United States: its construction of American values into a specific, mythically embedded ideology draws life from the conservative strain of individualist, exceptionalist politics in the United States.

2

Heat:
The Myth of the Militia
in the American Revolution

As many scholars have noted, a powerful myth shapes many Americans' interpretation of how the American Revolution was fought and won.[1] In this myth, gentle, selfless people (including women, African Americans, and even Native Americans) leave their homes (taking their weapons, of course) to volunteer to fight an oppressive foe. They have no ambition to impose their political will on others; rather, their dream is to be left alone to take care of their farms and families. They are motivated only by the kind of righteous rage against oppression that inspires heroism but avoids the oppression of others. And while they are overmatched in military terms, they find a way to harass and defeat their superior enemy. Then, when the war is over, these citizen-warriors depart the field of battle to return home and make their own "American Dream" rather than use their success to enhance their political or economic positions. Thus, according to the myth, American democracy was won by small groups of patriots who had the courage to face, and the wisdom to effectively fight, the world's most powerful nation.

This myth is deeply ingrained in American political life. Politicians invoke it in campaign speeches. Movies, books, and songs have all valorized the hero-citizens who drove the British from American shores. Ordinary Americans, from Nathan Hale to Ethan Allen to Molly Pitcher and more, have become icons of the Revolution, and of America. Schools, public buildings, and even roadways celebrate the militiamen and -women who are believed to have won freedom for the nascent United States. Perhaps most obviously, the battles at Lexington and Concord are taught to generation after generation of schoolchildren as the battles that started the Revolution—and as proof that militias armed with muskets and a spirit of freedom could defeat the world's most powerful army. Indeed, the date of these battles, April 19, 1775, is an important date both in American history and in the brief history of the modern American militia movement. As such, the myth has provided fertile ground in which the modern American militia movement has grown.

Notably, the Revolutionary myth of the militia has grounded the modern movement despite the fact that it is not a very accurate depiction of how the American Revolution was won. In reality, militia forces were not effective on the battlefield. They were a source of constant concern for the Revolution's military leaders. Most officers in the American army, including George Washington, repeatedly complained that militia forces were ineffective. These complaints were grounded in experience: in an era in which military forces stood in tightly packed rows a few hundred yards apart and were assailed by several exchanges of musket and artillery fire before finally charging across the remaining open ground to attack their enemies with bayonets, most militia units broke ranks and ran when confronted by the first volley of fire from their better-armed, better-trained, and more disciplined British opponents. Battles involving militias thus usually turned into destructive, demoralizing routs.[2]

Not only were the militias not particularly effective in battle, they were also often poorly armed, if they had weapons at all. As a result, Washington and other officers regularly complained about the militias' lack of equipment.[3] In the context of the needs of a professional military, then, the militias were a drain on their already scarce resources—and a drain that was untrustworthy and underprepared. While some militia units might serve as sharpshooters or scouts, in general they were not an important part of the Revolutionary War effort.

The militias were, as a rule, simply not suited to eighteenth-century warfare. Instead, by the end of the war the standing army Washington created looked in demographic profile very much like the standing army of any European nation. Instead of being beaten by the militias, then, the British were defeated by organized, professional armies—and navies. After the hard winter in Valley Forge, the American army professionalized: it trained repeatedly in tactics of eighteenth-century warfare, it moved to three-year enlistments to guarantee that it had the experienced manpower to engage British forces, and it acquired stores of muskets and artillery appropriate to fighting on contemporary battlefields. It was this professional army, in combination with the presence of a professional French army, that engaged British units in the later years of the war, substantially keeping the British tied to their coastal bases.[4] And, importantly, it was only after a French fleet arrived off his base on the Yorktown peninsula in Virginia that Cornwallis felt compelled to surrender his army to Washington: so long as the British navy had been able to keep his forces supplied by sea, Cornwallis had been content to wait for an opportunity to attack the American forces or to transport his troops by sea to another location. Whatever role the militias played in harassing enemy communications, it was not the reason the United States won its revolution.

However, *after* the war the militia myth became a convenient way to resolve certain political tensions. It then served as a foundation for the transformation of American culture in ways that ultimately inspired the modern militia movement. This chapter explores the construction of the militia myth in order to explain its contemporary use.

Creating the Myth of the Militia in the American Revolution

Given the relative unimportance of militias in the Revolution, it is fair to ask how and why the myth of their significance has grown to the point that it can ground contemporary political activity. Three factors can be seen to have particular importance in explaining the militia story. One is the empirical success that some militia units had during and after the war. A second is the way later political, social, and economic actors reinvented the history of the American frontier and the American Revolution during the mid- and late 1800s—a reinvention that has been continually reasserted as "fact" ever since. Of crucial importance were early political and cultural leaders who wished to serve their ideological agendas, later interpreters of the militia experience, and the development of a cultural acceptance and emphasis on guns. The third is the way this reinvented story resonates with particular values, ideas, and assumptions that ground American political culture.

Militia Acts: The Foundation of the Myth

It is important to admit that some militias did have limited success during the Revolution and in early American history. Indeed, the mythology that has been created about the militias' significance would have been very difficult to construct in the absence of any positive militia acts. For instance, examples of militia effectiveness during the Revolution are relatively easy to list. The citizens who fought British forces at Lexington and Concord, Daniel Morgan's sharpshooters, Francis Marion's swamp fighters, and Ethan Allen's Green Mountain boys all achieved noteworthy accomplishments during the war. Militia units harassed British forces and made their operations more difficult than they otherwise would have been. These successes, while not typical of most militia units, served as useful examples that future militia advocates could inflate to epic significance.

In addition, during the early years of American history the militias performed a function that generally assured their popular status: crime control, whether defined as stopping violence committed by citizens against one another (and their property), by Loyalists fomenting rebellion, or by slaves in rebellion. Militia units performed these functions from well before the beginning of the American Revolution through the middle of the nineteenth century.[5] Accordingly, the notion of the militia saving the community was culturally well entrenched even before later actors drew on this imagery and developed the myth of the militias in the Revolution.[6]

Constitutionalism and
the Construction of the Myth

While these examples of militia success are part of the explanation for the myth's growth, they are not sufficient to account for its broad acceptance in society. Of more importance were the ways the leaders of the new American polity constructed the myth to fit their political preferences. The radical Republican objection to standing armies was of particular significance in this context. For radical Republicans—opponents of centralized political authority like James Madison, for example—standing armies were dangerous for both practical and civic reasons. Practically, standing armies gave central political authorities the power to impose their will on citizens, thereby threatening individual liberty. This likelihood was further enhanced when the economic and social characteristics of professional armies were recognized: drawn from the relatively poorer parts of society, career soldiers were thought to lack the commitment to individual rights and freedoms that social "betters" had.[7] In a revolution aimed at the protection of individual rights, a standing army was therefore a problem.

Civically, Republican theory held that individual freedom could be guaranteed only when individuals controlled all power—including military power. Thus citizens needed to be armed for their own protection against even a state in whose name a war was being conducted: the state was as much a potential enemy as some foreign power, especially if it had a permanent army. Additionally, free men fighting in their own defense could be expected to fight more effectively than hired "mercenaries": the defense of liberty would encourage greater effort than would salaries. Citizen armies were believed to create and protect citizen polities.[8]

The fear of central political authority and the reluctance to establish, equip, and maintain a permanent military are well-known facets of the American Revolution and its political aftermath. George Washington, for example, constantly struggled to assemble and maintain an army capable of fighting the British. In addition, the initial document defining American government after the war, the Articles of Confederation, contains no provisions for a standing army or navy. Its successor document, the U.S. Constitution, establishes an elaborate set of procedural and formal limits on the scope of the central government's powers—in part because it allows for the establishment of professional military institutions. Antiprofessional, pro-militia sentiments were thus at the heart of the early American political experience.

Intellectually, the militias' inadequacy during the Revolution presented the designers of the new nation's government with a challenge: their practical experience emphasized the importance of permanent, professional military institutions even as their ideology

insisted that such forces were dangerous. In response, even Federalist supporters of a strong central government and professional
military forces came to assert the significance of the militias—particularly the right of private citizens to own guns that could be used
in defense of liberty—in their constitutional theory. Two quotes
from the *Federalist Papers* can illustrate this move. Writing in defense of the establishment of a standing army, for example, Alexander Hamilton, as strong an advocate of centralized government
power as could be found among the Constitution's creators,
nonetheless insists that militia power could be used to check the
power of a professional military by using tactics that mimicked
those allegedly used effectively by the militia during the war:

> If the representatives of the people betray their constituents, there is
> then no resource left but in the exertion of that original right of self-de-
> fense which is paramount to all positive forms of government. . . . If the
> federal army should be able to quell the resistance of one State, the dis-
> tant States would be able to make head with fresh forces. The advan-
> tages obtained in one place must be abandoned to subdue the opposi-
> tion in others; and the moment the part which had been reduced to
> submission was left to itself, its efforts would be renewed, and its resis-
> tance revive.[9]

James Madison makes similar arguments, even going so far as to
claim, against all immediate experience, that the Revolution was
won by the armed militias:

> Let a regular army, fully equal to the resources of the country, be
> formed; and let it be entirely at the devotion of the federal government:
> still it would not be going too far to say that the State governments with
> the people on their side would be able to repel the danger. . . . To [this
> army] would be opposed a militia amounting to near half a million cit-
> izens with arms in their hands, officered by men chosen from among
> themselves, fighting for their common liberties and united and con-
> ducted by governments possessing their affections and confidence. It
> may well be doubted whether a militia thus circumstanced could ever
> be conquered by such a proportion of regular troops. Those who are
> best acquainted with the late successful resistance of this country
> against the British will be most inclined to deny the possibility of it.

This is virtually guaranteed, Madison continues, because U.S. citizens have "the advantage of being armed, which the Americans

possess over the people of almost every other nation."[10] The myth of the militia thus became a tool with which early political leaders, even those who advocated relatively centralized political power and who had experienced the inadequacy of the militias during the Revolution, could resolve the needs of modern political systems for organized militaries while answering the demands of republican ideology.

Popular Culture and the Construction of the Myth

The early political valorization of the militia was followed in later years by creative writers and filmmakers who turned the militia myth into cultural fact through works of fiction and historical imagination. Michael Kammen has found, for example, that the militia myth and its variants—stories of individuals reluctantly taking action and then overcoming their enemies—have been central components of popular literature and culture in three distinct periods of American history: the 1820s–1840s, the 1890s–1950s, and the 1970s–present.[11] (Kammen's chapter was published in 1978; however, as films like *The Patriot* [discussed at the end of this chapter] and many others suggest, the contemporary period is sympathetic to the militia mythos.) In the earliest period, novelists like James Fenimore Cooper romanticized the actions and importance of individual frontiersmen during the Revolution.[12] Claiming that he was writing "history,"[13] in books like *The Spy* (1821) and *The Last of the Mohicans* (1826), Cooper tells stories that place quiet, competent volunteers as central figures of the Revolution. In the second period, novelists like Robert Chambers and William E. Griffis insisted that romantic treatments of the Revolution were actually better histories of the Revolution than were academic tomes: only fiction, they argued, could capture the spirit of the people who made a new America.[14] Authors (and, once the technologies developed, filmmakers and television producers) of the third period reconstructed and re-presented these themes in powerful and appealing ways in novels and on television and in the movies.[15] Works of popular fiction have thus taken the plastic material of the Revolution and helped to mold it into its present, mythical form.

Importantly, it is not even necessary for a work of popular fiction to focus on the Revolution to recognize it as a manifestation of the militia myth. While the American Revolution has served as the foundation for some motion pictures, it has not spawned as many films and television shows as has the western genre. But what is the plot of a typical western? While there are many types of westerns—hero, antihero, spaghetti—as presented in *High Noon, Shane, The Outlaw Josey Wales,* or *The Alamo,* the mythic story is instantly recognizable: a reluctant hero is forced to take his gun to defend his family, country, or other valuable thing against some evil intruding force. By remaining strong and true to (usually) his moral principles, the lonely hero overcomes great odds and achieves success. The hero then returns to private life. It is the classic hero's adventure set in the Old West and adapted to militia sensibilities. Thus a modern version of the militia myth survives and repeats through historical and technological contexts that earlier generations of militia mythologizers might never have imagined. The story never changes, just the cast.

Gun Culture and
the Construction of the Myth

This evolution and cultural transmission of the militia myth is even more evident when the development of the gun culture in the United States is recognized and integrated into the myth. While gun ownership was common, at least in relatively rural areas, through much of American colonial history, guns were not celebrated as an essential part of American political life until after the Civil War. Largely because of Samuel Colt's influence, guns were heavily advertised throughout the United States in the period from just before the Civil War through the 1880s and 1890s. This advertising had the effect of generating a market for guns: whereas prior to the war many Americans had not owned guns, after it gun advertising (seeking to enhance the market for a product that had been cheaply mass produced during the war but that faced a significant oversupply problem in the war's aftermath) promoted gun ownership as popular and appealing—even defining one's status as an American. Colt, in particular, worked hard to link the "taming" of the West with his weapons, and he engaged in numerous dubious schemes to compel the military to buy his guns just so he could make the romanticized claim that his were the pistols and rifles that had settled the West. "God created men," a popular slogan of the day insisted, "Colonel Colt made them equal."[16] Guns and gun ownership, then, were depicted as heroic tools for a society of equals.

Notably, this marketing scheme neatly linked the already developed myth of the militia with American political culture in the context of contemporary political circumstances. Guns were seen as the equalizer in a society undergoing rapid industrialization, with all the class-based inequities that inevitably accompany the concentration of wealth in corporate hands. Thus citizens could believe that they remained equal, free to pursue their individual destinies, because they, like their forebears, had weapons with which to challenge and defeat central political authority. Guns made the militia myth real.

The spread in gun ownership was accompanied by the development of an ideology legitimating their proliferation. The most important force in shaping this new ideology was the National Rifle Association (NRA). Formed in 1871, the NRA in its earliest days was intended to serve as a social club in which Civil War veterans could maintain their shooting skills. This instruction in the accurate use of handguns was particularly resonant at this time given the amount of labor unrest in the period—like their ancestors, these Americans could use guns for crime suppression and public safety.[17] Thus, as the NRA grew, it spread a message that gun ownership, whether for purposes of self-defense or sport, was important for every American.[18]

Over time, however, the NRA's mission to educate citizens to own and use guns as a part of their civic duty to the nation evolved into a harder, antigovernment form. Of crucial importance in enacting this change was Harlon Carter. In the 1970s, just before the rise of the contemporary militia movement, Carter led a movement to take control of the NRA. Moving beyond defending the right of citizens to own guns for sport or hunting, Carter's NRA increasingly drew on arguments expressing fear and outrage over the power of the federal government. Like proponents of radical Republican theory at the time of the writing of the U.S. Constitution, the NRA and other gun rights advocates insisted that government was threatening private liberties—especially, of course, the right to own guns. In response, they offered gun ownership as the answer to the question, How can ordinary citizens protect themselves from an increasingly repressive government? Guns could be used to protect individual rights and liberties against the authority of an intrusive government. Like the founding militias, then, contemporary citizens could stare down their government and demand justice and freedom.[19]

This pattern of NRA defense of guns on grounds of personal freedom has become a commonplace in contemporary America. Newspaper editorials, letters to the editor, television talk shows, and websites ranging from the NRA's own to ones less well known, such as www.gunssavelife.com, are awash in similar arguments about the linkage of guns and freedom. Perhaps the most vigorous recent articulation of this theme came from NRA president and actor Charlton Heston in 1997. Making an argument that runs counter to the bulk of historical evidence, Heston insisted, speaking to the National Press Club:

> Just about everything I hope is good about me—who I am, what I've tried to do—can be traced back to those smoking muskets and the radical declaration of independence by those ragtag rebels. Wearing threadbare coats and marching on bleeding feet, they defeated the finest army in the century, and they gave the world hope. Within them flowed an undertow of personal freedom, a relentless sense of what is right, so irresistibly strong they simply could not resist it.[20]

Importantly, guns were central to the militias' accomplishments:

> Our ancestors were armed with pride, and bequeathed it to us—I can prove it. . . . Because there, in that wooden stock and blued steel, is what gives the most common of common men the most uncommon of freedoms. When ordinary hands are free to own this extraordinary, symbolic tool standing for the full measure of human dignity and liberty, that's as good as it gets.
>
> It doesn't matter whether its purpose is to defend our shores or your front door; whether the gun is a rite of passage for a young man or a tool of survival for a young woman; whether it brings meat for the table or trophies for the shelf; without respect to age, or gender, or race, or class, the Second Amendment right to keep and bear arms connects us all— with all that is right—with that sacred document: the Bill of Rights.

"And no amount of oppression," Heston rages, "no FBI, no IRS, no big government, no social engineers, no matter what and no matter who, they cannot cleave the genes we share with our founding fathers."[21] Thus, militia plus guns equal freedom. The individualism and exceptionalism at the core of American political culture is linked to gun ownership as the means by which freedom and liberty can be protected at home while being spread around the world. That this formula has never been true is not the point. Political and social actors from the time of the Revolution to the current day have worked hard to construct it for their own purposes. Thus it is understood to be true and is the mythic stimulus to radical political action even today.

The "American" Militia Myth

To illustrate the way the militia myth has become informed by, and deeply ingrained within, American political culture, the movie *The Patriot* serves as a useful foil. In 2000, Mel Gibson, a quintessential Hollywood good guy in movies ranging from the low-budget *Mad Max* to his Academy Award–winning *Braveheart*, starred in *The Patriot*. Loosely integrating events from the lives and careers of Revolutionary War figures Francis Marion and Daniel Morgan, the movie chronicles the events that lead a reluctant citizen-farmer to join the fight against the British invasion of South Carolina during the American Revolution. It shows the hero, Gibson, begin as an opponent of fighting, organize a militia unit after one of his sons is murdered by a British officer, become the unit's leader, use his skills to win the battle that ends the British advance through the South, and then witness the British surrender at Yorktown. In so doing, whether consciously or not, it also articulates a version of American history and culture that is central to the modern militia movement's identity and self-asserted legitimacy. Accordingly, the movie serves as a useful place from which to summarize and express the continuing power of the militia myth in American political life.

As the film opens, Benjamin Martin (Gibson) is a member of the South Carolina legislature debating whether to send troops to join George Washington's forces in the North. Despite (or perhaps because of) his prior military experience in the French and Indian Wars, Martin is a strong opponent of joining the fighting. He reminds his fellow legislators that the war will be fought among their homes and families, that it is impossible for them to protect their children from the sights and sounds of violence. Instead, he advocates negotiation and peace. Despite the passion of his appeal, he loses.

Once the legislative session is over, Martin emerges from the statehouse to find that his oldest son has joined the force South Carolina is forming to send north. While he is opposed to this choice, Martin accepts it and returns home to his plantation. By implication, he will not bother the British so long as the British do not bother him.

With the British invasion of South Carolina, however, Martin's noninterference policy is shattered. When Martin's oldest son is wounded in a battle near the family homestead, he stumbles home for care. Dozens of other wounded American soldiers also make their way to Martin's plantation. When British forces occupy the plantation, their commander, Colonel Tavington, orders that all American prisoners be killed, that Martin's oldest son be taken to prison and hanged as a spy, and that the plantation be burned. In the ensuing clamor, one of Martin's younger sons is shot in the back and murdered by Colonel Tavington.

In response, Martin undergoes an immediate character transformation. His placid, pacifist self is replaced with righteous rage. He orders his daughters to take the youngest children to a relative's home; he then takes his two oldest remaining sons and attacks the British squad escorting his oldest son to prison. Catching up with this group in the woods, Martin makes use of the skills he had learned in the past and, with the help of his sons, kills all the British soldiers and rescues his oldest son. This killing is brutal, involving not only muskets but axes and knives, as Martin rescues his son from his unjust fate. It is also, the film makes clear, justified as the only way to save a wrongly accused man.

Now a confirmed partisan, Martin organizes a militia that hides in the swamps of coastal South Carolina and makes highly successful, if brutal, hit-and-run raids against British units and supply lines. The militia is mostly composed of farmers who, like Martin, would have preferred to be left alone but who were swept up in the fighting as British forces abused their rights and liberties. In addition, one is a slave who ultimately hopes to win his freedom. Another is a local preacher, linking God to the project of universal human emancipation. As fierce and as angry as these men are, then, the film clearly depicts them as justified in their rage. Such men are not killing for killing's sake. Instead, they are honorable, righteous men motivated to act in defense of their values and freedoms.

In the film, two factors limit the effectiveness of Martin's campaign: the superiority of the organized British military against its American army opponents, and the tactics of the British cavalry commander, Colonel Tavington. British forces defeat the American army in successive battles, and Colonel Tavington's cavalry conducts a savage campaign to punish supporters of Martin's forces. In a penultimate symbol of Tavington's ruthlessness and moral corruption, the film depicts him ordering the inhabitants of a small town into a church, which is then locked and set on fire. In another scene, Tavington kills the son Martin had rescued earlier in the film. This campaign undermines the militia's effectiveness by attacking the civilians who support their operations.

Tavington's tactics do not force the militia to quit, however. Instead, they re-form to avenge their losses. They are driven to defeat the British oppressors who have harmed their lives so completely.

Moreover, the organized American military's fortunes begin to turn when Martin and his militia forces join their operations. While most militiamen are seen to run away after facing the first volley of fire from British troops, Martin's soldiers provide effective service. In the crucial battle that is shown to stem the British advance through the South, for example, Martin conceives a plan in which the militia's propensity to retreat is turned against the British: when Colonel Tavington leads his troops to attack the apparently retreating militia, his cavalry is drawn into a trap and slaughtered. Martin himself kills Tavington with a final, savage bayonet strike through the stomach. Martin's catharsis is evident: having destroyed the evil that Tavington represents, he can go home and enjoy the life he always sought.

Once Cornwallis surrenders, Martin returns home to rebuild his life—a life, it is clear, that he would never have left had the British simply left him alone. Arriving back in South Carolina, he finds his old militia compatriots, including the now-freed former slave, working to rebuild his house. One informs him that they knew they had to start rebuilding the country somewhere, his house seemed like a good place to start. The war, then, is over. Martin can let go of his rage and make a new life and family, free from the prevarications of an oppressor government.

A number of dimensions of *The Patriot* express values, attitudes, and beliefs that appeal to and inspire members of the modern militia movement. Moreover, many of the film's themes are popular within the broad parameters of American political culture. In particular, questions of motives, tactics, and outcome that are central to *The Patriot* are also crucial to understanding the contemporary militias—and the way(s) the new militias have affected and will affect the broader American polity.

In terms of motive, Martin's actions manifest a version of proper political action that will be seen as central to the American political experience—and that modern militia members use to justify their actions and beliefs. Martin, for example, wishes only to be left alone. He has no ambition, no imperial desires. Instead, if he is allowed to farm his land, he will interfere with no one else's life. When aroused by an aggressive, immoral, irredeemable government agent (Colonel Tavington), he is enraged. This rage, however, rather than reducing his ability to act effectively, makes him firm, confident, and successful. But once the source of the rage is gone— in this case, the British army that would not leave him alone—he cares only about returning home and going about his business independent of others' actions. His actions are seen as pragmatic, appropriate, and moral. As such, he is the archetypal individualist— a man interested only in pursuing his personal goals, with no desire to impose his preferences on others.

A second major theme of *The Patriot* that is culturally relevant and serves as a foundation for modern militia action and ideology is that of tactics. The American army, importantly, is shown to be overmatched. When American forces confront well-disciplined, experienced British forces, they nearly always lose. The militias, however, when properly used, are a powerful and effective force. This means that when militia forces are included as part of conventional stand-and-shoot battle plans, they tend to fail. But when unleashed to harass enemy lines of communication and supply, the militias are very effective. Even the mighty British army—argued to be the most powerful, most experienced and best trained army of the era—cannot handle the militias. Indeed, it is because of the army's frustration with the local militias that Lord Cornwallis, commander of the British army, is seen to unleash Colonel Tavington's antimilitia raids. The militias, then, can counter, frustrate, and challenge the power of even the world's most powerful military.

The Patriot also teaches that not only can militia tactics be annoying but they can also defeat a well-organized, powerful foe. For example, Colonel Tavington's antimilitia raids ultimately fail. Even his cruel step of murdering a village full of civilians by burning them to death in their church does not deter the militia's activities. Instead, a reinvigorated militia eventually defeats Tavington and exploits its predilection for fleeing the battlefield to draw the British into the trap that checks their advance through the South. Despite the power and viciousness of the enemy, then, militia tactics can lead to victory.

Cumulatively, *The Patriot* takes the liberalism and exceptionalism of American political culture and links them to the Revolutionary myth of the militia all over again. Martin as mythic hero— and thus a cultural example of ideal behavior and values—is an individualist and a democrat. He believes in the power of hard work and individual morality. His courage provides a model around which his community can form for action. He has a vision of the proper structure of society and is willing to act aggressively, even ragefully, to defend and construct his preferred way of life. Then, at the height of his power, his innate goodness and trustworthiness demonstrate themselves and he goes home, leaving behind the trappings of power he accepted only as a necessity. He will again be what he apparently always wanted to be: a gentleman farmer, husband, and father—an American icon.

The militia myth, then, makes sense in the context of American political culture. It is constructed in, and shaped by, terms and values inherent within the broader U.S. political culture. It promotes an understanding of what it means to be a "good" American that, as the succeeding chapters of this book make clear, motivates action in line with evaluative criteria that are clear and powerful for modern militia members. Thus, since contemporary militia members believe these "right" values to be under assault from other parts of the political system, they wish to impose sanctions on the broader community in order to promote their idealized polity. Ultimately, the existence and activities of the modern American militia movement are a sign that the Revolution is not over. Its values, or at least a version of its values, remain points of pride, contention, and action for many Americans. It is for this reason that the rest of this book examines how and why this Revolutionary story has, and will, influence American politics for years to come.

3

Friction:
Militia Ideology and
the Rationalization of Rage

It is to the task of understanding the ideology of the contemporary militia movement that this chapter is dedicated. As will be seen, this ideology is linked to a tradition of right-wing populism in the United States; however, it contains some characteristics, particularly its advocacy of gun ownership and violent resistance to government authority, that deserve special attention. Moreover, militia ideology has the potential to significantly influence U.S. politics given both its dimensions and its cultural location. Militia ideology may seem absurd to most Americans, but it makes sense to militia members. It also makes sense to millions of other Americans. Unless this fact is recognized, the militia movement cannot be understood.

Dimensions of Ideology
in Right-Wing Populist Movements

To speak of "right-wing" ideology opens up a number of Pandora's boxes in the realm of ideology studies, and while it is not the purpose of this chapter to provide an exhaustive critique of ideology and right-wing politics, some definition of terms and concepts will be useful here. In general, following Sara Diamond, "right wing" is used to refer to those groups that generally support the state as an enforcer of political, social, and economic order but that oppose the state when its policies promote the distribution of wealth and power downward through society.[1] This careful definition recognizes that so-called right-wing groups may oppose the state under certain conditions and admits a wide range of groups to the general category of rightist organizations: for example, the Ku Klux Klan, white supremacists, militias, John Birchers, Christian conservatives, and, importantly (see chapter 7), conservative members of the Republican Party. Thus, while this book examines the militia version of right-wing ideology in America, militia ideology should not be taken to represent the whole range of rightist ideologies in American politics. Moreover, as will be examined in more detail in chapter 7, the common foundation and theoretical linkages among militia and other right-wing ideologies make the militia movement more influential than it perhaps would otherwise be.

In addition to a common position regarding appropriate (and inappropriate) government action, rightist ideologies—particularly those with a populist tone—can be seen to share additional characteristics that link them across groups. Chip Berlet and Matthew N. Lyons have recently outlined a useful set of dimensions that right-wing populist ideologies generally share. *Producerism* is the delineation of those who are productive in society versus those who are not, with the obvious political effect that producers are good, while others are not. *Demonization and scapegoating* are interactive concepts in which some "other" is dehumanized and then blamed for the bad things that occur in individuals' lives. *Conspiracism* elevates the scapegoat to the role of an organized plotter engaged in systematic acts of evil to deny rights and freedoms to the "good" people in society. Finally, *apocalyptic narratives and millennial visions* presage the holy war that many groups believe is necessary to purge the evil from social life and promote the coming of the new age.[2] While not all rightist groups share all of these ideological characteristics in the same intensity, they all tend to embody significant components of these dimensions, linking them together through multiple points of agreement.

As a last point of introduction, populism can be defined as a movement in which groups promote the people as the ideal moral and political force in society even as they express hatred of—and indeed often scapegoat—the elite.[3] In this tradition, ordinary citizens are seen as just and trustworthy; however, elites pervert the decent and moral intentions of the mass to serve some power-hungry, narrow purpose. Importantly, populist movements can emerge from the left, right, or center of the political spectrum. This book focuses on one right-wing populist movement, the militia, and its interconnections with other groups and dimensions of American politics. It should not be assumed, however, that *all* populist groups are right-wing.

Combined, these discussions of right-wing politics, populism, and the characteristics of rightist ideologies can serve as a useful starting place for an examination of contemporary militia ideology. Moving immediately into such a project, however, would lead to a lack of attention to the historical and theoretical foundations on which militia members build their worldview. While this book does not intend to provide a comprehensive history of right-wing movements in America, social movement theory makes it clear that it is important to understand that the particular dimensions of militia ideology emerged from a specific context. A description of this context is crucial to understanding both contemporary militia ideology and its relationship with broader patterns of American political life. Accordingly, a brief history of rightist movements in the United States is offered here so that the particular genesis and motives of the militia can be understood better.

Right-Wing Populist Movements in American History

While Berlet and Lyons argue that the Jacksonian era (1820s–1850s) constitutes the first example of rightist populism in post-Revolutionary U.S. political history, the rise of the Ku Klux Klan (KKK)—a racist, antigovernment group whose ideology drew supporters from a broad spectrum of U.S. society both in the South and elsewhere—after the Civil War provides a better model of early right-wing populism on the militia model. The first Klan, organized in Pulaski, Tennessee, in 1865 or 1866, insisted that racial segregation was just, argued that any African Americans who exercised authority or took property constituted a threat to the "proper" social order, and resisted federal "reconstruction" of the South. Northerners became the scapegoats for the overturning of the social and political order associated with Reconstruction. Since the Union army could not be attacked after the war ended, the Klan manifested its anger and rage against the beneficiaries of federal intervention: blacks. While the Klan's founder, former Confederate general Nathan Bedford Forrest, formally disbanded the Klan in 1869, claiming that its purpose had been "perverted" by racists more intent on savagery than defending the appropriate social order, the pattern of scapegoating by race and hating central government authority had been set for subsequent groups' use.[4]

In the decades that followed, other racist and ethnocentrist movements rose in the United States. Whether it was the anti-Chinese movement of the late nineteenth century,[5] or the imposition of temperance and associated values on central and south European immigrants at the turn of the twentieth century,[6] various groups have promoted views that scapegoat often powerless groups and seek to impose "right" values on them. Then, when post-Darwinian ideas of "race suicide" were introduced during the Progressive Era, leaders such as Theodore Roosevelt worried that white people might be losing their strength and capacity to rule the world as they were exhausted in the burgeoning factories built during the industrial revolution.[7] Scapegoating by race was thus a well-entrenched dimension of right-wing populist thought by the turn of the twentieth century.

Right-wing populist ideologies added anticommunist, anti-immigrant, pro-fascist, and anti-civil-rights components to their theories during World War I. The rise of communism, the integration of African Americans into the industrial labor force in the North, the passing of repressive, "pro-American" anti-immigration and sedition laws by both federal and state governments, and the emergence of fascism provided concepts and language that right-wing populists could use to define their political ideals and shape their political actions. Thus, for example, groups like the American Legion articulated near-fascist views of the importance of white racial supremacy and military preparedness even as they insisted that Jews and Communists were making an assault on the kinds of traditional values whites held most dear. Similarly, the Federal Bureau of Investigation (FBI) under J. Edgar Hoover became an institution convinced that "America" was under attack from Communist infiltrators and acted as if any protest—even civil rights or union protest—could only occur under Communist, and often Jewish, sponsorship.[8] (Interestingly, the FBI would adopt the same position during the 1960s civil rights protests—it investigated protesters, rather than the crimes committed against protesters—on the grounds that the protests were Communist-sponsored efforts to undermine the American regime.)[9] The second Ku Klux Klan was also formed in this period, and, while race remained its central focus, its ideology expanded to include a defense of "Americanism" against immigrants, Jews, and any group not white, Protestant, and of north-European heritage. Thus, an ideology that had been focused largely on internal enemies in the nineteenth century was adapted to recognize the international position—and vulnerability—of the United States in world affairs.[10]

Movements since World War I have continued to emphasize the role of international actors in undermining American life. For example, Henry Ford expressed his racist and anti-Semitic views by using one of his newspapers, the *Dearborn Independent*, to publish articles derived from the forged anti-Semitic work *The Protocols of the Elders of Zion;* a collection of these articles published under the title *The International Jew* sold over five hundred thousand copies in the 1920s. Similarly, he used his factories to socialize workers into proper "American" attitudes: foreign-born workers were taught English and appropriate political values in Ford-run schools. Such actions, he thought, were crucial to defending America from its potential demise.[11]

The New Deal period, too, was suffused with rightist populist thought. In its earliest days, Franklin Roosevelt scapegoated big business as the foundation of the contemporary economic crisis—a typically leftist position. However, many of his programs, most notably the National Recovery Administration, included controls on labor in terms of employment rights, freedom to organize into unions, and wage limits. During the same period, the radio priest Father Coughlin, who began his career as a political liberal, combined anti-Semitism with antiunionism to build a model of a corporatist state in which all members participated and kept their place: a core element of fascism. Similarly, groups like the Liberty League and the KKK argued that Jews and Communists were responsible for the stark economic state of affairs. Even the anti-interventionist movement that delayed U.S. entry into World War II was grounded on right-wing populist thought: the United States must stay out of the war, the anti-interventionists argued, because it was only by defending properly American values at home that the nation could avoid being corrupted by alien cultures.[12]

   The rise of the Cold War and its associated competition between
the West and the Soviet bloc provided the next impetus for right
wing populism in the United States. Practiced by Joseph McCarthy
during the Red Scare of the 1940s and 1950s, its ideology was espoused aggressively by the John Birch Society and the Liberty
Lobby. Rightist thought in this period took core ideas derived from
fascism, Henry Ford, and *The Protocols of the Elders of Zion* and developed conspiratorial explanations of contemporary U.S. social
and political problems. For Birchers, collectivism associated with
megacorporations was destroying the natural liberty that the pio-
neer lifestyle had engendered among Americans. Instead of individuals doing for themselves, Americans were being dominated by
business and intellectual elites more interested in the needs of international capital than of the American people. Then, building on
the ideological foundation laid by Henry Ford, fascists, and others,
Birchers claimed that Communists dominated the international
conspiracy—although they did not blame the Jews. Instead, it was
the Liberty Lobby that added anti-Semitism to the international
conspiracy in the American context, claiming, with Ford and the
Protocols, that Jewish control of the international banking order
gave them the power to manipulate the international political
order to their benefit and against the interests of ordinary Americans.[13]

   Cumulatively, the historical elements of right-wing populist ideology outlined so far—anti-Semitism, anti-Communism, racism,
ethnocentrism, individualism, and conspiracism—can be labeled
the "old" right. From the 1820s through the 1970s, right-wing populist movements combined different elements of these strains of
thought in varying combinations to create their particular version
of the "right" political and social order. Starting in the 1970s, however, innovative elements emerged in right-wing populist thought
derived from fundamentalist and evangelical Christianity. React-
ing to the rise of secular humanist politics in the 1960s and 1970s
that had led to government decisions like the ending of prayer in
school and the constitutional protection of abortion rights, evangelical and fundamentalist Christians began to participate in politics to promote their preferred policies. Importantly, they combined
several dimensions of old right thought with a religious spirit in
advancing their program. Thus the international conspiracy of
old—Jews and Communists—was understood to be an explicitly

secular effort to undermine America's true, Christian heritage. Similarly, collective business structures like megacorporations that were the source of John Birch Society concerns about the destruction of natural American liberty and freedom became central components of Christian right thought as fundamentalists and evangelicals came to believe that such corporations were the agents of secular values and so were part of the international conspiracy against their ideal America.[14]

In addition to linking traditional conservative values with religious dictates, the Christian right introduced apocalypticism and millennialism to right-wing populist ideologies. Millennialism refers to the end times, the time when the Antichrist is to rise, according to Christian doctrine, and Armageddon—the Apocalypse—is to occur. Armageddon is a good thing for Christians since it signals the return of Christ and his kingdom on earth. However, Christians differ as to whether Christ will return only after Armageddon (postmillennialists) or will return only when Christians have taken action to establish and enforce Christ's law on earth (premillennialists). Premillennialists tend to argue that Christian values must be imposed on the world at large, since such imposition is actually an act of love: by establishing Christian law in practice, premillennialists insist, they are helping sinners enter the Kingdom of Heaven.[15]

One other dimension of much of Christian right thought deserves consideration here: its racism and anti-Semitism. Some extreme strains of Christian theology, such as Christian Identity and Catholic Marianism, argue that whites are God's chosen people, that Jews are the agents of Satan, and that an international conspiracy of Jews and others are attempting to destroy white Christians on behalf of the Antichrist.[16] Such values are obviously closely related to those of old-right conservatism and have provided another link between activists of the old and new right.

A last, non-Christian development in rightist populist ideology deserves discussion: the rise of survivalists and white supremacists in the 1970s and 1980s. These two groups took many elements from both old- and new-right thought, added materials relevant to contemporary politics, and formed a new branch of right-wing populism in the United States. Survivalists, for example, linked apparent Soviet expansionism in places like Nicaragua, Angola, and Afghanistan to the continuing chaos in American cities—crime, drugs, and, not coincidentally, racial and ethnic diversity—and created an apocalyptic vision of the nation's likely future that clearly related to that of the Christian millennialists. The world would soon come to an end in a nuclear nightmare, survivalists held; only those who escaped to rural areas and prepared for Armageddon would survive both the war and the teeming hordes of crazed urbanites that would invade the heartland once the war had ended. White supremacists similarly linked the crime and drug problems of the nation's diverse urban centers with the federal government's largely successful efforts to destroy the KKK during the 1970s. For white supremacists, the government was a conspirator in destroying the racial and political superiority of "real"—white—Americans. Thus white Americans needed to resist the egalitarian policies of the government and needed to work to protect the racial purity and superiority of the white race. Only then, supremacists argued, could America be saved from its corrupted government.[17]

While many Americans might prefer to think that the various movements described in this section are deviations from "normal" American politics and values, they are not. Right-wing populist groups have simply taken the material of American political culture and constructed it in ways to promote their racist, ethnocentric, and religious values. For example, individualism suffuses each of the movements described here: it is individuals, not the government, who are seen as responsible for protecting their well-being and status, for example. Indeed, government actions aimed at softening the suffering or difficulties of individuals—bilingual education, civil rights laws, affirmative action, or even simple welfare—are used as evidence that the government has a plan to destroy the "real" liberty of the deserving, hardworking class of (white) Americans on behalf of undeserving, unproductive racial minorities and ethnic newcomers. Moreover, the millennialism of Christian thought neatly links to the exceptionalism of American political culture: the conflict over government policies becomes a struggle for control of the destiny of all of humanity in the continual story of good versus evil. Individualism and exceptionalism, then, stand at the core of right-wing populist thought. Such groups, as social movement theory suggests, both are framed by, and find life within, the context of the culture from which they emerge.

It is in the context of this history of right-wing populist ideology that militia thought must be understood. As will be seen, much of militia ideology parallels, draws on, and is informed by rightist populist thinking. However, militia members have added new dimensions, like the sanctity of the "sovereign" citizen and the primacy of armed resistance to government, to this intellectual tradition. These new ideas, mated to principles that have broad significance throughout U.S. society and to institutions like the conservative wing of the Republican Party, have the potential to influence the entire political system well into the future.

Militia Ideology

As was noted in chapter 1, Paul Ricoeur suggests that, when analyzing ideology, it is important to focus on its distortive, legitimating, and integrative functions.[18] Within the terms of this project, it is also important to link the content of specific ideologies to the cultural conditions that support their construction. This section will undertake such a task in relation to militia ideology, particularly focusing on the ways militia members describe the world of politics (distortion), justify their existence (legitimation), and promote their ideal vision of the way things ought to be (integration). These factors will then be linked back to the model of American public political culture offered in chapter 1.

Before beginning this examination, however, it is important to admit that accessing a set of core texts from which to derive militia ideology is not really possible. Unlike traditional political theory, where thinkers' works are usually compiled in books and articles that are generally accessible to others for review and commentary, most militia thought is expressed by diverse individuals in varying formats ranging from the Internet to newspapers to speeches made at group meetings. Thus, a central problem in interpreting militia thought is gaining access to appropriate texts for consideration.

Further, as is suggested by the review of right-wing populism in U.S. history offered above, militia thought inevitably links to, draws on, and blurs into other traditions from traditional conservatism to racist xenophobia. Determining that a text is an example of militia thought alone is difficult at best. This is particularly the case with a line of thinking associated with, but arguably separate from, militia ideology: the Patriot or common law movement.

Accordingly, it is important to decide how one is going to access and interpret militia thought within these complicating conditions.

Here, the question of access is largely answered through use of the Internet. Major militia groups, such as the Militia of Montana (MOM) and the Michigan Militia, have had a constant Internet presence since the movement rose in the early 1990s. Hundreds of other Internet sites exist, and while they may all be created by individuals representing separate groups, there is a remarkable degree of coherence among the sites in terms of the values they advocate and the programs they promote. These sites, in combination with interviews in newspapers, magazines, and other sources, constitute a set of texts available for interpretation and review. All such information will be appropriately cited throughout this chapter for anyone interested in following or challenging the interpretations offered.

The question of whether the text comes from a "militia" group or something else is answered by arguing that the notion of scientifically separating a militia text from other types of rightist ideologies is largely inappropriate. Indeed, the likely influence of the militia movement in U.S. politics and culture derives from its interconnections with other right-wing groups and institutions. Specific interpretations may be subject to challenge—this is the point of providing appropriate citations for the information presented. Keeping clear lines of demarcation among groups whose ideologies interact would miss much of the richness and significance of militia populism.

Distortion

According to Ricoeur, distortion is the process by which ideologies shape empirical reality to fit defined conditions and parameters. In other words, ideology misrepresents the real world. Importantly, distortion in this context is not meant as a pejorative term. Instead, since *all* ideologies necessarily mold reality to fit the parameters of the theory, and since everyone has an ideology, it follows that no one or group understands "truth" in the face of others' lies. Distortion is used as an analytic concept, as a way of drawing attention to the specific patterns of meaning individuals who share an ideological perspective ascribe to events, actions, ideas, and values.[19]

The specific distortions central to militia ideology center on three themes. The first is the corruption of the proper role and scope of powers of the U.S. federal government. The second is the rights and powers of individuals in political affairs. The third is the power and significance of armed resistance in American political history.

The Shadow Government and the Conspiracy to Destroy America

In simple terms, militia ideology holds that agents of what is variously termed the "Shadow Government" or the "New World Order" have corrupted the government of the United States. Evidence for this corruption is, for militia members, evident in the overreaching policies that the federal government has enacted since the end of the Civil War. Cumulatively, militia ideology insists that agents of the Shadow Government have perverted the institutions of American government away from their original purposes. Accordingly, American government has become illegitimate and must be resisted.

As evidenced in websites and interviews, militia members argue that "the Constitution that has protected our rights and liberties for more than 200 years is now in greater danger of being overthrown than at any time in our history." But it is not "Drug lords . . . Terrorists. . . . Hungry hordes of foreigners . . . Economic or ecological collapse . . . Nuclear proliferation" or "Space aliens" that is the source of this threat to American governance. Instead, it is government itself: "We have the evidence that for more than 60 years much of the legislation that has been passed, and much of what officials have done, is in substantial violation of the Constitution. Federal and State governments, especially the Federal, have assumed powers that have no foundation whatsoever in any of the provisions of the Constitution."[20]

As outlined by the militia, the federal government has inappropriately expanded its powers in the face of the many complex problems it has faced: war, communism, civil rights, and the like. Acts like the passage of the Fourteenth Amendment; the creation of the income tax in the Sixteenth Amendment; legislation creating the Federal Reserve Bank; the policies and programs associated with the New Deal; the centralization of political, economic, and military authority under federal control during World War II; the development of the national security state as the Cold War took

shape in the post–World War II years; the rise of centralized national media controlled by only a few major corporations; and the
civil rights movement gave the agents of the Shadow Government
opportunities to expand the powers of the national government
beyond the limited boundaries originally intended by the
Founders.[21] (The specific understanding of the proper role of the
federal government offered by the militia will be addressed later in
this section.)

Take, for example, the concept of emergency powers. Adopted
by Congress through established institutional procedures to provide government with the power necessary to respond to crises like
war (including a nuclear strike) and national disasters like floods
or tornadoes and for other purposes, emergency powers are, for
militia members, nothing but a pretext for the expansion of the federal government's authority into the private lives of ordinary citizens. "They have adopted legislation such as an amendment to the
Trading with the Enemy Act and various Presidential directives
such as the 1933 War and Emergency Power Order which treat the
People as the enemy of the Government, and orders which illegally seek to suspend the Constitution under ill-defined 'emergen-
cies.'" Or, as the same document later explains, "They have adopted secret legislation and appropriations of funds, and kept official
activities and documents secret, ostensibly for the purpose of 'national security' but in fact often for the purpose of concealing their
crimes and preventing the prosecution thereof."[22]

Other apparently innocuous developments in U.S. legal and constitutional traditions are also seen as tools for the inappropriate expansion of federal power. Clauses of the Constitution such as the
ones that allow Congress to regulate interstate commerce have
been warped by the Shadow Government to its insidious ends:
"They have exceeded their limited authority to regulate interstate
commerce to improperly encompass prohibition thereof, criminal
prosecution for violations, or to regulate or prohibit activities that
are not commercial, or have not yet crossed a state boundary . . . or
which 'affect' interstate commerce."[23] Similarly, treaty commit-
ments to foreign governments or—worst of all—the United Nations, are seen as "selling out" the American way of life: "Doing
nothing assures domination to the United Nations. Communism
will achieve its dream of ruling the world. We know this because
the New World Order, the beast of Revelation 13, appears in an-

other prophecy in Revelation 17. In Revelation 17:3 the beast is red. Red is used by God in another prophecy on Communism. And why not? Red is the official color denoting Communism—Red China, and Red Russia."[24]

Perhaps no other policy exemplifies federal government abuse of authority better than gun control. Militia members insist gun ownership is legal. They also argue that any government attempt to limit gun ownership is an unconstitutional trampling of fundamental political rights. Finally, and most ominously, militia ideology holds that unless the people have guns, government can abuse human rights and individual liberties.

The militia theory of the legality of gun ownership centers on a creative interpretation of the Second Amendment to the U.S. Constitution. Rights, for example, are seen as sacrosanct: "[R]ights are God-given and governments are formed to protect rights, not to grant them or take them away." Consequently, "the right to bear arms is not something that the government can legitimately legislate away through gun regulation, registration, licensing, taxation, or prohibition."[25] Thus, the right to keep and bear arms is absolute, and no amendatory clause— "A well regulated militia, being necessary to the security of a free state," the first clause of the Second Amendment—can limit that right:

> Infringe means to encroach upon and does not necessarily mean to totally do away with. There are many ways that the right to keep and bear arms can be infringed: regulation limits gun ownership by controlling the production and sales of firearms. Licensing means that an individual is permitted to own or carry weapons. Registration means that an individual's possession of a particular weapon with a serial number is recorded. (Gun businesses are regulated, gun owners are licensed, and guns themselves are registered.) Taxation restricts gun ownership, particularly among the poor, by increasing the cost. Prohibition is either an outright ban of gun possession or the limitation of guns that can be bought.[26]

The right to own guns, then, is basic, and no government action may interfere with this right.

This dry, dispassionate accounting of the foundation of gun rights in America does not really capture the intensity with which militia members advocate their rights to ownership and their hatred of government intervention against this right. More often than providing detailed legal justifications of gun ownership, militia websites and commentators articulate a vision in which a populace stripped of guns is laid helpless before a hateful, vicious government. Many sites make claims similar to, or in fact directly link to, a site titled "Gun Control and the First Million Mom March." This site presents rhetorically inflammatory language regarding the evils of gun control while linking prior efforts at gun limitation to events like the Holocaust, Stalin's massacres in the Soviet Union, and other examples of genocide worldwide. "All You Squeamish Bleeding Hearts—Pay Attention!!!!" the site rages. "Puke or pee in your pants if you must, but Pay Attention!!!!" This demand is followed by pictures, ostensibly from German sources, of naked men and women waiting to be slaughtered in the Holocaust. The caption describing these pictures reads: "Their disarmed husbands were sent to Nazi labor camps. Then these terrified moms, many holding babies, were forced to wait in line before being slaughtered by German soldiers and Ukrainian collaborators." Lest readers miss the point, the caption continues: "On May 14, 2000, the so-called 'Million Moms' marched to stop civilians from owning guns. Here's what happens when they get their wish"—the site then shows Holocaust victims in a mass grave. "These moms paid the price for gun control," the caption concludes.[27]

Militia ideology links more than just the Holocaust to gun control. The following extended quote demonstrates the breadth of their understanding of the significance of gun ownership in defending individual life and liberty.

Well over 56 million innocent civilians have been murdered, and billions have been "neutralized" in fear of brutalization by their governments this last century as a result of "Gun Control" laws . . . .

CONSIDER THIS . . . This is just part of the known tally. . . .

In 1929 the Soviet Union established gun control. From 1929 to 1953, approximately 20 million dissidents, unable to defend themselves, were rounded up and exterminated.

In 1911, Turkey established gun control. From 1915–1917, 1.5 million Armenians, unable to defend themselves, were rounded up and exterminated.

Germany established gun control in 1938 and from 1939 to 1945, 13 million Jews, gypsies, homosexuals, the mentally ill, and others, who were unable to defend themselves, were rounded up and exterminated.

China established gun control in 1935. From 1948 to 1952, 20 million political dissidents, unable to defend themselves, were rounded up and exterminated.

Guatemala established gun control in 1964. From 1964 to 1981, 100,000 Mayan Indians, unable to defend themselves, were exterminated.

Uganda established gun control in 1970. From 1971 to 1979, 300,000 Christians, unable to defend themselves, were rounded up and exterminated.

Cambodia established gun control in 1956. From 1975 to 1977, one million "educated" people, unable to defend themselves, were rounded up and exterminated.

That places total victims who lost their lives because of gun control at approximately 56 million in the last century. Since we should learn from the mistakes of history, the next time someone talks in favor of gun control, find out which group of citizens they wish to have exterminated.[28]

Militia ideology makes it clear that the United States is not exempt from this problem of corrupted governments slaughtering their own citizens. First, many sites insist that modern gun control legislation is grounded on similar legislation passed in Nazi Germany in 1938.[29] Further, as was noted earlier, the federal government is depicted as an evil, power-seeking entity controlled by corrupt agents of the New World Order: "When a government no longer fears the people, atrocities become possible such as the murder of members of Randy Weaver's family by U.S. Marshals and FBI agents. Emboldened by the lack of resistance when murdering women and children in Idaho, the Feds moved to Waco, Texas and slaughtered nearly 100 people, including four of their own agents."[30] "It's time to state it plainly," another site asserts,

guns in the hands of honest citizens save lives and property and, yes, gun-control laws only affect the law-abiding citizens. Take action before it's too late, write or call your State and Federal Representatives and Senators.

It ain't about controlling guns in the hands of criminals, folks, it is about CONTROL of you and me by the REAL CRIMINALS—The International Oligarchy!! ULTIMATE CONTROL!!

Defend Liberty and the Constitution for the United States of America and the Second Article of Amendment! Your very life depends on it!!![31]

"Had the Feds feared a militia as active as the one in Lexington on

April 19, 1775," notes a different site, "it is entirely possible that the massacre of Branch Davidians in Waco, Texas on April 19, 1993 would never have occurred. Long live the militia! Long live freedom! Long live government that fears the people!"[32]

Taken together, the increase in federal government power in the twentieth century has created a condition in which the American dream has been perverted into a totalitarian nightmare, according to militia ideology. "What had developed was beginning to look more and more like the system of political control that prevailed in the Soviet Union, in which the real decisions of government were made not by the official organs of government, but by the parallel structure of the Communist Party, backed by the KGB. In competing with the Soviets, we had taken on their methods and attributes of political control."[33] Or, in a pick-your-totalitarian-state-as-founder argument, another site exclaims, the federal government is Nazi-inspired:

> The National Socialists and their offspring, the Democratic Party of today in the 21st century, have called for nearly all of the "uplifts" brought into play over the last 68 years and unctuously baptized as the "New Deal"—employment by the United States for the unemployed, help from the Federal Treasury for the needy, public improvements to provide work, nationalization of utilities and some industries, "development" of many fields not before thought to be within the competence of government, insurance for health, accident, old age, death, and other things insurable, and practically anything else that anybody wanted.
>
> "A Chicken in every pot!!" (While they totally raided the henhouse ⁄ and financially enslaved the entire population of the nation.)[34]

Ultimately, then:

> Our government has adopted its own policy in complete disregard to our Constitution and Bill of Rights that government is to be served by the people, rather than the government serving the people. The Government has assumed the role of a dictatorship, telling the people only what the bureaucracy thinks the people need to know. We have become a controlled society. Every aspect of our lives fall under government control media: radio, television, newspapers, education, food, religion, medicine, health, utilities, industry, commerce, finance, insurance, standing armies, law enforcement, courts, and taxes. We have been conditioned to accept the socialist principles of communism fed to us by the

federal government, which now enshrines our local churches, school boards, city governments, county and state governments.[35]

The mechanism by which this Shadow Government maintains control is the occupation of key positions throughout government, the economy, and public life. "Shadow control . . . consists largely of the placement of shadow agents in key positions in all of the institutions that are to be controlled."[36] These include significant executive, legislative, and judicial branch positions; the staffs that support these positions; the intelligence agencies; military agencies; the Internal Revenue Service; police departments; major corporations, especially banks, insurance agencies, public utilities, security services, and credit bureaus; major media, both print and broadcast; communications networks like telephone and satellite services; organized crime; educational institutions, especially higher education; public interest groups focusing on civil rights, gender rights, and labor issues; international organizations like the United Nations, the International Monetary Fund, and NATO (the North Atlantic Treaty Organization); and select foreign governments. Cumulatively, the Shadow Government is seen to "bring most of the assets and revenues of the economy under the control of fewer and fewer people."[37] With such power, then, the relatively few people who are inside the conspiracy can manipulate hundreds of millions of people in ways that undermine individual rights in favor of the new oligarchy.

Why does this conspiracy exist? Among other reasons, militia ideology argues that the Shadow Government seeks "the disarming of the people." This would be a precursor to the overthrow of American democracy itself: "There are indications that after things settled down, the Shadow Government would allow the establishment of a parliamentary system that would provide a façade of democracy. . . . Such a system is not a republican form of government, based on the Rule of Law, or a representative democracy, but merely a tool for control by an oligarchy." Then, with their power augmented by "the development and use of mind control technologies, both electronic and chemical, which allow the elite to disable or discredit dissidents and keep the people compliant and productive," the Shadow Government can enact any evil plan its members can concoct: "There is also suspicious circumstantial evidence that part of the plan is the release of diseases, of which

HIV/AIDS is one, to reduce world population, selectively."[38] In the end, then, militia ideology insists that the federal government has become the enemy of the American people.

Limits on the Federal Government: Sovereign Citizens
and Constitutional Intent

An additional distortion embodied in militia thought involves the proper role of the federal government in political life, especially in relation to the true rights and freedoms of particular—usually white and male—citizens. In simple terms, militia groups argue that the federal government was created with limited powers, and no change to those powers can be legitimate without an amendment of the Constitution—and in some cases, not even then. This is particularly the case in relation to the rights of sovereign citizens, those individuals whose rights the Constitution was intended to protect, that never can be violated.

As outlined in militia thought, the federal government was understood to have a very limited role in the lives of American citizens. Focusing extensive attention on the Tenth Amendment, which states, "The powers not delegated to the United States by the Constitution, nor prohibited to it by the States, are reserved to the States respectively, or to the people," militia groups offer very simplistic analyses of constitutional interpretation, reinterpretation, original intent, and authority. As one site puts it:

> In Judge Cooley's Book, Constitutional Limitations, on page 706 it says: "In the American Constitutional system, the power to establish the ordinary police regulations has been left with the individual States and it cannot be taken from them, either wholly or in part, and exercised under legislation of Congress. Neither can the National Government through any of its departments and officers, assume any supervision of police regulations of the States."
>
> What is meant by 'police powers'? The States' powers were health, education, welfare, family affairs and police protection. . . . Collectively they are referred to as 'the police powers of the States.' Clearly and unmistakably our founding fathers intended the States to be in full control of health, education, welfare and police protection, and not subject to federal government interference.[39]

Or, as another site puts it, while the federal government is granted certain powers by the Constitution—for example, to regulate interstate commerce and immigration, to fix the standards of weights and measures, to coin money, to pay the debt, to raise and employ military forces, and, significantly, to "lay and collect import duties"—the government is also denied significant powers, of which the primary one is "[n]o exercise of powers not delegated to it by the Constitution."[40]

Militia ideology backs up this "strict constructionist" interpretation of constitutional law with an interesting understanding of limitations on the amendment process. For the militia, no interpretation or amendment that violates the original intent of the founders can be legitimate even if it is passed through legal channels:

> In Article V there is the right to amend but not to make new. It would not be an amendment to abolish the Constitution and adopt the Communist Manifesto or the laws of another country. An amendment has to be germane to the instrument; it must be something already in the Constitution or it fails the test of an amendment. . . .
>
> What this means is, no one can alter the 10th Amendment nor twist it to suit their own purpose, nor can the federal government constitutionally and legally do anything which is not in its delegated powers.[41]

Thus, whether passed by constitutional amendment or legal interpretation, policies like the income tax, federal enforcement of civil rights law, the abandonment of the gold standard, or other "modern" government programs like welfare are unconstitutional because they violate the intent of the founders:

> It may be argued that these actions were taken by 'duly elected' or appointed officials on behalf of the people. To this we say no governing body, who have taken an oath to protect and defend the constitution, has the right or the authority to alter or change the express directives of that constitution, except by means provided for within the constitution itself. Changes in the name of 'States of Emergency,' 'Executive Order,' 'Treaties,' 'Initiatives,' 'Acts,' 'Proclamation,' 'Presidential Directives,' 'Strategic Alliances,' or any other avenue outside of constitutional amendment, properly ratified by the people of the several States, represent a violation of oath of office and establishes those involved as enemies of 'We the People.' In addition, no governing body or majority can amend or legislate away the unalienable rights of the people in any case without the original intent of the founders, who themselves broke from a government that was involved in the same, being stimulated in the hearts, minds and actions of the liberty loving segments of the citizenry.[42]

This vision of limited government is further linked to an understanding of the particular rights and freedoms held by a special
class of citizens—sovereign citizens. Sovereign citizens are those
whose forebears entered into the social contract that created the
U.S. Constitution: "The Republic has Citizens of its own called
American Nationals. Those are the Sovereign Citizens who qualify
as such by being Members of the Posterity referred to in the Pre-
amble and can only be the Natural Born or Naturalized White Inhabitants of each state whose forefathers delegated by solemn
agreement certain powers to the Congress of the 'United States.'"[43]
(The tension between militia groups' insistence that they are not
racist and this vision of the demographic characteristics of the sovereign citizen will be addressed in the last section of this chapter.)
Such citizens hold a unique position in the polity in that they are
not bound by the laws of the national government since their true
identity was as citizens of states that merely delegated powers to
the national authority: "By metaphysical refinement, in examining
our form of government, it might be correctly said that there is no
such thing as a citizen of the United States. . . . In the Constitution
for the United States, the term was used to identify state Citizens
who were eligible under the suffrage laws to hold office, and they
were required under the Constitution to have primary allegiance to
one of the several states."[44] Thus, since states originally had the
right to nullify acts of the federal government (an argument militia
members assert to be true with little legal grounding), federal laws
that violate the contract between the government and the "posterity" of the founders cannot apply to citizens of states that made the
original constitution.[45] At most, militia ideology holds, the federal
government has authority over territory it directly controls—that
is, the District of Columbia—or over people, like African Americans, who have become citizens of the United States since the adop-
tion of Constitution.[46] Others must be left alone by the national
government.

Ultimately, then, it is not the national government, or the state
governments, or the Supreme Court, or political practice, or any
other force that determines the proper limit on federal government
authority over the lives of private citizens. It is sovereign citizens
who, as the posterity of the original contract makers, get to decide
what is and is not appropriate government action. Moreover, anything that these sovereign citizens decide is inappropriate is, ipso

facto, wrong, unconstitutional, and corrupt—an assault on the fundamental values of the nation. Thus, as was discussed earlier, the importance of guns in militia thought: when attacked, one has the right of self-defense, and in the case of American politics, one's defensive acts will have the additional virtue of reestablishing the nation on its true and righteous path.

The Power of Armed Resistance

A final noteworthy distortion expressed in militia ideology is an inflated sense of the capacity of militia action to resist and overcome the federal government. This belief derives from a misreading of the American Revolution and an understanding of the role the militia was expected to play in political life.

As might be expected given the discussion of the militia myth in American political history offered in chapter 2, militia ideology idealizes the role the militia played in the American Revolution. In a fundamental misreading of the reality of the Revolution, for example, one site insists:

> When the Reverend Josiah Clark met the British forces at Lexington on April 19, 1775, he was serving as the elected commander of a well-regulated militia. He had well-regulated his men many a Sunday afternoon following church services. The British had made the importation of powder (semi-automatic rifles?) illegal and General Gage had sent his men to confiscate colonial stockpiles, along with other war material such as muskets and food stores. . . .
>
> The militias of the communities outside of Boston had been alerted from Boston the night of April 18. Paul Revere was one of these messengers, although he was captured before he got very far. The British were defeated rather soundly by the militia at Lexington and the other companies that came from surrounding areas answering the call.[47]

Or, as another site explains, "Do we believe Paul Revere's militia unit was part of the organized government of his time? We think not! It was clear to the early patriots that the militia was independent of the organized government and made up of the people who stood ready to repel a tyrannical government from denying the rights of liberty under the Constitution."[48] This same site continues, "Furthermore, the founders of our government believed that power should remain in the hands of the people to stop the usurpation of power of government. For this expressed reason, they believed in the militia system where all citizens should keep and bear arms."[49]

What worked for the founders will work today, contemporary militia members insist. In the "Can we win an armed conflict?" subsection of a longer document, one militia text evokes the language of radical Republican political theory as it lays out a strategy that mirrors the logic of guerrilla warfare:

> Suppose you join us. Suppose we mobilize. Can we win? The enemy police and military forces under the control of a growing autocratic government will have and wield great might. . . . But we can win! Initially, the potential enemy will be greater in numbers, have superior firepower, better training, more equipment, and closer coordination. But we have three things in our favor that they do not have: the people, our own advantages, and a cause.[50]

There are, for example, "between 100 and 200 million firearms in the hands of private citizens of this country. . . . who, almost by definition, would side with the Constitution rather than the government in a struggle."[51] Indeed, even police and military forces would join the crusade since they "love their personal liberties." "So it would not be long until we are the ones with superior numbers and perhaps even superior firepower," the document asserts.[52] Thus, like radical Republican theory, militia ideology insists that militia members will have advantages like dependable supporters, motivated fighters, superior knowledge of the area of conflict, and better communications than the government, thus mirroring conditions in the Revolution and advantaging the militia in a real conflict.[53] Finally, the cause for which the militia fights—freedom and liberty—will guarantee the superior performance of militia warriors: "But while the patriot will not desire to risk or sacrifice his life in vain, he 'has' to fight to win. He will be willing to go beyond the call of duty because he is energized by an idea, not by self-preservation or selfish ambition."[54] As another writer vividly insists: "Let me give a VERY powerful fact that every high ranking officer knows. . . . [I]n 400 years of recorded military history NEVER has a corrupt government defeated an indigenous guerilla force. In a nut shell, what that means is that the power rests with the people!"[55]

Taken as a whole, militia ideology offers a distorted vision of the corruption of the federal government, the appropriate relationship among federal, state, and individual authorities, and the capacity of militia members to challenge and defeat organized military and police forces. This vision serves to place militia members in a central position in the political system both in terms of their power—they, as sovereign citizens, have authority to defy the government—and as moral agents—the militia are exposing the corruption that has undermined real American democracy and, as will be discussed in the next section, are working to save America from its current occupiers. Accordingly, militia ideology valorizes militia members as moral actors aimed at saving the community and reconstructing the nation in terms established at its founding.

However distorted this image is, it is important to understand that it makes sense in the context of American political culture, especially to conservatives. Just as the myth of the militia links idealism and exceptionalism to political practice in a way that makes armed citizens mythic heroes and models for action, militia ideology links individual freedom and the protection of American liberties to gun-owning citizen leaders. It is up to us as individuals to save America, militia ideology insists. We have done it before, and we can do it again. Thus, the distortions inherent in the movement's ideology tend to encourage other citizens imbued with the militia myth to join the contemporary movement's ranks: it builds on the preexisting biases of culture and prior social movements in a way that provides a plausible explanation for current political problems and an inspiring model for political action.

Legitimation

Ideology also serves to legitimate one's own worldview, according to Ricoeur. Thus, while ideologies necessarily distort reality, they also offer terms by which their adherents (and any converts) can recognize the appropriateness of their point of view. In militia ideology, the legitimation function is manifested in militia members' insistence on the legality of their operations and the justice of their goals.

Militia sites insist that contemporary militias, organized by private citizens and operating without formal government sanction, are legal and important. The legal argument takes two basic forms: an interpretation of the Bill of Rights (particularly the Second Amendment), and an analysis of U.S. law as it relates to the concept of militias. The constitutional argument, for example, rests on an "original intent" understanding of the place of the militia in U.S. life. "Opponents of the individual right to keep and bear arms have greatly misunderstood the initial clause of the Second Amendment," one site explains.

> For many in our time, it is inconceivable to think of anything being well-regulated without a law mandating the regulation and a bureaucracy to conduct the regulation. In the 18th century, the word regulation did not at all require government involvement. The actions of the American colonists make it plain that a well-regulated militia was well-rehearsed and well-drilled without the control of the government.[56]

Another site explains, "What the Second Amendment also does is recognize the right, power and duty of able-bodied persons (originally males, but now females also) to organize into militias and defend the state."[57]

> 'A well regulated Militia' does not refer to the regular army. It would be absurd to recognize the federal government's prerogative to raise an army in the Bill of Rights since: (a) It is presumed that all governments raised armies. (b) Since Article II amends the Constitution which already recognizes this prerogative. And (c) since the Bill of Rights is in its entirety a limitation upon, not an empowering of the federal government. Nor does it refer to a state's national guard. Had the Framers meant state militias, they would not have connected the militia with the right of the people to bear arms. It does mean a well-organized army of the people by the people. The word militia originally legally meant (Virginia Bill of Rights, Section 13) and still legally means (U.S. Code, Title 10, Section 31) the whole able-bodied citizenry of the country, not the formal armed forces of the United States. Therefore, 'A well regulated Militia' is a well organized citizens' army, not a well-controlled standing army.[58]

Citizen militias, then, are understood to be constitutionally protected.

For any who might doubt the constitutional interpretation legitimating the militia, the ideology also appeals to contemporary law—in specific, U.S. 10 section 311, incorrectly cited in the last quotation. (Ironically, that this is a federal law passed by a corrupted government does not make it illegitimate in militia thought. As is suggested by the notion of the sovereign citizen, so long as the citizen decides the law is not in violation of constitutional rights, it is acceptable.) Section 311 states:

> (a) The militia of the United States consists of all able-bodied males at least 17 years of age and, except as provided in section 313 of title 32, under 45 years of age who are, or who have made a declaration of intention to become, citizens of the United States and of female citizens of the United States who are members of the National Guard.
> (b)The classes of the militia are
> (1) the organized militia, which consists of the National Guard and the Naval Militia; and
> (2) the unorganized militia, which consists of the members of the militia who are not members of the National Guard or the Naval Militia.[59]

Thus, drawing on this code and diverse other laws, militia ideology insists that citizen militias are legal and appropriate:

> The 'unorganized' or reserve militia is a legal and lawful part of the armed forces of this nation. It is a military organization recognized by the Second Amendment of the Constitution; Title 10, Section 311 USC; the Dick Act of 1903; the National Defense Act of 1916; and affirmed by numerous court decisions.
> There is no ambiguity. The 'unorganized' citizens militia is not the National Guard or the state 'select' militia under the governor, or part of the 'organized' armed forces of the federal government. It is literally the entire body of armed citizenry.
> Although the 'unorganized' militia can be called up for lawful (Constitutional) purposes, it is not under the jurisdiction of any state or political jurisdiction. It represents the authority and power of the People over the government and stands as the last defense of the citizens of this country against domestic tyranny.[60]

As the last paragraph of the previous quotation suggests, there is more to the legitimation function in militia ideology than the appeal to constitutional or legal authorities. The self-asserted goals and purposes of the militia are also central to their understanding of their significance in American life. Of particular importance to the militia is their belief in their role in preventing the federal government's abuse of authority and their vision of an ideal America.

Militia ideology legitimizes the power of gun-owning private citizens against any competitive authority. Militia ideology holds that the militia is the ultimate line of defense for American freedoms against a tyrannical government. As the North Carolina Citizen Militia explains:

We believe that the truths and ideals represented in the Declaration of Independence, our Constitution and Bill of Rights express the core beliefs at the very heart and soul of America and her citizens. Therefore, the militia is pledged to uphold the ideals expressed in these documents and does not owe its loyalty to any political party, individual, or organization. We believe that America, and her republican form of government, administered with fairness, honesty and integrity, is worth saving. . . .

The primary purpose of the North Carolina unorganized, or reserve militia, therefore, is to defend the Constitution of the State of North Carolina and the United States against all enemies, foreign and domestic. Further, it is to uphold and guarantee all Constitutional guarantees as documented by the Bill of Rights to ensure that all citizens regardless of race, color, religion, sex or national origin retain the inalienable rights and opportunities established by the Founding Fathers of this great nation.[61]

As another site explains, "MILITIAS ARE NOT ANTI-GOVERNMENT. . . . MILITIA MEMBERS ARE NOT CRIMINALS. . . . MILITIA MEMBERS ARE NOT EXTREMISTS. . . . No militia participated in the siege at Ruby Ridge, Idaho, in 1992. . . . No Militia set fire to any religious group's communal home in Waco, Texas, in 1993." Instead, "The Militia seeks to preserve and practice . . . rights and liberties."[62] Other sites mirror this language: "The Free Militia's 'agenda' is the Bill of Rights. Our purpose is solely to defend these rights for ourselves and our neighbors."[63] "[T]he People, as the militia have the right to fight, if necessary, oppressive government, to prevent the usurpation of the Constitution (the supreme law of the land), by anyone, including the federal government."[64] And finally, as an example, "Like it or not, the only reason a civilian or unorganized militia exists is in order to keep government in check in order that the government may remain in the hand of the people."[65] In the end, then, legitimate power rests in the hands of ordinary, gun-owning citizens, not in the federal government.

Beyond simply asserting their right to protect the Bill of Rights, militias also assert a positive program, sometimes directly, sometimes through exposing the "wrongs" of contemporary society. While there is no single set of goals to which all militia groups aspire, those encompassed in the following list clearly embody much of what the militia wants. Importantly, it is precisely because they see this list as reasonable and constitutional that the militia see their formation and action as necessary and legitimate:

We the People of this great Republic:

- Demand the immediate removal of all foreign troops stationed on the sovereign soil of the united States of America.
- Demand that the War Powers Act, the Emergency Powers Act and the Federal Reserve Act be rescinded.
- Demand an end to the unconstitutional practice of Executive Orders which carry the force of law, and a rescission of all such Orders.
- Demand any acts and agencies derived from the War Powers, Emergency Powers, or Federal Reserve Acts or Executive Orders be dissolved.
- Demand the immediate removal of the United States from the foreign body known as the 'United Nations.'
- Demand an end to all United Nations funding both military programs and all other UN programs.
- Demand a rescission to all acts, and legislation that in any way infringes on the right to keep and bear arms.
- Demand a rescission to all acts, legislation and agencies that exceed the powers described in the constitution according to the 10th amendment.
- Demand that all educational concerns be returned to the several states directly and that all federal involvement in the same cease.
- Demand all local government and educational institutions to disavow the blackmail and social restructuring of federal funds.
- Urge all citizens to become self sufficient as individuals, as families, as localities, as counties and as states.
- Urge all liberty loving citizens to prepare, with God's help, to take the same course of action that our forefathers took in fighting tyranny.[66]

Our goals are just, the militia thus claims, and we have the legal and constitutional rights to operate. Thus, militia ideology insists, their existence—and their actions in support of their goals—is legitimate.

As was the case with the distortions inherent in militia ideology, the legitimating functions of militia thought also draw life from the broad spectrum of American political culture. The idea that individuals are the true sovereign authority in any polity clearly derives from liberal thought and is a core component of both the individualism that lies at the heart of American political culture and the Revolutionary myth of the militia. Moreover, this individualism is linked to a good-versus-evil struggle that draws on the language of Christian millennialism in defining the exceptionalist purpose of the American experiment. The individual's rights and powers must be sacrosanct if the polity, and thus American liberty, is to survive. The militia is, and must be, legitimate. In a culture suffused with pro-individualist liberal and exceptionalist values, a program legitimated in terms like those offered by the militia has the potential to find many supporters.

Integration

For Ricoeur, integration refers to the way ideology promotes group identity in a complex, often hostile world. This function links distorted visions of reality to legitimacy claims in a way that validates the adherent's identity. In other words, the worldview expressed and legitimated by specific ideologies causes followers to understand themselves as members of a group privileged to know the truth and empowered to act upon that knowledge.

This constructive power of ideology is fundamental. In defining who a person is, the integrative power of ideology provides a model of behavior and action that establishes one's values and ideals as right and proper and moral. It establishes "us" versus "them" and links this dyad to a moralistic construction of the "right" kind of society. Moreover, it links one's preferences to particular relationships of power and privileges some set of power interactions as natural, necessary, and good while at the same time delegitimating alternative formulations. What "I" believe, then, who "I" am, is good, moral, and just; and I am like people who are like me. Everyone not a part of "us" is "them" and can constitute a threat to who "we" are.

In militia thought, this integrative function is most clear when members or ideologues define themselves as ordinary people acting in heroic defense of the "real" America. It appears clearly, for example, in a website offered by the California militia as it explains "Who We Are":

> Contrary to what you may have read in the newspapers, or heard on the radio, or even seen on the television news, we are not a group of 'goose stepping' anti-Semitic racists with single digit IQ's. And in spite of what the government, and its lackeys in the media would have you believe, we are not a bunch of mad bombers. We are not out to destroy the government. We are hoping to restore it.
>
> Our members represent every racial group, every major religion, and both sexes. Many of our members are college graduates, and a substantial number possess advanced degrees, while others lack a high school

diploma. Most of our people are veterans and many have actual combat experience. From professionals to laborers, and teachers to law enforcement officers, we have come together because we have something in common, something that transcends race, or religion, or sex. We love America. We know where she's been, and we fear where she's heading.

We are graybeards who remember the cops that walked a beat in our neighborhoods, and who knocked on the door when they wanted to talk to us. We are young blacks who tremble at the sight of a police car in their rear view mirror.

We are lawyers who still choke up when we read the Constitution, and we are factory workers and house-wives who refuse to believe that sacred document, the Constitution, has become obsolete.

We are ordinary people who have done an extraordinary thing. We have read the writing on the wall, and we have said no. We have read the writing and said 'Hell no!' 'Hell no, I'm not giving up my country,' and 'Hell no, I'm not giving up America,' not to the socialists, and not to the United Nations, not without a fight!

And we pray. And our prayer is that somehow those who would take away our liberty, that those who have placed themselves above our Constitution and the supreme law of the land will read the writing on the walls, and give America back to us before it's too late.

But most of all, we are Patriots, sworn to protect and defend the Constitution of the United States of America against all enemies foreign and domestic.

So who are we? We are your neighbor, your secretary, your doctor, the mechanic who fixed your car, and yes, maybe even the face that stares at you from the mirror every morning.

We are Americans.[67]

"Our strategy is simple," the same group offers on another page: "Prepare to rebuild America."[68] Similarly, another site explains, "Citizen militias are made up of ordinary Americans who love their country."[69] To be a good American, then, is to be an active militia member willing to sacrifice all for the good of the nation. Anything less makes one an agent of the evil that has occupied America's government and is working to destroy ordinary citizens as well.

This integrative vision is obviously embedded in particular relations of power and identity. The "us" in question is patriotic, gun-wielding Americans who are unwilling to have their rights trampled on in the name of physical comfort. "Them," clearly, is everyone else: anyone who fails to see that freedom is under assault from the actions of government. Importantly, this dynamic privileges the militia: its members are the "real" Americans whose actions and beliefs can be the foundation of liberty in the United States. It understands which is more important—the freedom to own and use guns, for example, or the opportunity to live a healthy life free from fear of hunger—and this preference becomes the "American" attitude. Such beliefs are then linked to a moral call for action: real heroes, real patriots, will fight the actions of those who would corrupt their ideals and limit the prospect of the realization of the American promise. This, in turn, establishes a particular political order—one that is embedded in masculine, racist values—as true and right for all Americans. Indeed, it is an order worth dying to defend—or create. Militia ideology thus builds its followers into promoters of the real American identity.

As has been made clear above, the terms in which militia ideology performs this integrative function are central to American political culture. Individual rights and liberties are seen as the central components of good citizenship. Such values are under assault from a government other, thus necessitating a struggle to maintain the American mission—government of, for, and by the people, in Abraham Lincoln's evocative rhetoric at Gettysburg. Real Americans—those who believe in individual rights and fear excessive government—must join the militia.

Militia Ideology and the Populist
Justification of Rage

Taken as a whole, militia ideology constructs a remarkable vision of an American politics corrupted by agents of the New World Order intent on destroying "the American way." However, this ideology offers a path of hope in the face of this crisis: heroic, real Americans who have the legitimate right to interpret and restore proper constitutional government can save the nation if they struggle together in the name of freedom and liberty. Fortunately, most Americans can participate in this militia effort—while only a few are sovereign citizens, all have rights and liberties that they can recognize and work to protect. Thus, in the end, the militia is an example of American values and truths in action. Together, the militia concludes, we can make America what it ought to be.

There are, obviously, many dimensions of this ideology that beg for analysis and discussion. Some of these—whether the government of the United States is actually occupied by an enemy elite, for example, or whether gun control is a Nazi-inspired plot to make it easier for government to kill ordinary Americans—are essentially unchallengeable: they are beliefs founded on a lack of evidence as much as truths established by proof, and no amount of counter-argument will convince followers of militia ideology that no conspiracy exists. Indeed, the absence of direct evidence is proof of its sophistication and power. Similarly, militia readings of the limits of constitutional reform—the notion that an amendment cannot fundamentally alter the nature of a document being amended even if appropriate procedures are followed, or the idea that some citizens are "sovereign citizens" due special places of importance in the constitutional system—can only be refuted with detailed discussions of constitutional history and legal theory that are likely to deflect this book from its project: understanding the cultural location of the militia and assessing its likely importance in U.S. politics. After all, it does not matter whether what militia members believe is true in a constitutional sense; it only matters that militia members believe that it is true. Thus, rather than undertake a point-by-point refutation of the details of militia ideology, this section addresses how militia ideology relates to the history of right-wing populism in the United States, how it differs from that populism, and what the impact of its ideology is likely to be on militia actions and behaviors in the future.

As Berlet and Lyons suggest, militia ideology is rife with producerism, demonization and scapegoating, conspiracism, and apocalyptic revelations and millennial visions.[70] In the militia version of right-wing populism, ordinary Americans—particularly white, non-(recent)-immigrant Americans—are good, productive citizens, whereas the agents of a corrupted government are the unproductive demons whose predatory laws and practices favor unworthy people and the interests of the international conspiracy. These evil officials, serving a political order directed from the outside, are promoting policies that will either destroy the citizenry's lives or, if certain members of the community resist, promote the final confrontation between the inheritors of the American tradition and its mortal enemies. Fortunately, from the militia point of view, this battle is likely to see the creation of a new America freed of its corrupted masters, since millions of arms-bearing ordinary citizens will eventually overwhelm and defeat the elites dominating the New World Order and their paid lackeys. Thus, militia ideology embodies principles of premillennialism in linking action in defense of a holy ideal to the construction of the Edenic state that will follow.

At least two dimensions of militia thought deserve special attention here since they do not appear in the ideologies discussed in the section of this chapter dealing with the history of right-wing populism in the United States. These are the significance of guns and the militia members' insistence that they are not racists or sexists even as militia thought privileges certain citizens over others. As will be addressed in chapter 7, these themes provide many of the linkages among the militia and the more mainstream groups in U.S. politics. They also define terms through which militia members insist on the nature and legitimacy of their actions in the political system.

As was discussed earlier, guns are central to militia thinking. After all, militia members argue, it is only their status as armed citizens that makes it possible for them to defend themselves from a predatory government. Moreover, it is only guns that make it possible for them to save the nation from the evil actions of the Shadow Government. To limit one's access to guns, then, is to limit one's prospects of defending either one's own interests or the nation's. Indeed, efforts at gun control can be seen as direct attacks on liberty itself. As in the militia myth, guns and freedom are inextricably, and necessarily, linked. Ultimately, then, militia ideology, in a way new to the tradition of right-wing populist thought, insists on the righteousness of the defense of gun ownership as a dimension of protecting and advancing American liberty.

Similarly, militia thought deviates from much of right-wing populist thinking in its insistence that militia members are not racists or sexists. The Missouri Fifty-first Militia, for example, states "Under no circumstances will the Missouri 51st Militia tolerate any criminal behavior or racism."[71] Other militia sites make similar ethical statements central to their statements of purpose and goals. Yet these statements run counter to the insistence on categories like "sovereign citizens," white males whose forebears created the Constitution and who therefore enjoy special rights in the political system. They also challenge the political reality that many avowed racists have used an insistence on "states' rights," "strict constructionism," and "original intent" to argue against civil rights laws that forced state and local governments to ensure women and minorities basic rights like suffrage, equal opportunity for work, and a decent education. How, then, do militia members square the circle and insist they are not racists even as they take acts and make arguments regularly associated with racism, and to what effect?

It is possible to construct militia arguments in a way that shades their racist components and paints members as civil rights defenders worthy of the nation's support. (Note that it does not matter whether others agree with this interpretation; it only matters that it makes sense to militia members.) In brief, from the perspective of militia ideology, only certain citizens are sovereign, and so only they have the right to assess, consent to, or nullify government's actions. However, all citizens have rights guaranteed by the Constitution. Yet, if an African American disagrees with an action of the federal government, he or she has no right to reject the decision since it is the national government that guarantees that person's rights through the Fourteenth Amendment. By contrast, those people whose forebears signed the original social contract that became the Constitution are in a position to evaluate and accept or reject the decision since their rights are protected by the original social contract that no government can harm. In militia ideology, then, the differential application of rights is not racist. It is constitutional. Further, this system is understood to guarantee everyone equal rights in practice—African Americans, women, and other minorities have the same right to free speech as do sovereign citizens. All that differs is where the final authority to judge the limits of rights lies. For the militia, it is in the sovereign citizen, whose actions in defense of human liberty will bring benefits and protections to everyone, including minorities. Thus, militia members insist, they are not racist. Indeed, they are the nation's truest defenders.

It is this last sentiment, that the militia are the nation's last, best hope, that establishes the final significance of militia ideology in American politics. Like their Revolutionary forebears, militia members become benevolent hero-warriors motivated by patriotism and human rights to make—or restore—America into its ideal form. They are all the more heroic because they are willing to use guns and face threats of death from a manipulative, evil government to save the nation. Indeed, militia ideology encourages its adherents to adopt a righteous rage directed at the evil of the Shadow

Government and intended to purify the nation as a whole. Rage is, in other words, both justified and purgative.

Accordingly, the militia takes a unique place among right-wing populist groups in that their ideology promotes an activist, violent agenda as a means of redeeming the nation and saving it for its true heritage. Moreover, the terms of their ideology position them close to many mainstream groups in U.S. politics and to the cultural values that many Americans have learned to value from childhood. As a consequence, it is important to realize that the militia is not made up of a bunch of "kooks" who can be gawked at and not taken seriously. Their ideas, and the ways these ideas link to those of the polity at large, have the potential to shape the politics of the United States for a long time to come.

4

The Spark:
Randy Weaver and the Standoff
at Ruby Ridge

It can be fairly said that the specific event that led to the rise of modern American militia movement occurred in August 1992, as Randy Weaver and his family engaged in an eleven-day standoff with agents of the Federal Bureau of Investigation (FBI), U.S. Marshals Service, and the Bureau of Alcohol, Tobacco, and Firearms (ATF) trying to serve a warrant for Weaver's arrest. The warrant, charging Weaver with failing to appear for trial in 1991 on a charge of selling an illegally sawed-off shotgun to a federal informant in 1989, provided the legal justification that brought federal agents to Weaver's isolated mountaintop cabin on Ruby Ridge, Idaho. Weaver's response, along with that of his family, generated support for his cause from local residents and from ideological allies across the nation. The events on Ruby Ridge, taken as a whole, laid the groundwork on which thousands of Americans would form militias.

Yet the events at Ruby Ridge were only a piece of the puzzle leading to the rise of the militia movement. Militias would not have formed after Ruby Ridge had not thousands of Americans already believed in the kinds of antigovernment, pro-individualist ideas that Weaver was understood to represent. As chapters 1, 2, and 3 explained, Weaver's standoff occurred in the context of a culture primed to believe that government was an inherently oppressive, dangerous force for evil. But Weaver himself was not a member of a militia when he barricaded himself into his mountaintop cabin, nor did he ever join one: his ideology stood squarely in the tradition of white supremacy that most militias explicitly reject. Ironically, then, while Weaver's standoff made the militia movement, he himself never wished for such an outcome.

Coming to Ruby Ridge

The path that brought Randy Weaver and his family—wife Vicki, older daughter Sara, son Samuel, and younger daughter Rachel—to Idaho in 1983 was long and indirect. The elder Weavers both grew up in highly religious families in rural Iowa, Vicki as a Mormon and Randy as a conservative Protestant. Both were imbued with visions of a harsh and judgmental God punishing those who violated his law while protecting true believers. Additionally, both were educated to the idea that the battle between good and evil was active and ongoing in daily human life.[1] God's judgment, then, was constant and was to be actively feared.

Such beliefs, as was noted in chapter 3, are fairly common in the United States. They exist within the broader orbit of right-wing populist ideologies and movements in the United States. Moreover, they do not in and of themselves cause one to hate the government, fear those of different races, and use violence to resist federal warrants. Nor can many other parts of their lives together suggest exactly what shaped the Weavers' lives in the way that led them to Ruby Ridge. Randy enlisted in the army in 1968, graduated from the advanced training program for the Special Forces but never served in Vietnam, and got a good job working for John Deere and married Vicki in 1971. They settled in Cedar Falls, Iowa, soon thereafter, and their first child, Sara, was born in 1976. Samuel followed in 1979, and Rachel was born in 1982.[2] They were a fairly ordinary family of conservative Christians.

If any single event can be seen to have led the Weavers down a new path of conservative Christianity and explicit racism—the values that would lead them to Idaho—Vicki's reading of Hal Lindsey's *Late Great Planet Earth* in 1978 is the most likely candidate.[3] Lindsey's book tells an apocalyptic story of the forces of good fighting the forces of evil in a great religious struggle. The forces of evil are represented by foreigners, especially those of color, Communists, and Jews who refuse to accept Jesus as Messiah; the forces of good are "true" Christian literalists who accept God's word as the absolute law governing their lives. At the end of Lindsey's book, Earth is consumed in apocalyptic fire, true believers are raptured to Heaven, and Christ returns to establish a new Garden of Paradise on Earth.[4]

While both Randy and Vicki Weaver had expressed racially tinged sentiments prior to reading Lindsey's work, they adopted more extreme positions regarding race and religion after 1978. They became what they called "Legalists": those who took the Bible literally. They rid their house of photographs on the grounds that such pictures are graven images; associated the coming of one world government and the Antichrist with the spread of computers; and stopped celebrating Christmas, insisting that it was a pagan holiday. In addition, Randy began denying the Holocaust. He and Vicki also began watching evangelical Christian television programming like the *PTL Club* and came to believe that a Masonic-derived conspiracy had made it possible for groups like the Illuminati, the Council on Foreign Relations, and the Trilateral Commission to take over control of the U.S. government on behalf of Jewish servants of the Antichrist. Moreover, Randy began aggressively expounding his views at work, where he had risen to a supervisory position. This brought him into conflict with his employees and his supervisors; their resistance and orders that he stop proselytizing at work intensified his sense that Iowa was no longer a safe and comfortable home, especially as the end times approached. Accordingly, the family left Iowa in 1983, intending to move to Montana and its perceived comparative freedom.[5]

Unable to find affordable land in Montana, the Weavers crossed the border into northern Idaho. There, they felt comfortable amidst the jagged, isolated peaks, distant neighbors, and almost entirely white population. They bought land on Ruby Ridge in September 1983 and worked through the winter to build a cabin on its most isolated point. The cabin, cobbled together with plywood and scrap from a lumber yard, was ready for occupancy in March 1984. The family then moved in to their new home, cutting themselves off from what are considered standard amenities for most Americans: electricity, indoor plumbing, and similar facilities.[6]

The Weavers' physical isolation from mainstream American society was mirrored by an increasing ideological distance. What had been a low-grade racism in Iowa became explicit in Idaho. Jews and minorities became preferred targets of Weaver family rhetoric; Randy was pictured in 1989 wearing a T-shirt with the slogan, "Just Say No—To ZOG." (ZOG stands for Zionist Occupied Government.) Beginning in 1986, Randy started attending the annual Aryan Nations World Conference held in Naples, Idaho. The Aryan Nations, led by Richard Butler, provided Randy with an outlet for his racist beliefs as well as further validation of them: whites were the true inheritors of America, Butler preached, and its land was naturally theirs. Unfortunately, the ZOG was destroying America through its control of the federal government and its agents. Thus, policies aimed at protection the rights of Jews and other minorities were really assaults on white people by national authorities.[7]

As Weaver's racism grew, so did his connection to the religious movement known as Christian Identity.[8] Christian Identity preaches that Jews are the children of Satan while whites—generally understood as people of north European heritage—are the true Israelites, the real chosen of God. Accordingly, the coming Armageddon would restore whites to their proper place at God's right hand in the Garden of Paradise. The final battle would pit God-fearing, literalist whites against Communists, Asians, Africans, and any white person who failed to follow God's law. Linked to the politics espoused by the Aryan Nations, Christian Identity served to prove that Weaver's racism was ordained by God and that any challenge to his way of life meant that agents of Satan were engaged in an effort to destroy his soul.

While these views are clearly outside the American mainstream, and indeed run counter to a public culture that celebrates the integrative ethos of Martin Luther King's "I Have a Dream" speech with a national holiday in his honor, it is worth noting that these ideas are fairly common in the United States. As was shown in chapter 3, many dimensions of Weaver's philosophy have been introduced, grown to prominence, and evolved throughout American political history. Thus, there was nothing distinctive about Weaver's thought or actions (through the mid-1980s) that would necessarily bring him into direct conflict with the federal government or that would make him a symbol around which a new political movement might rally.

In addition, it should be emphasized that Weaver was not a militia member in either form or ideology. He was a white supremacist and religious racist-nationalist. Moreover, his lifestyle was that of a survivalist trying to escape the corruption of contemporary society. He did not say, as militia members claim, that his intent was to save society. Thus, even when he came into conflict with the national government, it did not follow that Randy Weaver would become a hero to the newly emerging militia movement. Instead, as will be seen later in this chapter, it took a combination of federal government mistakes, a skillful legal defense, and the work of the self-appointed leaders of the emerging militia movement to make Randy Weaver the militia poster boy opposing the evils of the federal government.

Randy Weaver first came to the attention of the federal government in the mid-1980s when a neighbor who lived near Weaver's Ruby Ridge land moved out of the area and wrote several letters to the U.S. Secret Service, the FBI, and other agencies claiming that Weaver was warehousing guns on his property and had threatened the life of the president. These charges were eventually investigated and found baseless; however, Weaver did write a letter to the federal authorities to defend his antigovernment point of view. Weaver claimed that he bore no hostility to the government: if it left him alone, he would leave it alone. He would defend himself if its agents—and the evil they represented—came on his land, however. From the perspective of local federal agents, then, Weaver appeared to be dangerous but fortunately isolated.[9]

In the mid-1980s, however, something changed in the Weaver family. They reduced their isolation from their fellow citizens and moved to a rented house at the bottom of their hill. Randy ran as a Republican for Boundary County sheriff in 1988; he lost in the predominantly Democratic county by a wide margin despite a campaign tactic that included handing out cards with the slogan "Get out of jail free" printed on one side. It appeared that the Weavers were returning to more mainstream society.[10]

The year 1989 turned out to be pivotal in Randy Weaver's story. While attending the Aryan Nations World Congress, Weaver was again introduced to Gus Magisono, whom he had met at the 1986 Aryan Nations conference. Weaver believed Magisono to be a fellow white supremacist. In fact, Magisono was a private detective and sometime federal informant named Kenneth Fadeley. At some point in one of their conversations, either Weaver or Fadeley suggested that Weaver sell several sawed-off shotguns to Fadeley.

They agreed, and on October 24, 1989, Weaver handed Fadeley two shotguns that he had illegally shortened by five and one-half inches in his workshop. Fadeley gave Weaver $300 for the guns and promised to pay an additional $150 later. This was the only sale of weapons Weaver made, although there were subsequent discussions about selling more guns.[11]

In fall 1989, the Weavers returned to their mountaintop home and left whatever kind thoughts they might have had about their fellow human beings behind. They broke off multiple, long-term friendships, intensified the nature and frequency of their racist rhetoric, and even participated in an armed effort to prevent county agents from evicting a neighboring family from their home.[12] Their religious values turned more extreme as well: by the late 1980s, first Vicki and then Sara would spend the week they were menstruating in a movable shed built away from the home in order not to defile the home with their fluids.[13] Thus, when ATF agents approached Weaver in June 1990 and asked him to become an informant against white supremacists and other extremists (including David Trochmann, who Weaver did not know, but who would later form the Militia of Montana, one of the first militia groups) or be charged with selling illegal weapons, Weaver rejected their offer out of hand.[14] His belief that the government was the agent of evil trying to destroy "real" Christians left him little choice.

Unsurprisingly, the ATF attempt to turn Weaver into an informant deepened his suspicion of government. The family became more reclusive. Thus, when the government finally decided to arrest Weaver on the weapons charge, it had to get access to him. Reluctant to pursue him onto his hilly, easily defended property, which had only one winding, narrow access road, agents set up a capture scenario away from Weaver's home in January 1991. Out riding snowmobiles one day, the Weavers noticed a vehicle broken down by the side of the road. Because it was snowing, they stopped to help. When Randy walked to the front of the truck to talk to the person leaning over the engine with the hood up, the apparently stranded driver stood up, put a gun in Weaver's chest, and arrested him. Weaver was arraigned and released on a bond secured by his property the next day; Weaver later became convinced that if he were convicted, he would lose his land.[15]

Upon his return to Ruby Ridge, Weaver and his family made the decision that they would not leave the mountain again. They ignored a court summons that, importantly, mistakenly ordered him to report for trial on March 20; his actual trial date was February 19. By March 1991, then, Weaver faced a charge of failure to appear as well as the original weapons charge.[16]

The Weavers remained on their property for over a year. U.S. marshals and Weaver family friends made occasional efforts to convince Weaver to surrender; all were unsuccessful. The Weavers' fourth child, Elisheba, was born in October 1991.[17] Weaver was essentially self-imprisoned.

In March 1992, Weaver's story became national news. Several newspapers, including the *New York Times,* found out about Weaver's defiance of the federal government and reported on it. In response, the agencies trying to arrest Weaver—primarily the U.S. marshals and the ATF—held a meeting on March 27, 1992, at which they decided to intensify their efforts to capture the fugitive. They initiated Operation Northern Exposure—named for a popular television series filmed in the Cascade Mountains town of Roslyn, Washington—to observe Weaver's patterns, establish his routines, and create a plan to achieve his arrest with the least risk to his family and to the agents involved. By April, surveillance cameras were installed in locations around Weaver's home, and many ATF agents and U.S. marshals patrolled Weaver's land, establishing observation posts. Additionally, the FBI's elite Hostage Rescue Team was integrated into the planning process for Weaver's eventual capture.[18]

These operations were remarkably successful, and the government learned a great deal about Weaver's lifestyle. Moreover, the surveillance helped convince the investigating agents of Weaver's irreconcilable hostility to their work. Weaver and his family never left the house unarmed, one surveillance camera was stolen (its remains were found on Weaver's property after the standoff), and the family was heard shouting angry statements at the agents they presumed were watching them. When several agents of the ATF walked onto Weaver's land before dawn on August 21, 1992, then, they were well armed and concerned about Weaver's potential for violence. However, such operations were routine, and there is little credible evidence that the agents expected a confrontation that day. Indeed, nothing might have come of it if the Weavers had not owned a dog named Striker. Instead, the events at Ruby Ridge became the specific, proximate cause of the rise of the modern American militia movement.

Eleven Days in Idaho

Six U.S. marshals in full camouflage walked onto Randy Weaver's property in the predawn hours of August 21, 1992. They split into two groups of three when they came to a turn in the long driveway to Weaver's home that had come to be known as the Y. Three moved to an established surveillance post off Weaver's land but with a good view of his home; three others moved closer to the Weaver home for more direct observations. Finished with their work by late morning, the three agents who had been engaged in close-in observations of the Weaver household were walking down the dirt drive leading from Weaver's home when Weaver, his son Sammy, and a family friend named Kevin Harris, who had lived with the Weavers on and off since 1984, left the family home carrying rifles. They were following Striker, who appeared to be following a scent. Sammy raced straight downhill after the dog. Kevin Harris gave chase, and Weaver followed more slowly using the main access road.[19]

Lower on the mountain, the three U.S. marshals heard Striker's baying bark get closer and knew they were in trouble. They began running down the hill; however, at one point in their retreat they realized they were going to have to cross a clearing that afforded anyone higher on the hill a good chance to shoot them. Rather than retreat into a shooting alley, they took cover in nearby trees and hoped the dog and the family would miss them.

The tactic failed. One agent, Arthur Roderick, decided that he should shoot the dog to protect his fellow agents. Another, William Degan, emerged from behind a tree and confronted Randy Weaver, either by identifying himself as a U.S. marshal or not, depending on which account of the story one believes. As Weaver turned and ran back up the hill, Kevin Harris fired on Degan, hitting him in the chest. Degan died a few minutes later but only after firing seven shots of his own. Sammy, angered at Striker's death, cursed the agents but responded to his father's call to come back up the hill. As he ran back toward the cabin, he was struck and killed by a bullet from Marshal Degan's gun—a fact that federal agents did not know until August 24. Kevin Harris rejoined Randy Weaver and the Weaver family at their cabin and informed them that Sammy was dead.[20]

All of these events occurred very quickly. The firefight was over in minutes. Indeed, at least part of the ensuing confusion about who did what, who shot first, etc., can be easily attributed to the chaos of this few minutes. However, this fact did not make its way to the headquarters of the U.S. Marshals Service, the FBI, or the ATF. Instead, when the second group of agents sent to observe Weaver on August 21 reached a telephone and placed a 911 call that shots had been fired and that a federal officer had been shot and killed, command personnel believed that there was a running gun battle on Ruby Ridge. This belief was reinforced by the inability of the remaining U.S. marshals to pull William Degan's body off the mountain: they remained on the hill, ostensibly under fire, until after eleven o'clock that evening, when an Idaho State Police team went up the hill to assist in extracting Degan. There had been no gun battle, however; agents had remained on the mountain because Degan's body was too heavy and too wet from a storm that had come to the mountain. The remaining agents simply could not move him down to their vehicle.[21]

From the perspective of the commanders in Washington, D.C., however, the events that occurred on August 21 proved Randy Weaver's irreconcilable hatred of the federal government. From the perspective of those inside the Weaver home, the events, including Sammy's death, proved the federal government's irresponsible evil. Much of the tragedy that followed was grounded in these fixed, rigid worldviews.

As the U.S. marshals lay in the woods waiting for help on August 21, Richard Rogers, commander of the FBI's Hostage Rescue Team, was in transit from Washington, D.C., to Idaho. He ordered his team to join him there. On the way, believing the Weavers to constitute a serious and immediate threat to all officers with whom they came into contact, Rogers revised the FBI's rules of engagement governing the use of deadly force. Instead of simply permitting FBI agents to defend themselves or innocent persons through deadly force—the normal rules—Rogers drafted rules that allowed FBI agents to shoot any armed person in the Weaver compound on the grounds that the individual's being armed constituted an immediate threat to the life of all federal agents. Tentatively approved by Rogers' supervisor, Larry Potts, these rules were ultimately revised to allow and encourage federal officers to shoot and kill armed adults in the Weaver compound on sight *after* the FBI had made a surrender demand of Weaver; prior to this demand, the rules allowed the shooting of any armed adult male. (These final rules were never approved by Rogers's supervisors, who did not see the final draft before it was posted.)[22]

The rules of engagement became a central concern to the small army of federal agents who arrived near Weaver's property overnight from August 21 to August 22. They were particularly important to the snipers of the Hostage Rescue Team because they, as a practical matter, were likely to be the first agents to have a chance to shoot anyone on Weaver's property: well-trained, snipers could be more than half a mile away and out of view of the Weaver family while they took their shots. Arriving on August 22 and briefed on the new rules of engagement, the snipers deployed around the Weaver cabin late in the day on August 22.

Around 6 P.M. on August 22, FBI sniper Lon Horiuchi saw two men and one woman leave the Weaver cabin and head for the shed in which Vicki and Sara had lived during their menstrual periods. As Randy Weaver approached the shed, Horiuchi fired at him, wounding Weaver in the right arm. As the three people rushed back to the cabin, Horiuchi aimed another shot. He thought he was aiming at the same person he had hit before, but in fact he was aiming at Kevin Harris, who was rushing to return to the cabin. Horiuchi led the fleeing man enough to compensate for his speed and the wind conditions and fired just as the man dove into the cabin's front door. He later told his supervisors he thought he had hit and probably killed this second suspect.[23]

He had not. Instead, his second shot penetrated the door of the Weaver home and shattered Vicki Weaver's head. She was killed instantly. The same bullet and some shrapnel hit Kevin Harris in the arm and chest, wounding him severely. Weaver returned to his cabin without further injury.

An hour later the first FBI attempt at negotiation began. A telephone was taken up to the outskirts of the Weaver cabin by a robot controlled from an armored personnel carrier and dropped in front of the door. FBI negotiators called Weaver by megaphone and asked him to pick it up, and when he didn't, they repeatedly called the number to let the phone ring in the dirt.[24] No one ever answered.

Once negotiations were initiated, a pattern emerged in the standoff. FBI negotiators called the Weavers repeatedly; no response came from the family. Armored personnel carriers were stationed around the perimeter of Weaver's home; a microphone hidden in the telephone picked up muted sounds from the Weaver household; and searchlights were turned onto the Weaver home as loudspeakers asked Vicki to send her children out so they could be properly fed. (Agents did not know that Vicki Weaver was dead; believing that the FBI knew it had killed Vicki, the Weavers took these requests as cruel taunts from a vicious, untrustworthy government. The Weavers became convinced that the federal government intended to kill them too.)

One further piece of information convinced the Weavers that their deaths were imminent if they began negotiations with the FBI: the robot that had dropped the telephone in front of their door had remained parked next to the cabin. In what the FBI later claimed was an oversight, the robot was equipped with a 12-gauge shotgun aimed directly at the cabin's entryway. Seeing this, Randy Weaver concluded that he was dead no matter what he did and so refused to retrieve the FBI's phone.[25]

In the meantime, there was a great deal of commotion at the bottom of the hill. Federal agents had established a roadblock to prevent anyone from attempting to assist the Weavers. This barrier became a rallying point for skinheads, white supremacists, antigovernment libertarians, and anyone else in the area with an ax to grind against the authorities. They began a ten-day vigil in which Weaver supporters threatened agents, accused authorities of being "baby killers," and vented their rage against what they saw as inappropriate intrusion of the federal government in the life of a small mountain community and one of its families.[26] This small community of protesters stood as a portent of things to come as the militia movement developed.

The barricade also became ground zero for a large contingent of television, newspaper, and magazine reporters who, in the absence of any news from the mountain itself, interviewed protesters and took pictures of the growing contingent of federal agents, helicopters, and armored vehicles that were descending on Ruby Ridge. Weaver's message, thus, was carried to the nation even as he remained quiet on top of his hill.

The first break in the standoff occurred on August 24, when, in an effort to improve their view of Weaver's home, the FBI decided to move the shed near the home. Several agents entered the building, having come to the site in armored personnel carriers, and found Sammy Weaver's body wrapped in a sheet. This was the moment when agents learned that Sammy had been killed, and this provided them with a sense of why the Weavers might have been reluctant to come out and pick up the phone. After removing Sammy's body, the FBI asked Weaver to pick up the phone and provide any instructions for his care; while Weaver did not answer, the FBI's tone toward the family became more sympathetic and understanding after August 24.[27]

While the FBI's tone became more conciliatory after the discovery of Sammy's body, the rhetoric of rage among the protesters at the bottom of the mountain escalated. What had been alleged was made real. Children appeared at the barricade wearing hand-lettered signs asking whose child was next and reminding viewers that the federal government might do the same thing to other children that it had done to Sammy Weaver. Over the next few years, this powerful image of federal agents threatening the lives of children would become a legitimating and motivating symbol of the growing militia movement.

The next key moment in the standoff came on August 26 when Bo Gritz, a former colonel in the Special Forces and a leader of the white supremacist movement in the United States, arrived at the roadblock and offered his services as negotiator. Gritz claimed to remember Weaver from the 1960s, and Weaver, who had by this point engaged in several shouting matches with FBI negotiators, agreed to let Gritz come up to the cabin. Gritz made his first trip on Friday, August 29.[28]

It was on this initial visit that Gritz, and subsequently the FBI and local onlookers, learned that Vicki Weaver was dead. The reaction among the crowd of protesters stationed around the roadblock was angry and aggressive. More protesters arrived, and they seemed increasingly out of control and ready to act. The situation appeared to be getting out of control.[29]

In response, the FBI's negotiators became convinced that the standoff needed to be ended quickly. Agents decided that the longer they stayed in north Idaho, the more explosive the situation would become. Agents had already stopped and arrested a group of skinheads carrying weapons and trying to get through to the Weavers; they feared more would be coming. Gritz agreed, but noted that Sara, not Randy, was really the force holding the family together locked in the cabin. Sara would be the one who required convincing if the standoff were to end peacefully. Gritz asked for another chance to negotiate, and the FBI agreed.

There was not universal agreement among the FBI agents on the scene about how best to end the standoff, however. Agents of the Hostage Rescue Team reacted to the increasing tension on the barricade by becoming more aggressive and belligerent. In a move they would later repeat at Waco, Texas, leaders of the team insisted that unless the Weavers quickly left the cabin of their own free will, the team would assault the home and pull Weaver and Harris out.

The standoff began to come to an end when Gritz convinced Randy and Sara that if Kevin Harris died—his health had deteriorated badly as a result of the wounds he had received when Vicki Weaver was killed—Randy would be charged with murder for failing to let Harris leave the cabin. On August 30, Harris left the cabin, was arrested, and was taken for medical treatment before being placed in jail.[30]

Later that same day Gritz convinced the family that it was time to have Vicki's body removed from the house, where it had lain under the kitchen table since August 22. Vicki's body was taken out and turned over to the FBI on August 30.[31]

With Vicki's body gone, the symbolic rallying point that had kept the family together was removed. Randy Weaver's wound was very painful, and he needed medical treatment as well. Thus, when Gritz returned to the cabin on August 31, the family was responsive to his promise that the children would not be sent to foster care if Weaver surrendered that day. Instead, they would be allowed to live with relatives. Gritz had also received a promise from prominent defense attorney Gerry Spence that he would represent Weaver if Randy left the cabin peacefully. Weaver agreed, and shortly after noon on August 31, Randy Weaver walked out of his mountaintop home and submitted himself for arrest. The standoff was over.[32]

The Aftermaths of Ruby Ridge

When assessing the impact of the standoff at Ruby Ridge on the militia movement, it is important to consider its multiple aftermaths. There was, for example, an aftermath for Randy Weaver and his family. This was arguably the least important aftermath, but in it lay the seeds of many a future conspiracy theory. There was also an aftermath for the FBI, the U.S. marshals, and the ATF, although this finish would not fully manifest itself until after the fire that consumed the Branch Davidian compound in Waco had long since burned out and cooled. The militia movement, too, can be seen as an aftermath of the Weaver standoff, although its rise relates to a fourth, most important, aftermath: the way the events at Ruby Ridge resonated with millions of Americans inclined to believe that the federal government was an abusive, evil presence in their lives, particularly after the fire at Mount Carmel. This last aftermath will be more fully explored in chapter 5, but its outlines will be sketched here.

The Aftermath, the Weaver Family, and Kevin Harris

After ending the standoff, Randy Weaver was arrested and jailed pending trial. Kevin Harris joined him there once his wounds were treated. The three surviving Weaver children left Idaho on September 2 and moved to Iowa, where various family members would care for them as they finished their educations, this time in public schools.[33]

Weaver and Harris were ultimately charged with ten crimes: conspiring in creating the standoff, illegally shortening a shotgun, failing to appear on the original trial date; attacking federal marshals; murdering William Degan; firing at a U.S. helicopter; harboring Randy Weaver, a known fugitive; violating terms of bond release; and using a weapon in the commission of a crime. At trial, their defense attorneys, Gerry Spence (Weaver) and David Nevin (Harris), poked holes in the prosecution's case by wondering out loud, for example, how Weaver and Harris could, while hiding in Weaver's cabin, have conspired to force agents of the federal government to come to the Weaver land, surround it, and engage in an eleven-day standoff. Spence and Nevin understood that the Idaho jury was likely to be filled with citizens largely sympathetic to the idea that the federal government should not interfere with the actions of private citizens no matter what those people believed. Thus, while insisting that Idahoans were not racist, Spence and Nevin focused on the idea that the federal government intruded on a private citizen's property, entrapped the citizen into selling an illegal weapon, and generally abused its authority. Whereas the prosecutors focused on the evils of Randy Weaver's ideology and the link between his ideology and his actions, the defense made Weaver the victim—a case much easier to make with Sammy and Vicki's deaths.[34]

The defense case rested on more than just appealing to the jury's sense of the appropriate limits of federal authority, however. The defense also spun a conspiracy theory to explain the federal government's actions. Diverse elements added up to an apparent government plot to "get" Randy Weaver on his mountain. For example, the agents were carrying silenced machine guns. Why? If they were not planning a major confrontation with the family, why carry machine guns? The lawyers noted that the agents threw stones at one point in their walk off the mountain. Why did agents supposedly walking down the road on their way off the property stop and throw stones unless it was to see if they could attract the attention of one of the Weaver dogs and so draw the Weavers out of their home? After all, agents knew that every time Weaver heard his dogs bark, some family member investigated, and the person who followed the dog always carried a gun. Why did agents claim that someone had fired at a hovering FBI helicopter (the excuse Lon Horiuchi gave for firing at Randy Weaver and Kevin Harris on August 22) when no such shots were ever fired? Why did Horiuchi claim that he did not see anyone inside the Weaver cabin when he fired, even though on September 1, 1992, he drew a sketch of the door of the Weaver cabin as he saw it when he fired—a picture that shows the tops of two heads in the window? How could the government claim that its snipers were experts who would never miss a target and then claim that the shooting of Vicki Weaver was accidental? Why did the FBI resist turning over evidence like after-action reports from Horiuchi and their general plan of action? Why did the government fail to disclose that a member of the Idaho State Police Critical Response Team who had extracted the marshals from Ruby Ridge the night of August 21, 1992, had reported that the government had shot first by killing Striker, the dog? And, finally, wasn't the original gun charge a set up, anyway?[35]

Cumulatively, this conspiracy theory, along with the mistakes the government made in its prosecution and the skill with which the defense countered the prosecution's points, had two important effects. First, simply, it made the prospects of gaining a conviction against either Randy Weaver or Kevin Harris very unlikely. Indeed, when the jury finally got the case and finished its deliberations, it found Kevin Harris not guilty of all counts he faced—including, on grounds of self-defense, the murder of U.S. Marshal William Degan.[36] (Harris was indicted for the murder of Marshal Degan in state court in 1997; this charge was dismissed by a higher court on grounds of double jeopardy.)[37] The jury found Weaver guilty only of failure to appear, even finding him not guilty of the original weapons charge that started the chain of events that led to the standoff. In October 1993, Weaver was sentenced to eighteen months in jail and given a $10,000 fine. Having already served fourteen months, he was released on December 17, 1993, after a supporter paid the fine.[38] He returned to Iowa and filed a wrongful death civil suit against the U.S. government. It was settled in April 1995 for $3.1 million: $1 million for each of the Weaver girls and $100,000 for Weaver himself.[39]

Second, and far more important in the context of this book, the conspiracy theory laid out in Weaver's trial formed the foundation on which millions of Americans who were already inclined to believe in government's malfeasance could find validation for their paranoia. Indeed, the skillful way Spence, Nevin, and the other defense attorneys kept the intensity of Weaver's racist and religious beliefs out of the trial meant that Weaver could become a symbol of innocence before a rampaging government, an Everyman whose fate could, if unchecked, become yours—or mine. Vicki, too, moved from radical adherent of offbeat and offensive political and religious opinions to an innocent mother killed with a baby in her arms. Thus, people who might have been horrified by the federal government's actions at Ruby Ridge but who might also have been turned off by Weaver's racist, sexist religious ideology did not face that dimension of Weaver's life. Instead, people could read into Weaver what they wished. Weaver's story seemed to fit the patterns of demagoguery, libertarianism, and individual resistance to abusive authority that are and have been shared by millions of Americans. Weaver became an innocent in no way responsible for the events that shattered his family. The U.S. government took the role of King George's oppressive army; Weaver became the hero-farmer harmed only because he desired to live free of government harassment. As such, his story could be used to ground a new movement that, ironically, Weaver himself did not support.

The Aftermath and the FBI

The events at Ruby Ridge also had effects on the FBI—effects that were generally negative, ultimately serving the interests of conspiracy theorists. For example, several investigations were launched into the FBI's actions in Idaho. One was conducted by the FBI and focused specifically on the process by which the rules of engagement were articulated and acted on during the standoff. This investigation argued, and several courts later agreed, that these rules were violations of the citizens' constitutional rights and should never have been promulgated. The investigation also demonstrated the inadequate systems of communication and control that existed between Washington, D.C., and commanders in the field.[40] The report might have been viewed as a serious attempt of a federal agency to recognize the mistakes it had made. Similarly, its recommendations and findings—that no FBI officer should be allowed to develop independent rules of engagement on site and that several agents involved in standoff be reprimanded or demoted, for example—might have been viewed as a serious attempt to fix a troubled system. Unfortunately, the FBI classified this report and resisted releasing it even to Congress. Thus, it became a simple matter to assume that the report constituted a cover-up of the FBI's mistakes in Idaho. This perception was advanced when FBI Director Louis Freeh promoted the supervisor of the Ruby Ridge incident, Larry Potts, to the second-ranking position in the FBI: permanent deputy director. Many other agents involved in the standoff at Ruby Ridge received light, if any, punishment.[41]

The perception that the FBI was engaged in a cover-up was furthered in 1995 during a congressional investigation of the events at Ruby Ridge, as well as by a number of journalistic inquiries into the incident. These examinations revealed a number of mistakes, lies, and active attempts by agents to cover up what had occurred in Idaho. For example, in the hours after Lon Horiuchi had shot Kevin Harris and Vicki Weaver, the snipers who had been deployed around the Weaver home were recalled and left to sit together unobserved. For conspiracy theorists, this is taken as proof that the agents shaped their stories to fit a common theme. Additionally, another FBI agent, Michael Kahoe, pleaded guilty to obstructing justice when he destroyed an after-action report in which Horiuchi had described his actions on August 22.[42] Much attention was focused on Horiuchi's claim that he fired only because he saw someone on the ground fire at a hovering FBI helicopter. No such shots were ever fired, so Horiuchi's shots were legal only if the revised rules of engagement were legal. Courts established that these rules were unconstitutional, meaning that the FBI illegally shot American citizens. Moreover, Horiuchi's claim that his shooting of Vicki Weaver was accidental was repeatedly challenged, first by those who claimed that she was fully visible in the doorway of the Weaver cabin and second by those who argued that since the FBI had a prior report in which Vicki was alleged to be the moral leader of the family, her death must have been an intentional effort to break the family's will.[43] In light of claims by the attorneys prosecuting Weaver and Harris after the incident that the FBI withheld crucial information that would have assisted in convicting the two, a pattern of FBI obfuscation, denial, and irresponsibility emerged as fodder for the radical right. This image would be hardened less than a year later with the disaster in Waco—which, ironically, coincided with Weaver and Harris's trial.

Ultimately, in many ways Horiuchi became the public face of the FBI's oppressive evil for right-wing ideologues in the United States. From the right's perspective, here was a camouflage-wearing, sophisticated-gun-toting, highly trained representative of the evil federal government using his power to destroy the life of an otherwise innocent person. This anger manifested itself in murder charges against Horiuchi, a rare event for a government agent acting in accord with duly issued orders. The image of the FBI, in addition, had been profoundly tarnished. Elliott Ness was replaced with Lon Horiuchi, at least in the minds of the militia. The New World Order had a face and a mode of operation. (After years of indictments, court appeals, and a change in Boundary County prosecutors, all charges against Horiuchi were finally dropped in June 2001.)[44] For those Americans who believed that government was dangerous to liberty—a core cultural value—Ruby Ridge was proof. Horiuchi's actions thus made sense to those who hated government, even as the militia myth provided a model by which such evil actions could be resisted.

The Aftermath and the Militia Movement

As was shown in chapters 1, 2, and 3, the antigovernment, pro-gun, isolationist individualism and apocalyptic Christianity Randy

Weaver practiced was not unique in the United States. Moreover, once the details of the standoff at Ruby Ridge were presented in a way that emphasized Weaver's innocence and the government's evil, his story could serve as a rallying point around which hundreds of thousands of Americans could decide that they needed to organize a counterforce.

This potential was enhanced by the mistakes, lies, and cover-ups of the FBI and by the skillful way Weaver's lawyers and supporters stripped the most offensive religious- and gender-specific components of his ideology out of his story and instead cast Weaver in the role of the innocent victim of a government conspiracy. Thus, Randy Weaver and his family became symbols of Every Family U.S.A. rather than representatives of a kooky religion who sold illegal weapons. In this role, the government might target *anyone*, might kill *anyone's* wife as she held a baby in her arms. Accordingly, in line with the Revolutionary myth of the militia, thousands of Americans came to believe that if they did not defend themselves and their families against the federal government, the government would attempt to destroy them, just as it had Randy Weaver.

In a portent of things to come, one week after Randy Weaver surrendered, a white drifter opened fire on a black man and a white woman at a bus terminal in Spokane, Washington. The drifter had been enraged by the events in Idaho and had hoped to join the protests there, but he had arrived too late. When he was caught the next day, he explained that he had shot the two people—both of whom survived with permanent injuries—because white people and black people were not supposed to mix together.[45]

The movement grew from there. For example, on October 23, 1992, Pete Peters, a leader in the Christian Identity movement, sponsored a meeting of other believers to articulate a response to the incident at Ruby Ridge. The gathering, in Estes Park, Colorado, was attended by representatives from the radical right in American politics ranging from members of the Ku Klux Klan and the Aryan Nations to Gun Owners of America leader Larry Pratt. The outcome of the meeting was the creation of a common language in which the events at Ruby Ridge were to be presented and developed. This language deemphasized Weaver's racism and anti-Semitism in favor of a more neutral, antigovernment rhetoric. One of the organizers of the meeting, Louis Beam, thus constructed the Weavers as being victimized by "the tender mercies of a government gone mad."[46]

Further, attendees were encouraged to reduce the racist rhetoric in their ideologies in favor of terms that would be more popular in mainstream society.[47]

Style was not substance, however, for Peters's allies. As quoted by Morris Dees, Louis Beam gave a vitriol-laced speech aimed squarely at the evils of the federal government: "I warn you calmly, coldly, and without reservation that over the next ten years you will come to hate the government more than anything in your life. . . . The federal government in north Idaho has demonstrated brutally, horribly, and with great terror how it will enforce its claim that we are religious fanatics and enemies of the state."[48] Beam further urged those attending the conference to organize to fight the government while harking back to the myth of the militia in American political culture:

> We bear the torch of light, of justice, of liberty, and we will be heard. . .
> . We will not yield this country to the forces of darkness, oppression, and tyranny. . . .
> So if you believe in the truth, if you believe in justice, then join with us. We are marching to the beat of the same drum. The beat of that drum, like those heard at Valley Forge and at Gettysburg, has called good men everywhere to action.[49]

The public face of the movement, then, would focus on the victimization of innocent citizens by an abusive government. Motivating the membership, however, would be grounded on profound hatred of the national government.

In addition to providing a common ideological core around which groups might form, the Estes Park meeting also led to the creation of a new type of political protest organization in the United States. Larry Pratt reportedly called for the abandonment of traditional lobbying techniques and conventional political action in favor of the formation of small, armed militias that could resist government's illegal actions directly.[50] Beam then offered the notion of "leaderless resistance," a concept borrowed from the French Resistance of World War II that refers to each cell making its own choices about what to do, even as all cells agree on a general goal of action. Thus the militia need not be a highly organized, bureaucratized structure. Instead, multiple cells might form, and if the government were to destroy one, its members could not betray the members of other militia groups.[51] Taken together, the ideological and organizational innovations offered in the Colorado meeting laid the groundwork for the new militia movement.

The effect of this construction of the events at Ruby Ridge was to make it possible for hundreds of thousands of Americans to support the militia movement without feeling themselves to be racists, or wackos, or crazies. After all, it was the federal government that, by its own admission, had shot and killed an unarmed woman; it was (allegedly) the federal government that had lured a dog and a boy into a trap on their own land; it was the federal government that had (probably) entrapped Randy Weaver into selling illegal weapons in the first place. By obscuring the racism and anti-Semitism of Weaver's ideology, the Estes Park meeting constructed a template on which groups could form in a way that might draw support from the general community. Indeed, as was seen in chapter 3, the essential components of militia ideology correspond closely with the terms established in Colorado. Additionally, it was now possible join an actual group whose members shared your goals—in other words, as was discussed in chapter 2, individuals could join the same kinds of revolutionary militias that created America's freedoms. To be in the militia, then, was to be part of an organization dedicated to saving America from its abusive government, not to support the hate crimes of a few hard-right isolationists.

This ideological reconstruction of the Weaver family's values corresponded closely with the version of events that Gerry Spence and David Nevin presented at the Weaver and Harris trial in 1993. Thus, when the jury found Harris not guilty on all counts and Weaver guilty only of the failure-to-appear charge, it put a legal seal of approval on the new Weaver image. Moreover, this legal outcome meant that militia organizers could easily claim that the Weavers were innocent victims whose plight might portend one's own fate. The fact that the Weavers only came under government scrutiny after Randy was alleged to have threatened the life of the president, had attended several white supremacists' meetings, and agreed to sell illegal weapons—acts very few Americans would ever engage in—faded into the background. As constructed by skilled lawyers and canny political activists, Weaver's story became the tool militia leaders could use to motivate new generations of resistance to federal government actions.

The Trochmanns, friends of the Weavers who would, on January

1, 1994, announce the formation of the Militia of Montana, certainly focused on this antigovernment rhetoric in their construction of the events at Ruby Ridge. Carolyn Trochmann, for example, argued in an interview during the standoff that federal agents "provoked" the conflict by intruding on the Weavers' land.[52] "He just wanted to be left alone," she insisted in another interview, continuing, "He's willing to die for that."[53] Indeed, she pointed out, "Most of us are willing to die for that."[54] This is the case, she noted, because "[h]ere, we don't roll over. . . . Biblically, it's wrong whenever we allow the government to take another law from God."[55] All in all, she claimed, the Weavers were perfectly normal people who deserved to be left alone: "We read from the Bible, laughed, played games. . . . They were living one day at a time, and were not the least afraid to die."[56]

Other witnesses and protesters at the time of the standoff made similar arguments about the Weavers. "Randy Weaver just wanted to be left alone," noted Chuck Sandelin, a preacher in northern Idaho. "[B]ut the government went after his property, after his firearms, and now they're paying for it." "That man," Sandelin continued, "Randy Weaver, is a patriot, not a criminal."[57]

Similarly, Roke Sherman, an area resident, claimed that "Randy Weaver ain't a damn bit different than most folks living in this county. . . . He just wanted to be left alone."[58] Swiss immigrant and area restaurant owner Lorenz Caduff asked, "What's going on here? In Switzerland we saw the Wild West on television, but I thought that was a fantasy. Now it's happened right in front of us. It's very scary. My wife is screaming, 'I want to go back to Switzerland!'"[59] Even Bob Miller, managing editor of the *Bonner's Ferry Herald,* joined in the construction of the new Weaver myth: "While people do not condone Weaver's beliefs, there is quite a bit of support for his stand against the Federal Government. People think he was set up."[60]

Ultimately, in a move that suggests the way the Weaver myth eventually came to shape public opinion in large parts of the United States (for more details, see chapter 7), the perception that Randy Weaver and his family were victims of a corrupted federal government eventually found its way into the public discourse of elected Idaho politicians. Representative Helen Chenoweth, for example, a conservative swept into office as part of the Republican Party takeover of the U.S. House of Representatives in the 1994 elections that followed Ruby Ridge and Waco, intoned: "Mr. Speaker, the issue of how our Government is maltreating its citizens while ignoring the effects of its own unjust actions is very much on the minds of millions of Americans. . . . They are wondering just where our Government is placing its values when it gives the highest commendation possible to an individual for shooting a child in the back as he is running to the comforting arms of his father."[61] Senator Larry Craig made a similar, if less melodramatic, point when he noted:

> The virtual exoneration of the two defendants was seen as proof that the Federal Government had acted improperly. Fairly or unfairly, the public expected the Government's law enforcement experts to be just that— experts. Even one misstep would have raised questions. The cumulative effect of these blunders was devastating with public opinion in my State. Not only did they diminish the value of the physical evidence and the credibility of the law enforcement testimony, but they strengthened the popular notion of the case as an example of powerful, corrupt Government pursuing vulnerable citizens and trying to cover up its own misdeeds.[62]

Even powerful actors in government, then, articulated a version of the standoff that minimized Weaver's responsibility for the events on Ruby Ridge even as it legitimated the formation of militias pledged to prevent such abuses.

In a final irony, the ideological and organizational lessons that the growing militia movement drew from Randy Weaver's conflict with the federal government ran counter to Weaver's actual goals and desires. Even after moving back to Iowa after being released from prison, Weaver remained an adherent of the basic tenets of Christian Identity and its racist, anti-Semitic values. He became, at most, a reluctant hero for a militia movement that rejected the racism that was at the core of his ideology. The movement's Everyman thus was a creation of the militia's making, using the stuff of American culture and myths linked to right-wing populist thought, not Randy Weaver's. But his story, combined with the events from February to April in Waco and linked to long-established right-wing ideological principles in a culture convinced that private gun owners had defeated the world's most powerful army during the American Revolution, would lead to the rise of the modern militia movement in America.

5

The Fire:
David Koresh, the Branch Davidians,
and the Fire at Waco

What the standoff at Ruby Ridge sparked, the fire at Waco, Texas, on April 19, 1993, inflamed. Hundreds of thousands of Americans culturally and ideologically inclined to believe that the government was a corrupt agent of the New World Order found their proof in the deaths of at least seventy-five members of a religious movement known as the Branch Davidians. The events at the Davidian compound, known as Mt. Carmel, placed the Bureau of Alcohol, Tobacco, and Firearms and the Federal Bureau of Investigation—especially its Hostage Rescue Team—at center stage once again. Thus, believers in the evil of the federal government not only had evidence of what government might do to anyone who deviated from its rules—especially regarding guns—but also had proof of who the primary actors in the coming oppression would be. Ultimately, the formation of armed, trained militia groups would, for many Americans, seem the only way to resist a heavily armed and oppressive government—just as the militia had opposed and defeated the British army in the American Revolution.

Coming to Waco

Unlike Randy Weaver, who was a recent immigrant to Idaho when his troubles with the federal government began, the religious sect that came to be known as the Branch Davidians had been in Waco for almost sixty years when its final showdown with the federal government began. The group's leader in April 1993, David Koresh, had lived in Waco since 1981 and was a native Texan.[1] Thus, for those people who wanted an example of federal government intrusion in the lives of ordinary citizens who were tolerated in their community, the standoff and fire of February–April 1993 would provide a clear case.

As was the case with Randy Weaver, David Koresh and the Branch Davidians were not in a militia, nor did their ideas correspond very closely with those of the militia movement. Instead, the events at Waco were constructed to promote the militia cause by entrepreneurial leaders of militia groups and by sympathetic political and cultural figures.

The disconnect between who and what the Branch Davidians were and the role they were assigned in the emerging militia movement can be illustrated by an examination of Davidian thought and practices, especially under their final leader, David Koresh. The Branch Davidians are an offshoot of Seventh-Day Adventism. Adventism, founded in 1818 by William Miller, holds that the current generation of people are living in the "end times," that period of time just before Christ's tumultuous return to Earth heralded by the Battle of Armageddon and the rise of a new Eden. In addition, Adventism insists that the Bible is a living, contextually based work that requires the interpretation of a series of living prophets to be understood properly. Indeed, prophecy itself makes things happen: prophets do not just tell the future; instead, the act of linking past words to current contexts makes the words come true at a specific time. Finally, Adventists believe that 144,000 "branches"— individuals who properly understand the Bible and God's message—will serve at Christ's right hand when the new Garden of Paradise is created.[2]

The group that eventually became the Branch Davidians was founded as the Davidian Adventists in 1929 by Victor Houteff. While subscribing to the main tenets of Adventism, he added two dimensions to Adventist teachings. First, he argued that the church, which had already grown quite large, needed to be purified to achieve the 144,000 true believers who could serve during Christ's rule. Second, he taught that the new Eden would literally rise in Palestine, eventually necessitating a move there by the 144,000 elect Adventists. These preachings led to a schism between the Seventh-Day Adventists and the Davidian Adventists that caused a formal separation in 1934.[3]

In 1935, Houteff bought land near Waco for the purpose of building a religious complex. He called it Mt. Carmel. In 1955, when Houteff died, the surviving members of his group sold the original Mt. Carmel to buy another piece of property near Waco.[4] It was at this later Mt. Carmel that David Koresh and his followers died in 1993.

David Koresh was born Vernon Howell in August 1959. His mother raised him in the Seventh-Day Adventist church in Tyler, Texas, but in 1981 he joined the Branch Davidians in Waco. His insistence that their church was corrupt led to his expulsion by the Tyler Adventists in 1983.[5]

Despite the fact that Howell was a shy, retiring young man, he captured the attention of the Branch Davidians' leader, a woman named Lois Roden. Roden recognized Vernon as her successor in 1983, even though she had an adult son, George.[6]

Howell was, at this point in his life, an intense, profoundly religious person totally committed to Adventist theology. He was also a young man in love with his guitar and rock music. The possible tension between these passions seemed to manifest itself in an ideology of sexuality that would both complicate his life at the Branch Davidian compound and eventually bring him to the attention of law enforcement authorities. Specifically, Howell believed that sex and sexuality were evil even as he experienced sexual desire. This tension led him to justify his own sexuality while insisting that his followers—even married couples—abstain from sexual conduct. To achieve this position, Howell drew on passages in the Bible that suggest that the person who would lead the world to the Second Coming would be a "Sinful Messiah": an ordinary human rather than an immaculately conceived child of God. In engaging in sexual acts, then, Howell was preparing himself to create the conditions for the Second Coming. In denying his followers their sexuality, he was protecting their entry into the new Garden of Eden.

Howell legally married the fourteen-year-old daughter of a Davidian, Rachel Jones, in 1984. He would later illegally marry multiple women in the Davidian church even as he segregated most males from most females regardless of marital status.[7] These marriages were part of the justification later used to charge and attempt to arrest Koresh in 1993.

Howell's marriage to Rachel Jones provoked a schism among the Branch Davidians at Waco. Lois Roden, unsurprisingly, was upset on hearing the news, and her subsequent revelation that she had had an affair with Howell caused many followers to lose faith in his leadership. George Roden, Lois's son, took advantage of this situation to garner support to have Howell thrown out of the compound in 1985. Howell and his supporters left Mt. Carmel for property in Palestine, Texas, for the next several years. (Lois Roden died in 1986.)[8]

Being thrown out of Mt. Carmel was not the only important event for Howell in 1985. He also visited Israel that year. He later claimed that God spoke to him in Israel and told him that he, Vernon Howell, was the last prophet. His prophecies would foretell the Second Coming.[9] It was from this apocalyptic frame of mind that Koresh later negotiated with the federal authorities trying to arrest him.

In 1986, Howell announced a nonlegal marriage to Karen Doyle, the fourteen-year-old daughter of another Branch Davidian. He also married Michele Jones, Rachel's twelve-year-old sister, and fathered a child with her. This was followed by at least three more marriages in 1987.[10]

It is worth noting that each of these marriages was supported by most Branch Davidians. Convinced, like Koresh, that the coming end times would be prophesied by a sinful Messiah, they perceived his sexuality as proof of his having been chosen by God. His preaching that even married couples should live apart likewise was understood by the Davidians to be properly based in biblical interpretation. Thus, acts that would seem deviant and statutory rapes to outsiders were seen as appropriate and godly among Koresh's followers.

In November 1987, a series of bizarre events culminated in Howell's return to Mt. Carmel. In that month, George Roden dug up the remains of a former Branch Davidian and challenged Howell, if Howell was the last prophet, to raise the man from the dead. Howell reported the illegal exhumation to the police, and when the police demanded proof, Howell organized a raid on the Mt. Carmel compound to take pictures of the exposed corpse. Howell and his supporters were discovered by Roden and his allies on the night of their raid, and a forty-five-minute gun battle that led to several injuries ensued between the two forces. Howell and his fellow commandos were arrested and charged with attempted murder. In April 1988, all of Howell's followers were acquitted of the attempted murder charges, and Howell himself went free when the jury could not agree on a verdict. George Roden then became enmeshed in another legal controversy when he was accused of murdering a fifty-six-year-old man. Roden escaped conviction on grounds of insanity and was committed to a mental hospital. At this point, Howell returned to Mt. Carmel and became the dominant figure of the Branch Davidian movement.[11]

In 1990, Howell changed his name to a biblical one: David Koresh—David for King David and Koresh after King Cyrus, who freed the Jews from bondage.[12] He preached that he, not the historical Jesus Christ, was the Lamb of God who could open the seven seals of prophecy contained in the Book of Revelation. He argued that the entire Bible constituted the seven seals and that he was the final prophet who would interpret and thus cause the Second Coming. He insisted that the term "Christ" was a title, not a condition, and so he could be the new Christ. And, perhaps most important in light of the coming events, he taught that resistance to evil was required by the Bible and was a necessary precondition for the establishment of God's rule on Earth.[13] As such, his ideology was tightly linked to premillennialist Christianity.

Throughout this period the Branch Davidians recruited new members from around the world. The group drew an ethnically diverse membership and owned property in California in addition to the Waco compound.[14] Regardless of how far outside the mainstream of American religious movements the Branch Davidians were, then, they were moderately successful and reasonably well integrated into the communities in which they operated.

The Branch Davidians first came to the attention of federal law enforcement authorities in September 1990 when two Branch Davidians left the group and reported that Koresh was engaged in mass child abuse and was accumulating a vast stockpile of illegal weapons in his Waco compound. The child abuse charges stemmed from his multiple "marriages" to very young girls: despite the fact that the girls' Branch Davidian parents consented to his liaisons, many were with girls under the age of consent in Texas.[15] The weapons allegations were more complex but emerged from two practices the Branch Davidians had followed at least since George Roden had controlled the group. First, the Branch Davidians had made substantial amounts of money to support their activities by selling weapons, dried foodstuffs, and even a David Koresh line of camouflage clothing at gun shows. At any point in time, then, they might be storing a significant number of weapons on their grounds. Second, the group had purchased and probably installed a number of kits designed to convert semiautomatic weapons to fully automatic.[16]

Other information emerged that suggested Koresh was engaged in more at Mt. Carmel than simply teaching religion. A driver for United Parcel Service reported that he had seen a grenade and a quantity of black powder gunpowder in a package that broke open as he was delivering it. In January 1992, an Australian television program broadcast a lurid documentary of Koresh's sexual practices and religious extremism. This story heightened the federal authorities' attention to David Koresh and his group. By June 1992, the Bureau of Alcohol, Tobacco, and Firearms (ATF) began an investigation into Koresh's weapons sales and sent an undercover agent to join his group.[17]

It was on the basis of allegations made by the former Branch Davidians and the ATF's own informant that the local agent for the ATF filed an affidavit to get an arrest warrant for David Koresh. While the agency is charged with investigating weapons violations, much of its affidavit for a warrant to arrest Koresh focused on his sexual practices.[18] Once the warrant was granted, the agency decided that it would take an aggressive "dynamic entry" to arrest Koresh since neither he nor any of his followers were expected to give up quietly. Operation Trojan Horse was launched at 9:48 A.M. on Sunday, February 28, 1993.[19] The modern American militia movement was its outcome.

Fifty-one Days in Texas

Like their ancient Greek predecessors, the ATF agents intended to surprise their opponents and capture their goal quickly. Several dozen agents would be hidden in cattle trucks that would pull up close to the Mt. Carmel buildings as if lost. Then, when the Branch Davidians least expected it, the agents would deploy, execute a dynamic assault on the property, and arrest Koresh.[20]

Nothing went as planned. Surprise was never achieved; indeed, the Branch Davidians were well aware that the raid was coming at its appointed time. In an example of inept planning, for example, the undercover agent in the Mt. Carmel compound had been discovered as a plant early during his time in the group: he and a group of men in their mid-twenties and mid-thirties had moved into a house across the road from Mt. Carmel and claimed that they were college students renting the house, although they were too old to be ordinary students, drove cars that were far too nice for average college students, and were living in a house that the owner had promised neighbors to never rent. On the morning of the raid, Koresh told the undercover agent, Robert Rodriguez, that he knew the assault was coming and asked Rodriguez to leave the compound to try to stop the attack. Rodriguez informed his superiors of Koresh's foreknowledge an hour before the raid began.[21]

Other signs pointed to an attack. In the days prior to the raid, Waco's hotels had filled with heavily armed ATF agents. On the morning of the twenty-eighth, a television reporter stopped a local postman and asked for directions to Mt. Carmel. In the course of their conversation, the reporter told the mailman that a raid was being launched later that morning. The mailman, who was a Branch Davidian, immediately returned to the compound to warn Koresh. Finally, helicopters began circling the property at 9:30 in anticipation of the coming conflict.[22] Something was obviously about to happen.

In a move that would ultimately fuel many conspiracy theories, the ATF leadership's response to the news that their raid had been exposed was to go forward as fast as possible.[23] Thus, an assault that was entirely dependent upon surprise for success was to proceed in the absence of surprise against a group that agents believed were heavily armed and likely to resist. For conspiracy theorists, this is proof that the raid was deadly in its intent: if the ATF only wanted to arrest Koresh, they insist, the ATF would not have risked an assault. Getting fired upon, however, gave the ATF the right to use deadly force.

As the raid began, David Koresh opened the door of Mt. Carmel and called out to the agents to stop their assault. Agents fired at him, and he shut the door. Other agents then climbed onto lower parts of the building in an effort to break into the compound. Gunfire poured into and out of the building for several hours, ultimately killing four ATF agents and six Branch Davidians while wounding twenty officers and four Davidians. Koresh was among the wounded. A cease-fire was arranged by noon.[24]

On March 1, the Federal Bureau of Investigation (FBI) took over control of the scene at Mt. Carmel and deployed its Hostage Rescue Team (HRT) to Waco despite the fact that no one in the compound was a hostage. Special Agent in Charge Jeff Jamar asserted that the FBI would wait the Branch Davidians out no matter how long they stayed in their compound. However, as had been the case in Idaho, the HRT had a strong antinegotiation bias: as the name suggests, the HRT is designed to rescue people, not wait for negotiations to play out.[25]

Unlike Randy Weaver, David Koresh proved very willing to talk to the FBI's negotiators. Indeed, he would spend hours discoursing on his theories of biblical interpretation and his prophetic role in the coming days. Ultimately, FBI negotiators would grow tired of Koresh's long orations, referring to them as "Bible Babble."[26]

It is worth noting that the religious principles Koresh advocated, while well outside those espoused by mainstream Christian groups, are relatively common among right-wing religious traditions. As was addressed in chapter 3, millennialism and apocalypticism are common components of right-wing thought. Thus, while Koresh was promoting values that many Americans (including the FBI's negotiators) did not agree with or even understand, his approach to God was understood by millions of conservative religious leaders and followers.

It is also worth noting that little in Koresh's approach linked to militia ideology. His theory of sexuality, the notion of prophetic interpretation making God's plan manifest in the world, and the special privilege of 144,000 believers as an elite group with a special role in God's plan all fell outside militia ideology; at best, the 144,000 elect relate indirectly to militia ideology's emphasis on the importance of sovereign citizens. Thus, as had been the case with Randy Weaver, Koresh's role in the formation of the militia movement derived from how his ideology and actions were interpreted by others after the fact.

In retrospect it is clear that the FBI's negotiators and Koresh had profoundly different frames of reference regarding the purposes of the negotiations. For the FBI, the conversations were an opportunity to try to persuade members of the community to leave Mt. Carmel, as well as to convince Koresh to surrender. For Koresh, the phone calls were a chance to spread his understanding of biblical truth to the world. This disjunction in purpose manifested itself at many points in the negotiations, to deadly effect.

One such gap between the FBI's goals and Koresh's manifested itself early in the standoff. Koresh promised to surrender if he were allowed to broadcast a message on the Christian Broadcasting Network (CBN). This request was granted; however, Koresh reneged on March 2, claiming that God had told him to wait. For the FBI, this was proof that Koresh was a charlatan hiding behind a religious facade For Koresh, the FBI's failure to recognize the legitimacy of his position as the Lamb proved that he could not trust the agency to keep its promises to him.[27]

Despite this disjunction, the first week of the standoff was a productive one from the government's point of view. Twenty-three Branch Davidians left the compound, including most of the children who were not Koresh's own. While Koresh himself did not seem in a hurry to give up, the FBI had developed a relationship with his second in command, Steve Schneider, who engaged in negotiations that were more explicit than Koresh's were.[28]

During this period the FBI sent in a video camera and asked the Branch Davidians to describe their values and ideals. This tape, which was not released to the media during the standoff, showed groups of relatively happy, dedicated supporters of Koresh talking about their inability to understand why the raid was ever launched. It also showed Koresh surrounded by his children.[29]

As time passed, however, the FBI's tactics hardened. On the day of the raid, for example, several of the mothers at Mt. Carmel had stopped lactating. Their children needed milk. Thus, on the same day that many children left the compound, the Branch Davidians gave the FBI $1,000 to pay their bills and to buy milk for the remaining children. FBI negotiators took this as an opportunity to convince the Davidians to release more children in a milk-for-children exchange. The Davidians took this as a betrayal, especially when they learned that the released children were not being sent to live with relatives or being fed according to the strict dietary protocols that Koresh demanded. Negotiations soured on both sides.[30]

Shortly after the milk-for-children demand, the FBI cut off communications from the Branch Davidian compound to the outside world. This angered Koresh, who had used multiple interviews with various press sources to teach the world about the coming

Armageddon. Bradley armored vehicles then began patrolling the grounds of Mt. Carmel, and the FBI increased its psychological warfare against the Branch Davidians by turning spotlights on the buildings twenty-four hours a day and by playing tapes of annoying, aggravating sounds at high volume. The most shocking of these were the sounds of rabbits being slaughtered.[31]

As anyone familiar with Koresh's religious values might have expected, these attempts to pressure the Branch Davidians to leave the compound only enhanced their conviction that the end times were near. Rather than splitting Koresh from his followers, then, the FBI's actions encouraged the group's belief that government—the Whore of Babylon—was acting on the Antichrist's orders. As the FBI increasingly treated Koresh as a criminal, it established the truth of his arguments in his followers' minds.

Interestingly, there were no religious experts involved in the negotiations. While several academic specialists in millennialist religions offered their help in interpreting Koresh's "Bible Babble," the FBI generally refused their help. Instead, the government's negotiators relied on analyses offered by anticult activists and other criminal psychologists. These experts agreed that Koresh was an out-of-control thug hiding behind his religious rhetoric. Accordingly, when Koresh made a promise to leave—on April 14, he offered to surrender as soon as he had finished a commentary on the seven seals—the FBI assumed that the promise was just another ploy. Koresh's original promise to leave after broadcasting his message on CBN was taken as proof of this interpretation.[32]

On March 21, several Branch Davidians left the compound. Only three more would leave before the end.[33] The FBI began planning another assault on the property to arrest Koresh and anyone who had been involved in the original firefight. Armored vehicles destroyed several outbuildings in the compound, and by early April over 660 FBI agents, 35 ATF agents, 5 customs agents, 15 U.S. Army troops, 130 Texas State Police, 10 Texas National Guard members, and 30 Texas Rangers had arrived in Waco.[34]

It was in this context of a force buildup that Koresh's surrender offer of April 14 was made. Koresh claimed that he would surrender to authorities as soon as he finished his commentary on the seven seals; those who believe this claim note that by April 17 the community was almost out of water. By April 19, Koresh had finished his commentary on the first five of the seven seals.[35]

As the FBI planned its final assault, it had several consultations with U.S. Attorney General Janet Reno. These discussions included the plan to use CS (chlorobenzalmalononitrile) gas in an effort to force the Davidians to leave their home. CS gas burns skin on contact and causes mucous membranes to swell; nausea is a common side effect. Such suffering was expected to pressure the Davidians, particularly the mothers, to flee the compound with their children. However, neither Reno nor FBI Director William Sessions was informed that CS gas was not approved for use inside buildings. Nor was either official informed of Koresh's surrender offer. They approved the FBI's planned assault, which was scheduled for April 19, 1993.[36]

April 19 is a significant day in American and world history. It was on April 19, 1775, that local volunteers responded to Paul Revere's midnight ride and attacked a column of British troops trying to seize stockpiles of weapons in Lexington and Concord, Massachusetts. Some accounts give Adolf Hitler's birthdate as April 19, 1889. On April 19, 1943, the German army began its assault on the Warsaw ghetto.[37] And it would be on April 19, 1995, that Timothy McVeigh destroyed the Alfred P. Murrah Federal Building in Oklahoma City, Oklahoma, as an act of vengeance for the FBI assault on Mt. Carmel on April 19, 1993.

The FBI's assault on the Branch Davidian compound began early in the morning of April 19. At 5:59 A.M., FBI negotiators called the Branch Davidians, demanded their surrender, and informed them that a tank was going to inject tear gas into the compound. They also insisted that the tank's action was not an assault since the tank was not going to enter the building. At 6:04 A.M., a specially equipped Bradley fighting vehicle began knocking holes in the walls of the Mt. Carmel Center and injecting CS gas into the building through a long metal tube sticking over the front of the tank. It made holes and injected gas in several places throughout the complex.[38]

As the morning passed, no Branch Davidians escaped. Occasionally, gunfire came from the buildings; in response, FBI tanks inserted more gas. The plan was to move the people into the center of the building where they would not be able to fire on any approaching agents if an assault was necessary.[39]

Throughout the operation, the FBI had a sense of what was going on inside Mt. Carmel because several listening devices were stationed on or near the building. As tanks began inserting the CS gas, Koresh and other leaders were heard telling their followers to put their gas masks on. No gas masks were available for the children, however—a fact that the FBI knew and assumed would encourage the mothers to escape.[40] At 11:42 A.M., as more gas was being inserted, FBI tape recordings indicate that the Davidians began discussing whether, where, and when to start fires to try to destroy or trap the Bradley tanks in the compound.[41]

Although CS gas is flammable and would be highly concentrated as it was injected into the Branch Davidian compound, the FBI had not alerted the local fire department to the possibility that a fire might occur at Mt. Carmel. Thus, when fire did break out, there was no firefighting equipment on the property.[42] Whether firefighters could have stopped the blaze is an open question, of course, and if there were continuing gunshots coming from the building, it is not clear that the firefighters would have even made the effort. The lack of firefighting equipment on scene would be a central point in subsequent conspiracy theories, however.

The first fire was detected by an FBI observational airplane using forward-looking infrared radar (FLIR) at 11:42 A.M. It was not near any of the Bradley vehicles. By 12:07 P.M., three more fires were detected.[43] The flames quickly consumed the dry plywood building. In fire temperatures reaching 2,000 degrees Fahrenheit, the complex burned to the ground in approximately twenty-five minutes.[44] The FBI called for fire trucks at 12:12. By 12:22, two engines had arrived. They were not allowed to pass the FBI checkpoint until 12:37. Five minutes earlier an agent on scene had informed his superiors in Washington, D.C., that the building had been fully destroyed.[45]

While nine Branch Davidians ultimately survived, at least seventy-five were killed. (Since no one knew exactly how many people were in the building, no one knows exactly how many died. Estimates range as high as eighty-six.) Some appear to have been asphyxiated, some burned to death, and several others, including Koresh, died of gunshot wounds. The standoff at Waco was over.

The Aftermaths of Waco

As was the case with Randy Weaver's standoff in Idaho, the events that occurred at Waco were constructed in ways to legitimate and advocate the new militia movement. While the ATF raid, FBI negotiation, and final assault on the compound had immediate effects for the Branch Davidians, their families, and the agencies involved, their broadest effects were manifested in the rapid spread of the modern militia movement throughout most of the United States.

The Aftermath and the Branch Davidians

Eleven surviving members of Koresh's group, some of whom had left the compound before the final fire, were charged with murder, attempted murder, conspiracy to commit murder, and possession of illegal firearms—specifically, forty-eight machine guns and other destructive devices, such as hand grenades. They were tried in federal court since the agents killed had been U.S. employees. As the prosecution had done in Idaho, the Waco prosecution tried to prove that simply by going to Mt. Carmel, Koresh's followers had engaged in a conspiracy to kill federal agents. The number of weapons owned by the Branch Davidians was used as proof that the group was armed and looking for a fight.[46]

In contrast with the defense strategy in Idaho, the defense in the Waco case did not articulate an elaborate conspiracy theory to justify their clients' actions. That would come later, through the work of militia and other antigovernment leaders. Instead, they appealed to Texans' sense that gun ownership was natural and expected. The defense pointed out that the guns were an investment; testimony was offered that the guns had in fact increased in value. Defense lawyers also insisted that, under Texas law, if law enforcement authorities use unreasonable force in making an arrest, citizens have the right to self-defense. Thus, even though the Texas law did not apply in federal court, the defense was able to introduce the idea that the original ATF raid had been improper since agents did not identify themselves. Any subsequent violence against the government, then, was justified.[47]

In a sign of the deep public tension about the government's actions at Waco and during the trial, a controversy emerged during the trial involving a Texas-based interest group, the Fully Informed Jury Association (FIJA). The judge sealed the names of the jury pool in the Davidian case, and FIJA protested. As an organization, FIJA argues that juries have the right to nullify government acts and laws if jurors find that the government has behaved improperly.

The group demanded the opportunity to mail information to the jurors so they could consider this point of view. When the judge refused, FIJA members conducted daily protests outside the courthouse.[48]

The jury rejected the prosecution's case. The Davidians were found not guilty of most of the serious charges—murder, conspiracy, attempted murder, and the like. Several were convicted of possessing illegal weapons, others were found to be in violation of immigration law, and some were convicted of involuntary manslaughter.[49] Compared to the possible verdicts, the jury's decision was seen as a repudiation of the government's case.

The jury's verdict did not stand, however. The judge set it aside on grounds that the members had failed to follow his instructions. One charge, for example, was possession of illegal firearms in the commission of a crime. Thus, the judge reasoned, being guilty of possessing the weapons meant that the Branch Davidians were also guilty of committing a crime. Similarly, he reasoned that the process of acquiring the weapons proved that the Davidians had engaged in a conspiracy. In response, he sentenced five Davidians to forty-year terms, and one each to twenty-, fifteen-, and five-year sentences. Three were freed. In addition, each of the convicted Davidians was ordered to pay $1.2 million in restitution to the FBI and the ATF.[50]

The verdicts were upheld on appeal.[51] Today, several groups of Branch Davidians live on or near the Mt. Carmel grounds and contend for leadership of the group. One has run tours of the bulldozed facility. The group has largely disappeared.[52] However, the justification offered for their actions—that they were essentially innocent gun collectors who had the right to practice their religion free from government interference and who were brutalized by a corrupt government—had been established as fact for many Americans. As had happened with Randy Weaver, the extremism that led the Davidians to their marginal lifestyle was obscured. What was left was a story that, in combination with the evident errors of the ATF and the FBI, could become the foundation of the militia movement.

The Aftermath for the FBI and the ATF

Two major actions in nine months left both the ATF and the FBI subject to public scrutiny and review. Both the Treasury Department—home of the ATF—and the Justice Department—home of the FBI—prepared special after-action reports on the incidents. In 1995, congressional inquiries also followed, with Waco being investigated even before Ruby Ridge.

The Treasury Department and Justice Department reports were remarkably similar in their findings. Both essentially cleared their agencies of causing the terrible series of events that culminated in the fire. Treasury found the ATF guilty only of mismanaging the original raid and revealed that some of its agents had tried to cover up their mistakes. The FBI was not found to have violated rules or procedures in either the negotiations or the final assault; the lack of coordination between the negotiating and tactical units at Waco drew the report's major criticism.[53]

The congressional investigation was much harsher. Questions emerged, particularly from Republicans on three committees—the House Judiciary Subcommittee on Crime, the House Government Reform and Oversight Subcommittee on Criminal Justice, and the Senate Judiciary Committee—about whether the government had abused its authority in attacking people simply because they had offbeat religious ideas and happened to own guns. Moreover, holes in the FBI story were exposed: evidence had been destroyed or was missing, and the disjunction had become clearer between the FBI's negotiating strategy and the on-scene conduct of the Hostage Rescue Team using Bradley fighting vehicles to destroy Davidian property in the weeks before the final assault. (The details of the missing evidence will be addressed in the next section.) Some evidence appeared only under testimony, such as the fact that the FBI had recorded the events of April 19, 1993, from the FLIR-equipped aircraft. The tapes were not released even then. The fact that the FBI used pyrotechnic tear-gas grenades capable of starting fires during the raid would not emerge for years.[54]

The reputation of the FBI, and particularly of its Hostage Rescue Team, was seriously damaged in the aftermath of these events. Richard Rogers, commander of the HRT, was removed from his position in June 1993.[55] Subsequently, new strategies for dealing with extreme religious or ideological groups were implemented. These were grounded on a negotiate-for-as-long-as-it-takes model. Indeed, one of the ironies of the subsequent growth in the militia movement was that it came in response to a style of law enforcement the FBI largely abandoned after the catastrophe at Waco.

Yet the FBI's slow release of evidence like the FLIR tape and its use of tear-gas grenades on April 19 caused the incident to remain alive in the minds of antigovernment ideologues. As a result, in September 1999 Attorney General Janet Reno appointed former Senator John Danforth as independent prosecutor to investigate the government's actions at Waco, including allegations that FBI agents shot at Branch Davidians during the fire. (This part of the conspiracy theory will also be addressed in the next section of this chapter.) Danforth's report, released in July 2000, concluded that the government had done nothing wrong. By this time, however, the image of federal agents burning down Mt. Carmel and abusing their authority was already well established in American public opinion. Indeed, Danforth's report noted that 61 percent of Americans believed that the government started the fire at Mt. Carmel.[56]

The long-term impact of Americans' perception that the government caused the fire that killed the Branch Davidians will be addressed in chapter 7. The short-term effect, however, was inflammatory. As constructed by defense attorneys and leaders of antigovernment groups, the ATF and FBI became vicious symbols of the New World Order. This new political order was believed to be so savage that it would even kill innocent children to achieve its goals. Thus, regardless of which agency was responsible for what actions at Waco, and indeed regardless of whether Koresh himself started every fire and shot every victim in the Mt. Carmel complex, for those Americans convinced that government would take and cover up any action as part of their shadow agenda, Waco was proof.

The Aftermath and the Militia Movement

The militia response to the events at Waco began even as the standoff was continuing. Linda Thompson, an Indianapolis attorney who promoted militia values, sent a fax to sympathetic people in the name of the "Unorganized Militia." In this fax she asked militia members to assemble in Waco "with long arms, vehicles (including tracked and armored), aircraft, and any available gear for inspection for fitness and use in a well-regulated militia, at 9:00 a.m. on Saturday, April 3, 1993."[57] While few militia members actually responded—Thompson's former boss, Patriot leader Gary

Hunt, sent out a counterfax requesting that everyone stay home[58]—Koresh's transformation into a militia hero had begun.

Thompson would be a central player in constructing the myth of Waco. In this myth Koresh and the Branch Davidians, like the simple Americans of the Revolutionary myth, became innocent, God-fearing, ordinary citizens victimized by the evil forces of an oppressive, corrupted government. Thus, as had happened in the case of Randy Weaver, the possibility that Koresh and his followers were in any way complicit in the events at Mt. Carmel was ignored in favor of a new story that could galvanize sympathetic Americans to join the developing militia movement. Creative story-telling, entrepreneurial group leaders, government mistakes, and significant mainstream political and cultural leaders would combine to make Waco the symbol of everything dangerous about government. As such, it would make the necessity of a citizen militia obvious.

Thompson's primary role in the reconstruction of the Waco story came through her production of two videotapes about the events at Mt. Carmel: *Waco: The Big Lie* and *Waco: The Big Lie Continues.* These videotapes asserted many points that antigovernment advocates would take as "truth." For example, *Waco: The Big Lie* insisted that government tanks actually shot fire from their turrets, rather than just gas. The government is seen to want to kill the Davidians. The tape emphasizes the deaths of the children. Similarly, *Waco: The Big Lie Continues* shows an ostensible government memo that outlines plans to deliberately attack churches with machine guns. Without evidence, it claims that a gap in news coverage of the final raid must contain an edit of government wrongdoing. And, perhaps most remarkably, it notes that three of the four agents killed in the initial, February 28 raid had been bodyguards for President Clinton. The tape asserts that these men were shot through the head, at close range, "professional execution style" by other government agents.[59] Why this was done is left unexplained.

A longer video released in 1997, *Waco: The Rules of Engagement,* makes similar claims to Thompson's, but with greater presentation of evidence. The religious extremism of the Branch Davidians is completely downplayed, as is any reference to Koresh's Bible Babble. In fact, the video presents only the portions of the tapes made of the Koresh-FBI negotiations in which Koresh is attacking the government for assaulting his house; the hours of religious discourse are passed over. Of particular emphasis are portions in which Koresh and his supporters allege that gunfire came from the helicopters circling Mt. Carmel during the initial raid. Extensive use is made of a videotape the Branch Davidians made of themselves during the standoff; the Davidians are shown to be decent, caring people committed to their values and lifestyle. The program also presents extensive footage of the final assault recorded by the FLIR aircraft. It uses this tape to make the allegation, based on flashes apparently outside the Davidian compound, that FBI agents had fired at Davidians to force them to remain in the burning building and die. (Ironically, one of the HRT snipers in position around the Branch Davidian compound on April 19 was Lon Horiuchi, who had been a central figure in the Ruby Ridge incident and its aftermath.) The tape also alleges that ATF agents shot at Davidians from helicopters during the initial February raid. Such indiscriminate killing and inattention to life is shown to prove the government's indifference to the lives of its citizens.[60]

These and other allegations became the core of the "government did it" myth about Waco. Other events combined with the allegations made in these videotapes to "prove" the government's venality for those who desired such proof. Cumulatively, this list of events was constructed in a way that made the government guilty and the militia necessary:

- Three days after the fire, state troopers in Texas arrested reporters with the Associated Press and the *Houston Chronicle* and seized film they had shot of the burned compound.
- Texas Rangers were not allowed onto the Mt. Carmel property until after federal agents had completed their investigation.
- The Branch Davidian compound was bulldozed just days after the fire. This was ostensibly done so that the Texas Department of Health could work on the property; however, the department's work did not commence for a year.
- A safe found onsite with $50,000 in cash and precious metals was signed over to the FBI by Texas authorities; neither the safe nor the money ever appeared in FBI evidence lockers.
- Autopsies were performed quickly and carelessly. In one case, a fifty-year-old woman was identified as a ten-year-old girl.
- Koresh's commentary on the seven seals was withheld for months.

- The FLIR tapes were withheld for years, and only one tape has ever been released, even though antigovernment activists insist there must have been more.
- The FLIR video is alleged to show a second airplane operating at lower altitude over the compound. Neither the existence of that airplane nor any tapes or evidence it collected has ever been acknowledged by the FBI.
- A television camera with a long-range lens filmed what appeared to be an HRT member filming the final operation; that tape, if it exists, has never been released.
- The ATF began a shooting review thirty-six hours after its February raid; the person directing the review was ordered to stop his investigation on the grounds that it might produce Brady material—that is, material helpful to the defense that the prosecution is obliged to turn over.
- HRT's actions in bulldozing and running over cars and other property on the Branch Davidian compound is alleged to have destroyed evidence from which bullet trajectories and other information injurious to the government might have been collected.
- A Branch Davidian posted to an outbuilding on the property on the morning of February 28 is alleged to have been assassinated by government agents. Killed March 1, Mike Schroeder was pictured after his death wearing a blue wool watch cap. This cap, which might have contained gunpowder and other evidence if he had been shot at close range as in an execution, disappeared before his autopsy.
- Half of the front door of the main building at Mt. Carmel— the right side of a two-door opening—is missing. The ATF alleges that Koresh and his supporters fired through this door as the ATF launched its original raid. Antigovernment actors believe the right side of the door proves that ATF agents fired first.
- Tapes of the final hours of the Branch Davidians made by the eleven listening devices positioned around Mt. Carmel were altered to imply that the Davidians had started the fire.
- Only one alleged machine gun in the Davidian arsenal was ever examined by experts, and the defense was not allowed to have its own experts test the weapon.
- Surviving Branch Davidians and supporters allege that holes

in the roof of Mt. Carmel were made by gunfire from the helicopters circling the property on the morning of February 28.[61]

As noted earlier, independent prosecutor John Danforth rejected
most of these allegations in his report of July 2000. For militia
members and antigovernment sympathizers, however, such findings were irrelevant. Already disposed to believe the worst of
government and embedded in a culture that insists on the rights of
the individual—especially gun-owning individuals—against the
machinations of the government, the dual events of Ruby Ridge
and Waco were all the proof they needed. The movement exploded.

The Militia of Montana (MOM) was the first to form in the aftermath of the Waco disaster. Founded in February 1994 by the
Trochmann family—several of whom had been friends with Randy
Weaver before his standoff with the government in Idaho—MOM
was based in the small town of Noxon, Montana. Angered by the
government's actions at Ruby Ridge and using rhetoric clearly informed by the Revolutionary myth of the militia, John Trochmann
asserted, "Next time, we'll throw up fifteen hundred militia on a
moment's notice in a circle of protection." And if there is gunfire,
Trochmann further asserted, harking back to the Revolution, "it
will be the shot heard 'round the world."[62]

In addition to being first, the Militia of Montana was significant
because Trochmann and his allies marketed literature detailing
how to organize militia groups. The organization sold a "Blue
Book" for $75 that reprinted militia doctrine and articulated the
conspiracy theories that are core to the movement. MOM also developed and marketed a militia manual that included sections on
how to organize, lead, arm, train, and legitimate militia groups.
They sold a manual on how to escape from the concentration
camps that militia members insisted were being built around the
nation for the imprisonment of God-fearing, gun-owning Americans everywhere. And they sold a series of conspiracy-theory
videotapes, including *America in Crisis,* a tape in which Helen
Chenoweth, a former conservative lobbyist and recently elected
congresswoman, argued that environmental policies sponsored in
Washington were destroying property rights in favor of the interests of the "shadow government."[63]

The core market for the Militia of Montana's message was gun
owners fearful of government regulation. In the context of the re-

cently passed Brady bill, which for many gun owners constituted an unconstitutional limitation of their rights to buy and sell as many weapons as they wished, concerns over further limits on gun rights became a rallying cry around which the militia movement could form. As a political choice, this emphasis on gun rights was brilliant: Trochmann himself was a white supremacist who had met Randy Weaver through his association with the Aryan Nations.[64] In its public literature, however, MOM downplayed the racial components of its founder's message in favor of a politically more lucrative position. As is anticipated by the analysis of militia ideology offered in chapter 3, Trochmann insisted:

> The security of a free state is not found in the citizens having guns in the closet. It is found in the citizenry being trained, prepared, organized, equipped and lead [sic] properly so that if the government uses its force against the citizens, the people can respond with a superior amount of firearms, and appropriately defend their rights.[65]

The tactic worked: in 1995, Bob Fletcher, spokesman for MOM, claimed that the group had developed a communications network that could send messages to five hundred thousand people in thirty minutes. Further, the group claimed it sent out two hundred packets every week about how to create one's own militia.[66]

Montana remained a hotbed of militia activity even as groups other than MOM were formed. The North American Volunteer Militia, which was based in Indiana, also had members in Montana. They regularly threatened county and state officials with violence and death if the officials made rulings or interpretations that violated the group's sense of what was and was not constitutional. The Montana Freemen, a constitutionalist group with ideas similar to the militia's, threatened a judge who was hearing a case involving a traffic violation with trial in a "common law" court. The judge was sufficiently scared to have her children moved from her home several times in the belief that she was about to be kidnapped. She also received a briefing from local law enforcement officials about where she and her children should hide in the event her home was fired on by Freemen activists.[67] (The Freemen's ultimate standoff with the federal government will be addressed in chapter 7.)

What began in Montana soon spread nationwide. By 1995, militia groups were operating in at least thirty-six states.[68] One county in the state of Washington, Stevens, had two.[69] Most were small, but one, the Michigan Militia, founded in April 1994, became as important in the militia movement as MOM. Its leaders, Ray Southwell and the Reverend Norman Olson, had no strongly racist beliefs to deemphasize; however, they articulated the same government-conspiracy and gun-ownership-rights theories that were common to militia ideology. Moreover, these men, in addition to a third group leader, Ken Adams, were not shy: they appeared on Phil Donahue's television talk show to expound their beliefs. Accordingly, the Michigan Militia became the public face of the movement. Thus, rather than having to hide the racist roots of some militia leaders, like John Trochmann, the movement was fronted by individuals who could claim only that they loved the Constitution and wanted to protect their fellow citizens from the prevarications of the federal government. As Ray Southwell put it on the Donahue show:

> I'm afraid . . . at some point the government will cross the line and it will be neighbor coming to the aid of neighbor. Just like at Lexington and Concord. . . . There is one last hope to avoid armed confrontation, and that's if our state governments rise up and tell our federal government to back off. If the state does not rise up . . . the American people will.[70]

This message of noble Americans resisting evil just as their forefathers had in 1775 resonated in a culture educated in the militia myth and convinced of the centrality of guns in the American political experience. By late 1994, Southwell's group asserted that it had organizations in sixty-three of Michigan's eighty-three counties. It further claimed to have some ten thousand active members.[71]

The twenty-four months that passed between the destruction of the Branch Davidian compound in Waco and the bombing of the Alfred P. Murrah Federal Building in Oklahoma City would constitute the golden era of the militia movement. As will be discussed in the next chapter, while Timothy McVeigh's horrific act did not lead to an immediate reduction in militia-group formation and activity, it was a factor that set the decline of the movement in motion. But in 1994 and early 1995, those people convinced of the venality of government believed that they had found a legal, constitutional, American way of stopping the coming repression.

A brief chronicle of militia activities in the year following Waco can emphasize how many people rallied to the militia cause:

- In the summer of 1994, three hundred people in Catron County, New Mexico—a community with only twenty-five hundred residents—formed a militia to stop the federal government from enforcing regulations limiting cattle grazing on federal lands. In response, the Bureau of Land Management (BLM) ordered its agents to travel in pairs and decided not to attempt to enforce the new regulations. In 1995, BLM extended its travel-in-pairs order and recommended that all its employees in the West do so.[72]
- Linda Thompson, whose tapes *Waco: The Big Lie* and *Waco: The Big Lie Continued* had done much to popularize antigovernment conspiracies regarding events at the Branch Davidian compound, styled herself the "'Acting Adjutant General' of the Unorganized Militia of the United States." She called on the militia to arrest Congress on September 19, 1994. Charges ranged from continuing U.S. participation in the Federal Reserve system to passing the Fourteenth, Sixteenth, and Seventeenth Amendments to the Constitution. Congress members were to be tried in citizens' courts. The event was ultimately canceled after substantial discussion among militia groups.[73]
- Jim Rodgers, a militia leader in California, urged his group's members to attend local board meetings and intimidate members into complying with the group's wishes: "They're going to assume someone in the back has a rope."[74]
- A leader of a North Carolina militia known as the Citizens for the Reinstatement of Constitutionalist Government called on its members to stockpile what he called the "Four B's—Bibles, bullets, bandages, and beans" as part of the group's efforts to stop the shadow government.[75]
- The Florida State Militia published a pamphlet for distribution to its five hundred members that encouraged recipients to stockpile ammunition because it would soon be banned from the market.[76]
- Two Minnesota Patriots' Council members were convicted in 1995 of a plan to murder law enforcement figures and federal agents with the poison ricin.[77]

As had happened in Idaho, the events in Waco had been shaped by entrepreneurial movement leaders and cultural and political figures into a story that resonated with many Americans. Government was seen to be a corrupt captive of an evil New World Order and could not be trusted. The fact that the government was trying to extend its control over guns in the United States with measures such as the Brady bill was taken as proof that the government had evil intentions to destroy the liberty of innocents like Koresh and his followers: the raids at Ruby Ridge and at Waco, after all, had been undertaken to enforce gun laws. Thus, since government was evil and afraid of guns, it was obvious that only armed resistance to government's actions could save American freedom. And as the examples of Lexington and Concord were alleged to prove, Americans had used guns to defeat a powerful enemy before. Join us, came the militia call, and save America again.

This ideological strategy resonated with the liberalism and exceptionalism of American political culture. Individual rights were emphasized; the struggle between the forces of freedom and the agents of evil were cast into ultimate contests of right and wrong, truth and lies, with real consequences for Americans (both the Idaho and Texas confrontations ended in the evil government killing innocent Americans, after all, militia ideologues insisted); these ideas were linked together with a model of heroic, mythic action that has been deeply ingrained in American political life. In such a context, the militia movement found fertile ground for growth.

It would take Timothy McVeigh and the destruction of the Alfred P. Murrah Federal Building in Oklahoma City to make many of the Americans who heeded the militia's call begin to question their choice.

6

The Inferno:
Timothy McVeigh and the Bombing
in Oklahoma City

When Timothy McVeigh lit the fuse that led to the bomb that destroyed the Alfred P. Murrah Federal Building in Oklahoma City, Oklahoma, he manifested the values and attitudes of the militia movement enraged. Combining racism with extreme antigovernment paranoia, McVeigh and his fellow conspirators took an action that made sense to them in the context of militia ideology and values, even as most militia groups disavowed both the bombing and McVeigh.

While the horrible destruction of the Murrah Building made sense for many militia members, it began the process of undermining the militia movement. Like all infernos, it consumed the material that fed it and turned its fuel into something else. Millions of sympathizers were forced to confront the potential consequences of ideological rage unleashed. Yet, McVeigh's crime did not destroy the militia movement, for even two years later there were still hundreds of militia groups operating in the United States.

Coming to Oklahoma City

Many writers have examined how and why Timothy McVeigh, along with his coconspirators, Michael Fortier and Terry Nichols, could have conceived of the plan to destroy the Murrah Building. Commonly, these authors look to the childhoods of these figures, apparently hoping to identify some seminal moment that turned ordinary citizens into creatures of evil. Such explanations are usually unsatisfying because, frankly, most of the individuals who committed the crime in Oklahoma City lived relatively ordinary, if not always happy, lives as children. In other cases, authors look to drug use or post–traumatic stress disorder (PTSD) to account for the shift in attitudes that turned Timothy McVeigh, in particular, from a "normal," if somewhat gun-focused, young man into what one describes as an "all-American monster."[1] These explanations, too, are unpersuasive because they do not recognize the power of ideology to shape behavior, and thus they miss the real danger that McVeigh and his fellow conspirators represent: anyone with an extremist ideology may commit horrible crimes, not just those who are on drugs or who have fought in a war. The real problem posed by the militia or any fundamentalist group lies in its conviction that all truth and all justice are contained by its values, while all evil is represented by the "other." This problem is much deeper and more intrinsic in the whole of U.S. society than is drug-induced behavior linked to PTSD, and so is much more serious, as is discussed in chapter 7.

Timothy McVeigh was born April 23, 1968, in upstate New York. He was a personable, engaged child, active in school, with many friends. He was a good student, was known to pay attention in class, and had a good attendance record. Yet school never really interested McVeigh, and after his high school graduation in 1986 he did not go to college.[2]

Instead, what fascinated the young Timothy McVeigh was guns. He received his first rifle at thirteen and his first shotgun at fifteen. Unlike many of his peers, however, McVeigh did not hunt. He was interested in target practice. After graduating from high school, he began to focus on gun rights and to oppose any legislation limiting a citizen's right to own weapons. He also got a job as a security guard.[3]

In 1988, bored and with little focus to his life, McVeigh enlisted in the army. There, for a while, he would appear to find the direction his life ought to take. He also met eventual Oklahoma City co-conspirators Michael Fortier and Terry Nichols. And he read the book that would change his life, Andrew MacDonald's *Turner Diaries.*[4]

In his early days in the army, McVeigh was an exemplary soldier.

He worked harder, trained more seriously, kept his weapon and clothing cleaner, and lived more ascetically than any other soldier in his unit. When his fellow soldiers went off base to bars and strip clubs, McVeigh stayed on base, worked out, and hoarded his money. (As a consequence of this latter behavior, McVeigh became a "bank," loaning money, at interest, to his less-disciplined comrades.)[5]

Yet his asceticism caused McVeigh problems, particularly as he grew more racist on base. The restraint that kept McVeigh from joining his unit during their off-base partying caused most of his fellow soldiers to dislike him. In addition, the quiet racism that had suffused his thinking as a child in rural, almost exclusively white, upstate New York became explicit as he was confronted with the racially mixed, ethnically diverse army. McVeigh made numerous racist comments during his time in service, even after he was promoted to sergeant for his high-quality work.[6]

McVeigh's antigovernment philosophy, which until this point had been largely a matter of rage against gun control legislation, began to evolve to include a dislike of civil rights and other race-mixing policies. The army, after all, is one of the most integrated aspects of contemporary U.S. society. For McVeigh this meant that the government was engaged in racial homogenization—something he opposed. Thus, even as he excelled as a soldier, McVeigh remained isolated from his fellow soldiers, the institutional practices that made the army effective, and the policies of the government that created and funded the army in which McVeigh was finding success.

The relative isolation McVeigh felt within his unit was limited only by his friendships with Terry Nichols and Michael Fortier. McVeigh met Nichols in basic training. Nichols had been raised on a farm in rural Michigan and, after graduating from high school in 1973, had knocked around at a number of odd jobs and farming efforts before joining the army. He became an older brother to McVeigh. They spent hours together during the slack periods of basic training and then in regular military life. Many of their conversations reinforced their inherent racism.[7]

Michael Fortier was added to the mix when McVeigh and Nichols were posted to Fort Riley, Kansas, after completing basic training. A friendly, likable person, Fortier had been raised in northern Arizona before graduating from high school in 1987. He, too, was a racist and found kindred spirits in Nichols and McVeigh. They spent hours together during their time at Fort Riley.[8]

Whatever chance there might have been that McVeigh would give up his racist, antigovernment beliefs was ended when, during his time in the army, someone gave him a copy of *The Turner Diaries*, a hate-filled work by Andrew MacDonald (a pseudonym for racist leader William Pierce). *The Turner Diaries* tells the story of a federal government so corrupted by civil rights and antigun programs that a law (the Cohen Act, tellingly) is passed to eliminate all private gun ownership in the United States. This stimulates a rebellion on the part of white, race-loving Americans concerned for real freedom and liberty. (The government fails to stop this rebellion or find the guns that keep it going because the African Americans who have taken over the Federal Bureau of Investigation [FBI] under affirmative action are completely incompetent.) As part of this rebellion, race-loving whites launch a guerrilla campaign of terror and violence to destabilize the regime and bring real freedom for white men and women. Among these terrorist acts is the destruction of FBI headquarters by men who use a truck bomb packed with diesel fuel and fertilizer. Ultimately, these white supremacists gain control of nuclear weapons and launch a final assault that purges the world of the inferior races and saves it for white people.[9]

McVeigh became a strong advocate of *The Turner Diaries*. He urged fellow soldiers to read it and, once he left the army, traveled the gun-show circuit selling the book below cost in order to promote its message.[10] Guns, racism, and a hatred of a government that seemed to favor one group at the expense of another became the target of his attention.

In contrast with Randy Weaver and David Koresh, McVeigh espoused an ideology that corresponded closely with the values associated with the then nascent militia movement. His locating guns as the central focus of American liberty and concern that the government was abusing its powers in improperly mixing the races clearly link to the ideas and attitudes discussed in chapter 3. Even his racism, which was perhaps more explicit in McVeigh's daily life than militia ideology recommends, seems a manifestation of the general parameters of militia thought. Accordingly, his ideas, while outside the mainstream of American political culture and practice, were in line with conservative interpretations of right and wrong in American political life. Of course, in 1989 McVeigh could not have called himself a militiaman since, as a practical matter, the movement had not yet formed. But it would be from people who shared McVeigh's racist, pro-gun, and antigovernment attitudes that the militia movement would ultimately spring.

The path from Timothy McVeigh, successful if racist soldier, to Timothy McVeigh, terrorist, took five additional steps between 1989 and 1995. First, he grew even more lonely after Terry Nichols was discharged from the army and Michael Fortier's service in another unit kept him away for extended periods of time. This left McVeigh increasingly isolated from his fellow soldiers, and to fill the time, he focused more and more on right-wing magazines that espoused antigovernment, racist, and pro-gun positions.[11]

Second, McVeigh's desire to transfer out of the regular army and into the Special Forces was interrupted by the Persian Gulf war. As early as his original enlistment, McVeigh had hoped to join the Special Forces. (His enlistment officer tricked him into signing conventional papers; this was one of the sources of his hatred of the government.) By 1989, McVeigh began doing supplemental training to prepare for the rigors of Special Forces camp. His fitness test for entry into the Special Forces was scheduled for July 1990.[12]

Instead of reporting for his fitness test, however, McVeigh and his unit were ordered to Saudi Arabia as part of the buildup of forces that later fought against Iraq in Kuwait. By the time he returned from the war in April 1991, reporting for Special Forces training later that month, he was exhausted, bitter, and badly out of shape. He dropped out of the fitness test on the first day, convinced that his participation in the Persian Gulf war had ended his chances of entering the Special Forces. He was further convinced that the test was unfair, given his wartime service. He would never trust the army again. (It is not clear that McVeigh would ever have been admitted for Special Forces service: his psychological profile was reported to have indicated his unsuitability for the unique work Special Forces soldiers undertake.)[13]

McVeigh's service in the Persian Gulf war was the third step on his journey to rage. His participation was minimal, even though both he and his unit received special commendations for their service. At one point they were even assigned to guard the commander of U.S. forces in the gulf, Norman Schwarzkopf. While McVeigh was disappointed at the limited role he played in the war, he was in fact opposed to the war as such. He saw it as a sham war designed to make Republicans look good.[14] For McVeigh, any government that would send its army to fight in a war like that in the Persian Gulf could not be trusted.

Fourth, once he returned home from the gulf, McVeigh began to drift. He reenlisted but isolated himself physically from most of his fellow soldiers by living with a series of friends and acquaintances off base. He was so dissatisfied with army life that he finally filed for a discharge and left the army in January 1992. Moving home for a period, he drifted through a series of low-thought, low-energy jobs. He joined the New York National Guard and insisted to James Nichols, Terry's brother, that the federal government kept track of his location through a computer chip it had implanted in his buttocks one night while he slept. He quit the National Rifle Association (NRA) because he decided the organization was not vigorous enough in protecting Americans' gun rights. His concerns were those of gun rights and antigovernment conspiracies; nothing in "normal" life made such issues important or even put them on the agendas of his friends and family.[15] Thus, he was no more connected at home than he had been in the army.

The fifth and final step McVeigh took toward the Oklahoma apocalypse was deciding, in June 1992, to leave the National Guard, quit his security job, and move in with Terry Nichols in Michigan.[16] From that point on, he would live in a circle of antigovernment conspiracy theorists who watched the government raids in Ruby Ridge, Idaho, and Waco, Texas. Whether living with Terry Nichols and his family or Michael Fortier and his, whether living in Michigan or Arizona, McVeigh would enter a world of hate and rage against the government justified by—from his perspective— its race-mixing, antigun, antifreedom policies. Within this context, and for these people, the bombing in Oklahoma City would make perfect sense.

An Inferno in Oklahoma

In the second half of 1992, McVeigh moved to Michigan to live with Terry Nichols. It was there that he watched, with growing rage, the government standoff with, and final surrender of, Randy Weaver and his family in Ruby Ridge. McVeigh, already convinced of government's evil, had his beliefs confirmed during the Weaver operation.[17] He became totally convinced by the Weaver myth that government agents were solely to blame for attacking an innocent man and his family living lives of quiet solitude, practicing their religion, and freely owning guns. For McVeigh, if the Weavers could be the target of government oppression, anyone could be.

In the aftermath of Ruby Ridge, McVeigh interacted with many militia groups that began to form in the area and in nearby states. Drifting again, McVeigh stayed with friends or, for brief periods of time, in places he rented. If he found people to talk to, they were members of the militia and/or racist undergrounds in American life.[18]

What Ruby Ridge began for McVeigh, Waco finished. The government raids and ultimate destruction of the Mt. Carmel complex in early 1993 were all the proof of government's evil that McVeigh would ever need. He visited Waco during the standoff: he was videotaped at Mt. Carmel by a crew filming a documentary made during the siege. He visited Waco again after the fire had destroyed the Branch Davidian compound.[19] For McVeigh, something had to be done to stop such evil acts on the part of the government.

The rough structure of what would finally be a conspiracy to destroy the Alfred P. Murrah Federal Building in Oklahoma City was set sometime in 1993. In early 1993, McVeigh visited Michael Fortier in Kingman, Arizona.[20] McVeigh would spend most of the next two years in and around the Kingman area, although his drifting ways never fully ended until he was arrested for speeding and driving without appropriate license tags on his car in the hours after the bombing.

The conspiracy was both simple and time-consuming. McVeigh knew he had to gather sufficient funds to purchase the ingredients for his bomb, and he also knew he needed help to construct the bomb and carry his plan forward. He began placing ads in military surplus and right-wing magazines offering to sell replica antitank launchers to interested people; the real purpose of these ads was to identify and recruit fellow conspirators. In addition, McVeigh robbed banks and gun dealers to raise money; both Terry Nichols and Michael Fortier are known to have helped McVeigh at various times in these operations. McVeigh also established multiple aliases during this period and worked hard to cover his tracks by, for example, purchasing prepaid phone cards under a pseudonym and using these to conduct his dealing and trading operations.[21] Nonetheless, he was convinced the government was following him.

Final planning for the bombing of the Murrah Building began in December 1994. It was then that McVeigh began placing bulk orders for ammonium nitrate, a fertilizer that, when mixed appropriately with diesel fuel and ignited, can make a powerful explosive. These bulk purchases were stored in various facilities waiting for use. In addition, McVeigh and Fortier visited the Murrah Building over Christmas to examine their target.[22]

So why the Alfred P. Murrah Building? In *The Turner Diaries*, it is FBI headquarters in Washington, D.C., that gets destroyed, and indeed gets destroyed fairly early in the book. Given that McVeigh was fixated on *The Turner Diaries*, some contemporary conspiracy theorists assert that the operation could not have been undertaken by McVeigh: they insist he would have duplicated the actions of his hero. However, as a practical matter, FBI headquarters was far too heavily guarded in the aftermath of the attempt two years earlier to destroy New York's World Trade Center by a truck bomb. Additionally, and more significantly for McVeigh, the FBI office that led the Waco assault, as well as the office for the spokesman for the Bureau of Alcohol, Tobacco, and Firearms (ATF) who directed Waco operations, was supposedly in the Murrah Building. (The FBI office had, in fact, been moved since the Waco fire, and the spokesperson for the ATF during the Waco disaster no longer worked in the Murrah Building by the time of the bombing.) McVeigh and his fellow conspirators did not know this, however, and perceived the building to be a highly vulnerable, highly desirable target.[23]

It is also not clear that even had they known that the FBI and ATF offices of interest had moved, the conspirators would have changed their plans. In addition to some offices for the ATF, the Murrah building also housed the America's Kids Daycare Center, a credit union, and offices of the Oklahoma Highway Administration, the Social Security Administration, the Agriculture Department, the Department of Housing and Urban Development, the Secret Service, the Drug Enforcement Administration, the Marine Corps, military recruiters, and the General Accounting Office.[24] These symbols of a corrupt government were located in a building close to a busy public street—one from which it would be comparatively easy to launch a truck-bomb attack while anticipating maximum damage and the creation of maximum fear. Thus, if

McVeigh's intent was to kill, cause fear in the hearts of ordinary citizens, and harm agents of a corrupt government, the Murrah Building was an attractive target quite separate from its position as a home for the ATF and the FBI.

Unfortunately for the victims of the attack, it is possible to design and build a remarkably powerful bomb using relatively ordinary materials. As his heroes had done in *The Turner Diaries*, McVeigh made his of a mix of ammonium nitrate fertilizer and diesel fuel. These products were mixed in large blue barrels and loaded into the back of a Ryder rental truck; linked to a fuse, they would create a blast capable of shattering a nine-story building in seconds.[25]

Through early 1995, McVeigh and his fellow conspirators mixed their lethal broth and stored it. On April 12, McVeigh drove from Kingman, Arizona, to Junction City, Kansas. There, he sold his car and purchased an older, well-used 1977 Mercury. He then checked into the Dreamland Motel. The next day, he drove to Oklahoma City and left the car near the Murrah Building. He then called Terry Nichols for a ride back to Junction City. On April 17, McVeigh rented a Ryder truck in Junction City using the alias Bob Kling. (Some accounts say that McVeigh rented the truck with a second man, subsequently known as John Doe 2. His existence, or not, will be addressed in the next section of this chapter.) On the eighteenth, he drove the Ryder truck to Geary State Fishing Lake, where he and others were observed loading numerous blue barrels into the back of the truck. In all, twenty half-filled fifty-five-gallon drums went into the back of the truck. When he and his compatriots were finished, the truck was carrying nearly five thousand pounds of explosives, and its floor had been extensively drilled to pass fuses to the various components of the bomb.[26]

At 8:30 A.M. on April 19, McVeigh asked a passerby for directions to a street corner near the Murrah Building. At 8:40 A.M., a parking meter reader saw a bright yellow truck near the property. At 8:55 A.M., three people saw a man fitting McVeigh's description standing next to a Ryder rental truck. At 9:00 A.M., a driver had to hit his brakes to avoid hitting McVeigh as he crossed the street between intersections. At 9:02 A.M., the bomb exploded, ripping the face off the building and ultimately killing 168 men, women, and children.[27] Timothy McVeigh had had his revenge against his hated government. Ironically, he also began the process of undermining the modern militia movement.

The Aftermaths of Oklahoma City

As was the case with the events at Ruby Ridge and Waco, the horrible crime of the bombing in Oklahoma City is relevant here only because of the way(s) it influenced the militia movement. In order to explore this point, this section examines the aftermath for the participants, the affected communities, and the broader militia movement. As will be seen, there is not a linear relationship between the bombing in Oklahoma City and the decline of the militia movement.

The Aftermath for Timothy McVeigh and the Other Conspirators

One hour and seventeen minutes after the bomb destroyed the Murrah Building, Timothy McVeigh was stopped outside Oklahoma City for speeding and driving a vehicle without license tags.[28] As McVeigh was leaning over to give the officer his driver's license, the trooper noticed a bulge under his jacket. He ordered McVeigh to exit the car and remove his jacket. McVeigh warned the trooper he had a gun. The officer then arrested McVeigh for speeding, driving without tags, driving without insurance, possession of an illegal weapon, and transporting an illegal weapon. McVeigh was taken to the Noble County jail.[29]

Tellingly, the driver's license McVeigh gave the state trooper listed a false birthday: April 19, 1972.[30] That date—April 19—was as central to McVeigh's thinking as it is in militia ideology. In addition to memorializing the events at Lexington and Concord in 1775, and those in Waco in 1993, the particular April 19 of 1995 was significant to Timothy McVeigh for two reasons. First, it was National Militia Day, as every April 19 since 1993 had been. Second, April 19, 1995, was the day scheduled by the state of Arkansas for the execution of Richard Snell, a white supremacist who had been convicted of murdering a white male he thought was Jewish and an African American Arkansas State Police officer.[31]

In the immediate aftermath of the bombing, national attention focused on likely suspects. A consensus rapidly formed that this attack must have been the act of Middle East terrorists. In response to this assumption, the FBI threw out a substantial dragnet that, at its most extreme, led to the searching of a Palestinian man waiting for an international flight at the Detroit airport, the search of his bags when they made it to Rome, and his detention and questioning in London, where he flew after missing his original flight.[32] It seemed impossible that an "American," especially a white person, could commit such a horrible crime. Meanwhile, McVeigh languished in jail, waiting for a bail hearing.

The process that led to McVeigh's arrest for the Murrah Building bombing began with an axle. The rear axle of the Ryder truck McVeigh had rented was found intact near the blast site. Its vehicle identification number was still legible. With this information, the FBI was able to trace where the vehicle was rented and to whom it was rented—Robert Kling, one of McVeigh's false identities. With the Kling name, the FBI was able to establish McVeigh's real identity.[33]

Once they knew who they were looking for, the FBI conducted a computer search to see if they could find McVeigh. They found that he was in jail in Perry, Oklahoma. His bail hearing was imminent. An FBI agent called the local facility and asked that McVeigh be delayed from attending this hearing. Local prosecutors got the bail hearing judge to agree to a delay, and McVeigh, who was prepared to be released, was told he had to wait.[34]

Once the FBI agents arrived, their interview with McVeigh did not mirror the stereotypical "third degree" depicted in popular culture. Agents asked McVeigh if he knew why they were interviewing him. Without any further prompting, he replied, "Yes. That thing in Oklahoma City, I guess."[35] All that remained for the FBI was to define the dimensions of the conspiracy. What remained for the American people was the struggle to understand why.

For Timothy McVeigh, April 19, 1995, was the last day he began outside a jail cell. Once arrested for the Oklahoma City attack, McVeigh was transferred to jail in Oklahoma City. After much litigation, his trial was moved to a federal court in Denver. This change of venue was undertaken because he was charged with one count of murder for each federal agent killed in the blast and because his defense attorney, Stephen Jones, claimed McVeigh could not get a fair trial in Oklahoma City.[36]

The evidence against McVeigh was extensive. Once his multiple identities had been exposed, tracing the fertilizer and fuel purchases, truck rental, and gun sales that were part of the conspiracy was comparatively easy. In addition, in return for a promise he would not face the death penalty, Michael Fortier agreed to testify against McVeigh. He was able to detail gun thefts (and sales) as well as fertilizer purchases that were central to the conspiracy.[37]

McVeigh was convicted of murder on June 2, 1997. He was sentenced to death and transferred to federal prison in Terre Haute, Indiana. After his appeal for a new trial was denied, he was executed on June 11, 2001, the first federal prisoner to be put to death since 1963.[38]

McVeigh's death did not end his story, however. His original date of execution was delayed by Attorney Géneral John Ashcroft when the FBI revealed that it had found thirty-five hundred pages of documents related to the investigation of the Murrah bombing that it had never turned over to the defense. While no evidence emerged from these documents that in any way suggested McVeigh's innocence—and he himself insisted on his guilt—the fact that they had never been disclosed lent continued credence to those conspiracy theorists who argued that the FBI would do anything it had to do in its relentless effort to destroy American liberties. Suggestions that the trial might be reopened were quieted only when McVeigh chose to prevent all appeals on his behalf.

In addition, as had been the case with the Randy Weaver trial, the defense in McVeigh's trial worked hard to establish McVeigh's innocence by articulating a number of conspiracy theories. These were quickly supplemented by right-wing antigovernment spokespersons. Stephen Jones, for example, argued that McVeigh was not guilty of the crime. After all, millions of people distrusted government—especially in the aftermath of Ruby Ridge and Waco—but distrust hardly constitutes motive. He derided Michael Fortier's testimony, noting that Fortier had a reason to lie and had been, until the time of the bombing, a heavy drug user. He also emphasized the government's failure to find "John Doe 2," a person who was originally alleged to have rented the Ryder truck with McVeigh. (The government's case insisted that John Doe 2 had visited the truck rental place; however, it identified him as a man who visited the next day and argued that the clerk who reported that McVeigh was accompanied by another man had made a mistake.) The possible existence of a John Doe 2 meant, Jones insisted, that there was a broader conspiracy involved in the attack, one that did not include McVeigh. He then supplemented this argument with a discussion of the comparative lack of forensic evidence against

McVeigh found by the FBI's crime lab: there were few traces of fertilizer or other bomb-making substances in McVeigh's clothes or hair. Thus, Jones concluded, McVeigh was not involved, and the government had focused on the young antigovernment activist as a convenient target for its case.[39]

While the jury was not convinced by these arguments, many Americans found them—and derivations of them—persuasive. As had happened in both Idaho and Texas, the events in Oklahoma City led to the rise and spread of a number of conspiracy theories about who was responsible for the bombing and why they did it. Most fed off the cultural assumption that government was an evil, oppressive force that had to be resisted if liberty and freedom for the individual were to be saved. For example, one theory alleged that the bombing was sponsored by, or at least had the tacit consent of, President Bill Clinton. Its actual aim, the theory held, was the death of a former Clinton Secret Service bodyguard who, along with an ATF agent killed in Waco, "knew too much" about Clinton's actions and behaviors. Combined, the federal actions at Waco and Oklahoma City saw the deaths of four people who had worked closely with Clinton while he served as governor or president. Thus, obviously—at least to those who were inclined to believe that those with power would do anything to protect and extend their positions—Clinton caused their deaths in order to shut these potential witnesses up.[40]

Other theories held that the United Nations was involved. The plot was part of a plan to destabilize the United States in order to encourage a UN coup. Or, alternatively, some government had to be involved in the plot because the bomb was highly sophisticated, well beyond the abilities of novices like McVeigh, Nichols, and Fortier to construct. Another theory held that two bombs were used to destroy the building. Evidence for this point was adduced from a seismograph taken by an office of the U.S. Geological Survey that showed two tremors.[41] The fact that the second tremor was likely caused by the building collapsing was irrelevant for conspiracy theorists. Primed to believe that the government was evil, they would use any evidence to prove the case.

Finally, another theory insisted that the government blew up the Murrah Building to frame the militia movement. Unable to stop it by other means, the federal government is understood to have destroyed one of its own properties, in the process killing both people it employed and many innocent children, in order to come up with a legitimate means to destroy the militia movement. McVeigh, then, was a patsy, and the movement had one more piece of evidence that the government would do anything to achieve its goals—evidence that, in the context of the liberalism and exceptionalism of American political culture, encouraged gun ownership, training, and an ideology of hate: if the government would kill children, the militia movement was even more important if American freedoms were to be protected.

McVeigh's fellow conspirators also faced justice. As noted earlier, Michael Fortier agreed to testify against McVeigh in exchange for avoiding the death penalty. His testimony was central to the prosecution's case, and he pleaded guilty to charges of failing to warn authorities about the plot, lying to the FBI, and transporting stolen weapons. His original sentence of twelve years in prison was overturned when a federal judge ruled that his punishment was based on federal rules governing first-degree murder when the appropriate guidelines were those associated with involuntary manslaughter. He was released from prison for time served.[42]

The case involving Terry Nichols was more complicated and bitterer. McVeigh and Nichols had had a falling-out before the bombing; however, Nichols faced trial as a coconspirator Also, the fact that McVeigh had been tried in federal court angered many Oklahoma City residents, who wanted both McVeigh and Nichols to stand trial in Oklahoma for the deaths of Oklahoma citizens, not just the deaths of federal employees.

As McVeigh's attorneys had done, Nichols's defense counsel tried to shift blame for the attacks elsewhere. They emphasized McVeigh's extremism in an attempt to suggest McVeigh's motives and distinguish them from Nichols's.[43] They also pushed the John Doe 2 theory, especially focusing on the remarkable differences in the physical characteristics of Doe and Nichols. They also introduced evidence that McVeigh had carried on a surreptitious communication with an "SC," Steve Colburn, an antigovernment ideologue who was also a chemist wanted on federal firearms charges.[44] Such themes reinforced the conspiracy theories already well entrenched since the bombing.

Nichols's case was further complicated by its outcome. Nichols was tried in federal court and found guilty of involuntary manslaughter and conspiracy to bomb the Murrah Building. The court did not find him guilty of either first- or second-degree murder, however.[45] He was subsequently sentenced to life in prison, a sentence that angered many in Oklahoma. In reaction, in March 1999, Oklahoma County District Attorney Bob Macy filed 160 first-degree murder charges against Nichols and promised to seek the death penalty. This led to a series of court battles over venues that remains undecided as of December 2002. In September 2001, Nichols offered to end his appeals of his federal sentence in return for avoiding trial in state court.[46] Through December 2002 no decision had been made regarding this pledge.

In the end, then, the trials and sentencings of McVeigh, Fortier, and Nichols served multiple ends. As had been the case in the trial of Randy Weaver, justice was formally handed out by the legal system. Due process of law was validated. Ironically, however, the impact among antigovernment extremists ran counter to the legal findings: no matter how explicitly the government followed its own rules for finding people guilty (or not, in Randy Weaver's case), the very fact of the confrontation was seen as proof of the government's insidious intent. This ironic outcome of the McVeigh trial can be seen in the impact it had on the militia movement itself, as explained below.

The Aftermath, the FBI, and Oklahoma City

For the FBI, Oklahoma City did not constitute an end to the agency's troubles. It was not until *after* Oklahoma City that the House and Senate conducted investigations of the agency's handling of the events at Ruby Ridge and Waco. (The political effects of these hearings will be addressed in the next chapter.) Further, questions emerged regarding the agency's possible mishandling of Oklahoma City crime scene evidence, particularly at its forensics laboratory. Later, the FBI's failure to disclose thirty-five hundred pages in documents relevant to Timothy McVeigh's trial would rise up as yet more evidence of the agency's incompetence and hostile motives, at least for those already convinced of the agency's venality. This, combined with the questions raised about the FBI's mishandling of the cases involving Randy Weaver and David Koresh, not to mention the conspiracy theories that hit the agency during the trials related to the two incidents, caused the FBI to lose

much of the political shine it had enjoyed as a crime-busting organization that captured Mafia bosses and Soviet spies.

Ironically, however, this image of the agency as a civil-liberties-
abusing failure was, by the time of Oklahoma City, largely inaccurate, at least in terms of the agency's response to the militia movement. As the cases of the Montana Freemen and Republic of Texas
show (see chapter 7), the FBI abandoned its aggressive, confrontational style when encountering militia and related groups. Questions of group motivation, ideology, and the need to isolate groups
from public support became paramount in the agency's operations.
Thus, since Waco, the FBI has not engaged in a violent raid against
a heavily defended militia or other site. This has undermined the
antigovernment activists' conspiracy theories: with confrontations
ending in peaceable arrests, violent resistance no longer seems like
self-defense.

Similarly, the FBI began an extensive intelligence-gathering operation across the United States in an attempt to undermine the
militia movement. As will be discussed further in chapter 7, this effort prevented many incidents of militia violence and brought
down many militia organizations. Thus, the FBI became very successful at dealing with the militia in spite of the agency's reputation. This reputation, however, endures, a fact that will likely shape
the prospects for a resurgence of the movement. This prospect will
be addressed in the epilogue.

The Aftermath and the Militia Movement

For the militia movement, Timothy McVeigh's act was both anticipated and the beginning of the end. For some leaders, it became a
symbol of the evils of the federal government. For others, it became
a sign that it was time to abandon the militia label and advance
their values in new ways. Regardless of their reaction, however, the
Oklahoma City bombing took place in a context that must be understood if the ultimate shape and decline of the militia movement
are to be more fully explained.

The months leading up to the Murrah Building's destruction
were tense ones in the movement. Early in 1995, the militia newspaper *The Register* reported that it had received a memo leaked
from the Bureau of Alcohol, Tobacco, and Firearms. The ATF was

purportedly on the verge of launching nationwide raids against militia compounds and members. While some militia leaders, like Linda Thompson, denounced the report as a lie, others insisted that it was true. Some even specified a date for the raids—March 25. In addition to planning raids on the homes of militia leaders and their supporters, the memo was also alleged to list a range of offices to be bombed and to provide the names of legitimate, uncorrupted law enforcement and judicial officers to be arrested. Government agents were expected to act as provocateurs whose outrageous actions would become the foundation of the government's subsequent arrests, killings, and repression.

In response, militia supporters sprang into action. Montana militia leader Calvin Greenup asked the militia to come to his property to shoot down any government helicopters that might bring agents coming to arrest him. John Trochmann of the Militia of Montana was arrested at a Montana courthouse with guns, armor-piercing bullets, and other weapons. A young militia member shot an Oregon State Police officer and the officer's passenger rather than place himself under the officer's control. The office of the Toiyabe National Forest Service in Nevada was hit by a bomb. The leader of the Escambia County, Florida, Militia's Alligator Chapter received multiple offers from fellow members to hide him in their homes. The U.S. Marshals Service informed John Bohlman of Musselshell County, Montana, that a group of militia were coming from Oregon to Montana to protest Trochmann's arraignment and to blow up a power station.

The government, too, responded to this increased activity. Power plants throughout Montana, Idaho, North Dakota, South Dakota, Washington, and Oregon were placed on heightened security. Other federal agencies increased their levels of preparedness. Some confrontation seemed inevitable.

In this context of heightened confrontation with a government they did not trust, the conspiracy theories articulated by the militia movement's leaders—or by McVeigh's, Fortier's, or Nichols's attorneys—in the aftermath of the Oklahoma City bombing made sense to militia members. First to explain the attack as a crime committed by the federal government was Mark Koernke of the Michigan Militia. On April 19, 1995, just hours after the bombing, Koernke said:

[W]e're one day closer to victory for all of our brothers and sisters behind the lines in occupied territory. . . . [O]ur enemy, the New World
Order crowd, has a tendency to turn every event on its ear, and they
have tried to do it once again. Of course, we all know that two years ago
on the nineteenth of April there was the final destruction of the Waco
church and home. . . .

[M]any of you are glued to your radios or are watching television to
observe what happened in Oklahoma City today. . . . [This] is yet another foot-stomp on the part of the New World Order crowd to manipulate the population. . . . We watched Bill Clinton make his public statement. . . . "We are going to hunt down these individuals who performed
this bombing in Oklahoma City." What is Bill going to do then? Punish
them the way he punished his murderers at Waco by putting letters of
reprimand in their files? . . .

For those of you who are skeptical . . . [t]hese people have butchered
our cities. They have killed whole population groups. They are greedy.
They are power-mongers. And they EAT THEIR YOUNG! So, for those
of you who don't think that there is a little bit of manipulation involved here—this is a propaganda campaign, and FEMA [the Federal
Emergency Management Agency], as we expected, is right in the middle of it.[47]

Similarly, Linda Thompson, who had rejected the idea that the
federal government was about to launch a series of raids against
the militia in March 1995, argued that "I genuinely believe the government did this bombing. . . . I mean, who's got a track record of
killing innocent children?" Bo Gritz, the white supremacist who
had negotiated an end to the standoff at Ruby Ridge, asserted that
the bombing had to be an act of government since the bombing was
clearly well planned and executed and used a sophisticated device.[48]

While some militia leaders resisted the urge to blame the government, others insisted government—even perhaps a foreign government—was involved in the attacks. Norman Olson and Ray
Southwell asserted that the attack was planned by the Japanese
government as an act of revenge for alleged American involvement
in a terrorist gas attack on the Tokyo subway system. (Olson and
Southwell later resigned from the Michigan Militia when their allegations were refuted; Olson started another group and argued
that the Michigan Militia was no longer radical enough to be true
to its values.)[49] Lyndon Larouche's political followers insisted that
the attack had been plotted by the British government.[50]

One other group found itself blamed for the attack: Jews. One militia flyer insisted "Clinton Ordered Oklahoma Bombing" on behalf of the Jewish conspiracy to control the world.

> With the help of his two co-conspirators, Attorney General Janet Reno, the cigar-smoking "butch" lesbian who owns 47 pet peacocks, ALL named "Horace," and the Communist-Jew FBI Director Louis Freeh (appointed the day BEFORE the suspicious death of Clinton crony Vince Foster), Clinton used Jewish CIA agents who had infiltrated certain patriotic militia organizations to orchestrate and carry out this murderous crime.[51]

Spotlight, a magazine run by the Liberty Lobby, claimed, "Timothy McVeigh was in close, and probably sustained long-time, contact with an agent of the Anti-Defamation League (ADL) of B'nai B'rith operating in McVeigh's immediate circle."[52] Whatever the responsible party—the U.S. government or some other—one thing was clear to the militia: the bombing was not their fault. Instead, it was an excuse that was likely to be used by a corrupt system to once again assault American lives and freedoms.

Tellingly, millions of Americans found these explanations of the bombing persuasive, or at least plausible. In a culture shaped by an insistence on the rights of the individual as a sacred pact, government could be framed as a force of evil and oppression quite easily. Thus, while many Americans might prefer to believe that the shock and horror of the events at Oklahoma City led to the quick demise of the militia movement, this is not what happened. Instead, while some groups did cease operations and many sympathizers pulled back from open support of militia values, the movement actually sustained itself for at least two years after Oklahoma City. Understanding this point is crucial to recognizing the complex factors associated with its ultimate decline and assessing the likelihood of its—or a similar movement's—return to the United States.

At the end of 1997, *U.S. News and World Report* chronicled activities undertaken by militias and associated groups like the Patriot and common law movements. In November 1995, for example, the leader of an Oklahoma militia was arrested while building bombs and planning to attack civil rights centers, abortion clinics, welfare processing centers, and even gay bars. From April through July 1996, a group calling itself the Phineas Priests robbed several banks and bombed the offices of the *Spokesman Review* newspaper in Spokane, Washington. Members of the Viper Militia, active in Arizona, were arrested in July 1996 for possession of 300 pounds of ammonium nitrate—the chemical Timothy McVeigh used to destroy the Murrah Building—and possession of illegal automatic weapons and blasting caps. In October 1996, agents arrested members of the Mountaineer Militia in Clarksburg, West Virginia. They were allegedly planning to destroy the FBI's fingerprint facility in West Virginia and possessed sufficient quantities of TNT, grenades, and the plastic explosive known as C-4 to make the threat credible. A militia member in Kalamazoo, Michigan, was arrested in March 1997 for providing an undercover informant with eleven pipe bombs as part of a plan to destroy local government offices, nearby armories, and a television station. Yuba City, California, was hit the following month by a blast that led police to an apparent militia storehouse of 550 pounds of a gelatin form of dynamite known as Petrogel. In addition, a number of antigovernment activists decided to attack Fort Hood, Texas, as part of a plot to stop the United Nations from, as the activists believed, practicing a coup aimed at overthrowing the government of the United States. The activists' plan was to be implemented on July 4; however, the group's members were arrested and their machine guns and pipe bombs were confiscated before the attack could begin.[53] Cumulatively, by 1997 there were more than nine hundred domestic terrorism cases open in the United States, compared to only one hundred open in 1995.[54]

Further, in a case to be examined in detail in chapter 7, a group of Montana common law activists calling themselves the Freemen confronted federal officials in an eighty-one-day standoff through the summer of 1996. Likewise, the Republic of Texas group declared war on the federal government in April 1997 (for details, see chapter 7).

There were other examples of the continuing impact of the militia in the late 1990s. By 1997, many federal and state agents indicated that they no longer felt safe trying to enforce laws and regulations across much of the West. Such officials reported being shot at, either in their vehicles or as individuals, as they patrolled. Similarly, collecting taxes became almost impossible in certain areas. Even firefighters expressed concern about having their helicopters shot down if they attempted to fly over militia members' property as part of a firefighting effort.[55] In addition, evidence emerged that, following McVeigh's own efforts, other militia associates worked to recruit members who were on active duty in the U.S. military. According to a confidential survey of 17,080 soldiers, 3.5 percent claimed to have been contacted by members of extremist organizations; 7.1 percent claimed to know a soldier who was a member of a right-wing group.[56]

One particularly insidious technique that emerged in militia harassment of federal, state, and local officials was the use of liens. Militia members would file false liens against the property or other assets of officials, and if the county clerk accepted the paperwork, sheriffs and other agents would discover that if they wanted to sell their houses, for example, there were huge outstanding claims against the property that had to be cleared. If militia members could not slip these false liens by a local clerk, they often used the threat of violence to force the clerk to accept the document: many county officials had vehicles shot, tires slashed, and threats made against their homes and families if they refused to place the county seal on a lien. The militia message, then, was clear: don't tread on me, or else.

The number of militia and patriot groups increased between 1995 and 1997, with 1996 being the year of greatest growth. By 1997, there were active militia movements in all fifty states.[57] Moreover, the groups and members that remained were, in the words of the Southern Poverty Law Center's (SPLC) *Intelligence Report*, "harder."[58] Adherents were clearly more willing to use violence against the corrupted government than had been the case two years previously. While Oklahoma City had diminished some public sympathy for the movement, it galvanized a new rush to antigovernment groups among the far right wing of American political life.

The year 1998 saw its share of militia-related violence as well. In March, for example, a southern-Illinois-based organization known as the New Order was broken up when several of its members were arrested in a plot to blow up a number of buildings as well as to commit murder. On the group's target list was Morris Dees, whose Southern Poverty Law Center works to expose and undermine racist, hate, and other right-wing groups across the United States. Similarly, the offices of the SPLC were to be destroyed, as was the Simon Wiesenthal Center in Los Angeles. Also in March of 1998, members of southwestern Michigan's North American Militia were arrested for plotting to destroy several federal buildings and murder several federal agents.[59]

Yet as the 1990s neared their end, the militia movement began to decline. As Kenneth Stern notes, some militia members left the movement in reaction to the Murrah Building bombing. Two groups shut down operations on April 19, 1995. Other organizations recast themselves as political action groups rather than as armed militias. Some established more intimate relationships with groups that are part of the explicitly racist right.[60] The number of militia and related groups declined from their peak of over 800 in 1995/1996 to 194 in 2000. Of these, only 72 fit the model of the militia explored in this book.[61] The reasons for this decline will be examined in chapter 7.

The Aftermath and Oklahoma City

It should be noted that there was an aftermath for the people of Oklahoma City as well. Until September 11, 2001, they were the victims of the worst act of terrorism in the history of the United States. As happened in New York City and at the Pentagon in the aftermath of the later tragedy, the site of the Murrah Building quickly became a shrine. People left offerings of pictures, memorabilia, and white and yellow ribbons to commemorate those who had died. On May 25, 1995, explosives were used to bring the remaining parts of the building to the ground.[62] On April 19, 2000, the site became a park featuring 168 stone chairs facing a reflecting pond. Each chair represents a victim of the blast of April 19, 1995. A central rectangular mass records the time 9:01, one minute before the bomb went off—the last minute the militia movement operated without serious challenge in the United States.

7

Embers:
The Decline of
the Militia Movement

The decline of the modern American militia movement was, like its growth, rapid. Born in anger after Ruby Ridge and Waco, it expressed its rage in the inferno in Oklahoma City. Like all fires, however, it consumed itself, leaving little more than embers, remnants that might flare up again if more fuel is added but that may go out if left alone.

As has been suggested throughout this book, the reasons for the decline of the militia movement are several. This chapter seeks to explain the decline in militia membership. It identifies four major factors that shaped the movement's cooling: alienation of many potential sympathizers by the extremism of its hard core; state actions that undermined group recruitment and operations, driving it underground; success in achieving key goals; and co-optation of certain militia principles by mainstream political forces. Combined, these factors shaped the contemporary state of the militia movement.

One of the least-investigated areas in social movement research is why movements decline. Whether because movements are more interesting when they are active than when they are over, or because the impacts movements have on the political and social system are considered more intrinsically important, the actual sources of the decline of movements have rarely been examined closely.

As Doug McAdam notes, there are three dominant theories of social movement decline: the classical, resource mobilization, and political process perspectives.[1] Classical theory predicts that movements will decline for a combination of three reasons: an oligarchy that is interested more in retaining power than in radical goal achievement emerges within the movement; the movement is increasingly institutionalized so that members have formal responsibilities that serve to reduce enthusiasm and spontaneous action; and the movement's leaders become more conservative over time, thus reducing their desire to challenge the established order.[2]

Resource mobilization theory lacks an explicit explanation of movement change and decline; however, one can be deduced from the theory's logic. Resource mobilization theory holds that movements emerge whenever the system provides sufficient resources for the movement's development. Such resources can include the emergence of splits in the dominant governing consensus within a community, the defection of large numbers of people from traditional patterns of political support and participation, or sudden problems that emerge that government cannot address. In such circumstances, movements can be expected to grow. Logically, then, if the regime becomes capable of handling the problems it is facing, or if popular support is withdrawn from movement proponents, the resources necessary to movement formation no longer exist, and the movement can be expected to decline.[3]

Political process theory holds three variables to be crucial in explaining movement decline. First is the organizational strength of the movement. A well-organized, well-supported movement can be expected to last longer than a weaker, less popular one. Second is the political context—the distribution of groups and individuals, capacities of state agencies to address movement demands, and the like that influence whether or not a movement can succeed, or even has a logical reason to exist. Obviously, when many individuals and groups support a movement's goals at a time when a state may lack the capacity to repress the movement and its supporters, the prospects for a movement's success are enhanced. Opposite circumstances can be expected to have dramatically different results. Third, how other groups respond to the movement also influences its survival or decline: when different components of the political system respond favorably to the group, it is more likely to succeed; when opposition is encountered, it is more likely to fail.[4]

As will be seen in the rest of this chapter, little evidence supporting a classical explanation of movement decline can be found in the case of the militia movement. The movement did not grow more conservative, nor was it institutionalized. Nor is it clear that resources had much to do with the movement's decline: if anything, the rise of the Internet made it easier for militia members to express their message, and the penetration of computers and Internet connectivity into mainstream society grew even as the movement declined. Instead, the movement's weakening can best be seen as the result of political changes that enhanced the popularity of the state at a time that movement radicalism undermined its appeal. However, the increased popularity of the state was in part the result of the state's acceptance of some of the militia's goals: once mainstream political forces began adopting parts of the militia message, potential movement sympathizers returned to traditional political participation. Moreover, the current reshaping of the militia movement is taking place in a context similar to the one that encouraged its growth, suggesting that the decline might not be permanent.

Extremism and the Isolation
of the Militia Movement

It is clear that at least part of the reason for the militia movement's decline lies in its extremism. The hateful ideology and enraged actions of many militia members, leaders, and groups alienated these organizations from the American mainstream over time.

As was noted in chapter 6, this change in public support for the militia occurred slowly. The movement continued to grow for at least two years after the destruction of the Murrah Building in Oklahoma City. This growth, however, can be seen to derive from a polarization of opinion about the militia in the United States: those on the extreme right were mobilized to join or support militia groups, while less ideological conservatives—along with most other Americans—recoiled from the movement in shock and horror. Over time, this polarization led to the marginalization of the movement, encouraging its decline.

Opinion polls focused on public perceptions of terrorism certainly support the claim that most Americans came to view the militia movement and its companion right-wing groups as a threat. (The polls discussed in this chapter were taken *before* the attacks on the World Trade Center and the Pentagon on September 11, 2001, and were focused on domestic rather than international terrorism.) Polls consistently demonstrated that in the aftermath of the Oklahoma City bombing, Americans became more concerned with being victims of terrorism, worried more about being in public places, and were less likely to consider work to be a safe place. Several polls, for example, demonstrated that the percentage of Americans who believed terrorism was among the most important, most serious issues facing the United States increased from as little as 33 percent in March 1993 to as much as 90 percent in August 1996.[5] Similarly, only a month after the attack, in May 1995, 25 percent of Americans worried about themselves, family members, or friends being a victim of terrorism; three years later, in August 1998, that number had risen to 32 percent.[6] The workplace, too, was increasingly perceived as a place of danger: whereas only 12 percent of Americans considered their place of business potentially dangerous in March 1993, 57 percent did in August 1998.[7]

Increased concern with terrorism was linked to decreased confidence in the ability of the government to solve or prevent terrorist activity in the United States. Where as many as 64 percent of Americans had a great deal of confidence or a good amount of confidence in the government's capacity to prevent terrorist attacks before Timothy McVeigh committed his horrible crime, the number had fallen to as low as 33 percent by August 1996.[8] When asked if there were any actions that the U.S. government could take to prevent future acts of terrorism, only 45 percent thought such actions were possible in April 1995; a year later, in July 1996, only 49 percent were hopeful.[9] Meanwhile, more Americans believed that internal groups were a greater threat to security than were external actors throughout the whole period 1995–1997.[10] Clearly, for those Americans not inclined to support the militia movement, its extremism and propensity to violence were frightening. In such a context, declines in support for extremist ideas could be expected.

There was a context for the public perception of the militia movement's extremism beyond Oklahoma City, of course. As the list of militia and militia-related activities in the aftermath of the bombing presented in chapter 6 suggests, there were many active, violent groups and individuals pursuing the militia agenda through the period 1995–1997. Perhaps the most aggressive and dangerous of these groups was an organization that called itself the Viper Militia. Active in Arizona in the late 1990s, the Vipers were actually thrown out of the Militia of Arizona for the extremism of their rhetoric. Viper members practiced using explosives, openly discussed the vulnerabilities of several federal buildings and suggested procedures for destroying each of them, and advocated "OPLAN American Viper"—a plan to use guerrilla war tactics against invading troops and agents of the oppressive federal government. Acts like assassination, sniper assaults, and biological and chemical warfare were addressed in OPLAN. When twelve members of the group were indicted on weapons charges and six were charged with conspiracy to provide bombs to promote civil disorder, they were arrested. One member had a personal collection of ninety-five guns. Another owned a .30-caliber machine gun he took to bed at night and called Shirley.[11] The actions of such groups contributed to public concerns about the extremism of the militia.

Meanwhile, activists in the movement were engaged in a process of purging and transformation. Some groups softened their rhetoric after Oklahoma City, while others became more extreme. John Trochmann, the leader of the Militia of Montana, for example, deemphasized the military war games his organization had practiced and instead reconceived his group as an educational tool. He began speaking at high schools, among other venues, in an effort to shape public opinion rather than fight the federal government. Similarly, the Michigan Militia emphasized the need to build new political institutions that could deal with the problems that would arise when, as the group predicted would happen, the U.S. government collapsed. Military training, when it occurred, was deemphasized in the group's activities.[12]

The remnants of militia groups often became more extreme, however. Even as the core of the Michigan Militia moved to soften its image, opponents of this change demanded increased radicalism from the movement. Norman Olson, the founder of the Michigan Militia who was forced from office when he accused the Japanese government of being responsible for the Oklahoma City bombing, resisted the more mainstream transformation of his former organization. "I've been trying to influence the militia in Michigan to be bold, to be decisive and stand their ground," Olson insisted. "The militia is getting more fierce and more angry as the days go by. I think they've broken free of the 'adopt-a-highway' and 'hug-a-tree' philosophy."[13] Anyone needing proof that the militia had grown too extreme needed only to consider statements like Olson's to find their proof.

Testimonials of former group members further served to establish the extremism of the movement. The story of Floyd Cochran, a former white supremacist who had lived at the Aryan Nations compound in Idaho where Randy Weaver had his racist beliefs encouraged and validated, is a useful example. Cochran, who had served as spokesman for the Aryan Nations and who had later been alleged to have been involved in a plot to kill a civil rights leader, began to doubt the group's message when it insisted that anyone born with a deformity should be put to death. Cochran had a son who had been born with a cleft palate. Over time, and after extensive discussions with civil rights activist Loretta Ross, among others, Cochran came to reject his racist past. He went on to speak against the Aryan Nations' message with an insider's knowledge.[14] Such messages carried great credibility among both those opposed to right-wing movements in the United States and potential sympathizers who were forced to confront the negative aspects of the groups' ideas and actions.

Cumulatively, American public concerns, group infighting, the exposure of group plots to commit violence, and even former members' testimonials can be seen to have contributed to the decline of the militia movement, at least in the sense that they can be seen to explain why the movement ceased gathering active or tacit supporters after about 1997. After all, extremism does not really explain why active members, particularly those who were extremists themselves, dropped out of the movement. Yet, given the precipitous drop in the number of active militia groups between 1997 and 2000 described in chapter 6, some explanation of why even extremist members of the militia movement abandoned it during these years must be developed. Extremism is only part of the story.

State Action and the Decline of the Militia Movement

Another dimension of the explanation of the decline in the militia movement is the way the state—especially the Federal Bureau of

Investigation (FBI) and the courts—reacted to militia activities in the late 1990s. A combination of improved detective work, more measured responses to confrontations, and various legal actions worked to undermine both the logic and the resources of some right-wing groups, including the militia. Thus, by the end of the 1990s, many potential movement supporters had nowhere to turn: many organizations had been broken up, and the actions of the FBI no longer seemed likely to inspire paranoia and hate.

In chapter 6 a list of militia activities after Oklahoma City was presented. Many of the events involved the arrest of militia members, usually before they were able to commit acts of violence. This was certainly the case with the Viper militia. Such arrests empirically demonstrated a change in U.S. government policy toward the militia that took place after the Murrah bombing. The Justice Department formed the Executive Working Group on Domestic Terrorism, which met every two weeks to share information and plan strategy for combating home-grown violence.[15] Rather than investigating militia crimes after the fact, then, the FBI turned toward the active infiltration of militia groups with the aim of stopping violence before it occurred. The use of informants, wiretaps, monitoring of gun and munitions sales, and the creation of special marking pellets that could be included in purchases of ammonium nitrate to track where products were bought and used followed Timothy McVeigh's crime. In support of these activities, an antiterrorism bill was passed in 1996 that enhanced the government's ability to install wiretaps, check mail, and monitor the movement of products like ammonium nitrate.

This federal activity was linked to investigations by state police. Information about arms and other shipments was shared at the federal, state, and local levels. FBI investigations stimulated greater attention to militia groups on the part of state and local police authorities.

This combination of federal, state, and local police work made substantial progress against the militia movement. It became increasingly difficult for even hard-core activists to plan violence, if for no other reason than the plotters could not be sure if one of their members was an informant. Tighter controls on the distribution, purchase, and use of ammonium nitrate limited the ability of militia groups to plan follow-up acts of terrorism to Oklahoma City. In such circumstances, membership in a militia group became more dangerous. Many members quit, and new members stopped joining organizations in large numbers.

The change in state responses to the militia movement entailed more than direct police work, however. In the aftermath of Waco, the FBI undertook a systematic review of its tactics and strategies in confrontations with armed, ideologically passionate groups. Rather than treating group leaders as criminals and group members as innocent victims needing to be freed from a hostage situation, for example, after Waco the FBI emphasized negotiation, patience, and the isolation of the group from the mainstream. In so doing, the FBI undermined the conspiracy theories espoused by militia and other right-wing leaders convinced that the FBI and the rest of the federal government were out to get ordinary, decent citizens. Ultimately, this change in policy made it more difficult for militia sympathizers to garner evidence for their hatred of the federal government.

Two major post-Waco events demonstrated the FBI's new, more patient strategy in dealing with the militia and similar groups: the standoff with the Freemen of Montana in the spring of 1996 and the confrontation with the secessionists of the Republic of Texas in spring 1997. The Freemen standoff lasted for eighty-one days in 1996, including the infamous date of April 19. In contrast with Ruby Ridge and Waco, it ended peaceably with the active help of other right-wing organizations.

The Freemen were followers of the common law movement, a variant of the militia movement. Believing themselves to be sovereign citizens not subject to the laws of the United States, they wrote millions of dollars in bank drafts and other bogus checks on the basis of liens they filed against local and state officials. They threatened local judges. They put $1 million bounties on the heads of Garfield County sheriff Charles Phillips and attorney Nick Murnion. When Edwin Clark faced a foreclosure proceeding on his ranch near Jordan, Montana, the other members of the group barricaded themselves on the property. They renamed the ranch Justus Township and declared themselves a sovereign territory not answerable to the laws and jurisdiction of the United States.[16]

The confrontation between the Freemen and the FBI began when two Freemen leaders, LeRoy Schweitzer and Daniel Peterson, were arrested in March on bank fraud and other charges.[17] When the Freemen retreated to the Clark ranch—Justus Township—with their children, the FBI's Critical Incident Response Group mobilized to capture the remaining fugitives.[18]

The people of Garfield County, Montana, were unsympathetic to the Freemen. Eastern Montana is an area of ranches and farms, and local residents generally believed that the Freemen had adopted their separationist ideas only in the aftermath of bad business decisions that cost many their property in foreclosure proceedings.[19] Thus, in contrast with the situation in Idaho where many supporters of the Weaver family came out to protest FBI activities, no such anger was expressed toward the FBI during the Freemen standoff.

Also in contrast with Ruby Ridge and Waco, the FBI moved slowly in handling the Freemen. The Clark ranch covered nearly a thousand acres, and FBI leaders decided that negotiations would be the primary focus of their actions. Moreover, in a move very different from what had occurred in Idaho and Texas, they noted that the Freemen were effectively contained so long as they remained on their property.[20] There was, in other words, no reason to take aggressive steps to end the confrontation.

There was yet another significant difference in the FBI's approach to the Freemen confrontation compared to events like Waco. Whereas the FBI had generally ignored the advice of religion experts in their negotiations with David Koresh and the Branch Davidians, the agency actively sought the advice, help, and intervention of several right-wing leaders to bring an end to the Montana crisis. Agents called on Bo Gritz, the former army officer who had finally brought Randy Weaver off his mountain in 1992, as well as Jack McLamb, a former Phoenix police officer who recruited police personnel to join the Patriot movement, to talk to the Freemen. The FBI also brought in Colorado state senator Charles Duke, a public supporter of militia and common law groups, to try to work out a deal with the Freemen.[21]

While none of these individuals was able to work effectively with the Freemen, another group, CAUSE, a legal firm that defends white supremacists and other right-wing group members, had more success. CAUSE leaders were brought to Montana at the government's expense, and a CAUSE-sponsored proposal put in motion the steps that eventually ended the standoff: A CAUSE leader suggested that the FBI take one of the leaders of the encircled Freemen to meet with the group's leader, LeRoy Schweitzer, who was in jail in Billings. FBI officials initially reacted in surprise. "Let me get this straight," one asked. "You want us to take a man who is technically under arrest, fly him in an FBI plane to a jail we hope to see him incarcerated in, bring him home, and then put him under siege again?" Incredulity was put aside, however, and the FBI agreed. After this meeting, Schweitzer wrote a note encouraging his followers to submit to arrest. The end came quickly. With an agreement that the Freemen would have the right to turn over documents to a Montana state legislator rather than directly to the FBI, the standoff ended in June 1996.[22] No one was hurt or killed in the longest standoff in U.S. law enforcement history.

The FBI's cooperation with right-wing groups extended beyond its decision to integrate such figures in negotiations. Both government officials and militia leaders across the United States urged members to stay at home or to leave their guns behind during the standoff. In contrast with militia leaders' insistence that, after Waco, the militia movement would mobilize to prevent any further assaults on citizens, many militia leaders called for the deescalation of the Freemen standoff. For example, John Parsons, a leader of the South Dakota–based Tri-State Militia, asked his fellow militia members to "stay home and let the negotiators and the people on the site handle this problem, so we don't have a Waco or a Ruby Ridge."[23]

The FBI's confrontation with the members of the Republic of Texas took a similar, if shorter, course. The Republic was led by its self-styled ambassador, Richard McLaren, and was based in the rural west Texas community of Fort Davis. Although the group had only twenty active members, as many as eight hundred people claimed citizenship in the Republic.[24]

Like the Freemen, members of the Republic of Texas insisted that they were not subject to the authority of the federal government because Texas had never legally joined the United States. Thus, for example, they were not obliged to pay taxes.[25]

The Republic of Texas's confrontation with the government began on April 27, 1997. In response to the arrest of one of their members, three members took two local people hostage. The group then declared war on the United States.[26]

As had been the case in Montana a year earlier, the local population was not sympathetic to the Republic. Likewise, authorities—in this case the Texas Department of Public Safety and the FBI—responded carefully. Their emphasis was on negotiations. For example, law enforcement officials made an early decision to return the arrested group member to the Republic compound in exchange for the group's two hostages. In addition, authorities used language that made McLaren and his followers comfortable, referring to the negotiations as diplomacy and McLaren's compound as an embassy. Agents agreed that McLaren and his followers could file any petition he desired with a federal court—a right any citizen holds but an issue that was important for the Republic leader. They agreed that he could petition the United Nations for support—yet another opportunity anyone has but a significant issue for McLaren. Finally, in an attempt to end the confrontation peacefully, negotiators focused on McLaren's wife, hoping that if she could be convinced to leave, her husband would follow. She left the compound at 11 A.M., Saturday, May 3; McLaren followed five hours later.[27]

Authorities took other steps to make sure that violence did not occur during the standoff. Officials asked many local residents to leave the immediate area around the Republic compound and stopped and arrested seven armed militia members in nearby Pecos, Texas. These activists were coming to intervene in the standoff, thus possibly exacerbating the crisis.[28]

The only violence during the standoff took place when two group members tried to leave the compound. They were confronted by agents from the Texas Department of Criminal Justice, and one was killed in the ensuing gun battle.[29] In contrast with Waco and Ruby Ridge, this shooting involved fugitives leaving or off their land, rather than individuals encircled on their own property.

There are other examples of changed government tactics in dealing with extremist groups. In September 1997, a woman from Roby, Illinois, who was ordered to undergo a court-mandated psychiatric evaluation barricaded herself in her house with a 12-gauge shotgun after confronting police who had come to escort her to her appointment. Despite efforts of local militia groups to construct the following standoff as "Roby Ridge," the incident was resolved peacefully after police cut off her electricity and gas and waited her out.[30] That same month, a white supremacist in Utah wanted on a weapons charge barricaded himself into his property in rural La Verkin, Utah.[31] Rather than raid the fugitive's home, Saint George police acted on a tip that the suspect was in a local apartment. When the man left, the police blocked his car and arrested him peacefully.[32] In 1999 it was revealed that the Clinton administration canceled a planned raid to break up a logging protest in Oregon in 1996 for fear the protesters would be hurt, thus deepening antigovernment sentiments in the region.[33] Even militia members urged patience in this new context: Bradford Metcalf, a militia member from Michigan who was arrested and tried for planning to blow up several federal buildings, told codefendant Kenneth Carter, "I really hope everybody keeps their cool." He hoped this was the case, he said, surprisingly, "because I want to clean these guys' clocks in the courtroom."[34] Such a statement makes sense only if militia members believed they could get a fair trial from the government—a sentiment that would have seemed inconceivable during the previously confrontational relationship between the government and the militia.

Cumulatively, the change in government tactics in confrontations with right-wing groups delegitimized the claims of those militia members who insisted that the government was engaged in aggressive plans to undermine citizen rights. Whereas Ruby Ridge and Waco provided the materials that made conspiracy theories make sense, the standoffs with the Freemen and the Republic of Texas made such theories seem overblown. Thus, a central premise of militia ideology was challenged, if not refuted.

A final dimension of the government-movement relationship that worked to undermine the militia was the use of court cases by private citizens to break up right-wing organizations. The most notable of these was a case filed against Richard Butler's Aryan Nations, the group through which Randy Weaver met the informant who facilitated the weapons sale that started the militia movement. In July 1998, Victoria and Jason Keenan were shot at by security guards while they were driving past the Aryan Nations compound. When at least five bullets struck their car, a punctured tire forced the vehicle to swerve into a ditch. Three Aryan Nations security guards forced the pair from the car and threatened to kill them. Through their attorney, Morris Dees of the Southern Poverty Law Center, the Keenans accused Butler and his organization of being negligent in the selection, training, and supervision of the guards. They asked for more than $11 million in punitive damages. A jury ultimately agreed, awarding the Keenans $6.3 million. The Aryan Nations compound was closed in 2000, and Butler lost the right to use the name Aryan Nations.[35]

The combination of enhanced police work, changed tactics, and the use of civil court cases to undermine the organizational capacity of right-wing groups had a powerful effect on the militia movement. Membership became dangerous in light of increased surveillance and more active arrests. The legitimacy of militia ideology was challenged by more careful government-group confrontations. And leaders of militia and other groups could face legal action if their followers broke the law; accordingly, leadership became as dangerous as followership. Much of the decline of the militia movement can be accounted for as a result of this new matrix of government action.

It is important not to grant too much credit to changed government tactics when explaining the decline of the movement, however. The idea that government action exclusively led to the decay of the militia, or even the notion that it was a combination of the government's policies and the movement's extremism, would lead to the false conclusion that the militia movement did not achieve any of its goals. As will be seen in the next section of this chapter, militia members and their more mainstream political sympathizers were very successful in realizing one important goal: many proposed new gun control bills were defeated in the aftermath of the rise of the militia. Ironically, then, the militia were at least tangentially successful in achieving a central purpose of their movement. In being successful, however, they undermined their own justification for their existence.

The Success of the Movement: Gun Control

As was shown in chapters 1, 2, and 3, no issue was a more important symbol to the militia of the federal government's evil than gun control. Gun control was seen as the first step in a developing plot to destroy the Constitution and impose foreign rule over the United States; guns were to be taken away so that private citizens could no longer defend themselves and their loved ones from the coming conspiracy-sponsored genocide.

In this context, major pieces of gun control legislation such as the Brady bill, passed in 1993, were anathema to the militia. The Brady bill, which established a waiting period between the purchase of a gun and the buyer's right to take it home, leaving a time for background checks of the purchaser, was extremely unpopular among militia groups. Its provisions, particularly the requirement that background checks be conducted to limit the chances that a convicted felon or other inappropriate person could buy a weapon, were seen by the militia as a violation in their private and absolute right to buy and sell as many guns as they wished.

It is worth noting that as unpopular as gun control legislation was among the militia, it was equally popular among the vast majority of American citizens. In the aftermath of widely publicized school mass murders in Columbine High School in Littleton, Colorado, in April 1999 and Santana High School in San Diego, California, in June 2001, along with many other similar incidents, polls regularly showed that two-thirds of Americans supported stricter gun control laws.[36]

One area in which additional legislation was proposed lay in an attempt to close the gun-show exception to the Brady bill's waiting period. In the Brady bill, sales of guns between private individuals at gun shows were exempt from the background check requirements. Other attempts were made to create a system that could support instant background checks, thereby avoiding the problem at gun shows that clients might wish to purchase guns but, if forced to wait, would not be able to complete the sale since the gun show might have moved on to another location by the time the background check was complete. These changes, which seemed acceptable and useful to most Americans, particularly after Columbine and the other school shootings, were vigorously opposed by militia groups and other gun-rights supporters on the grounds that they violated the Second Amendment's protection of the rights of private citizens to own guns.

No piece of federal gun control legislation has been passed by the U.S. Congress since 1994—the same year the militia began its mass mobilization in American political life. While it is not possible to directly tie the rise of the militia to the failure of gun control legislation—even bills that have substantial support among the general population—it is possible to trace the process by which passing additional gun control legislation was stopped. The role of militia groups, and more particularly the mobilization of their sympathizers, throughout the United States made passing more gun limitations politically difficult. As a consequence, one of the main issues that energized the militia lost significance as the 1990s progressed: in undermining gun control legislation, the militia achieved one of its major objectives. In so doing, it also lost part of the foundation on which its relevance rested. The movement's decline, then, was the partial result of its success.

A major push for anti-gun-control mobilization began in 1995, when National Rifle Association (NRA) executive vice president Wayne LaPierre sent out a fundraising letter to the organization's members. This letter invoked militia rhetoric and strong antigovernment attitudes as it drew a metaphorical line in the sand against further gun control in the United States. "Dear Fellow Americans," the letter begins, "I've worn out a lot of shoe leather walking the halls of Congress. I've met key leaders, I've talked with old allies, I've met with new Congressmen and many staff leaders. What I'm hearing concerns me." What concerns LaPierre, the letter goes on to say, is that the government is using legislation like the Brady bill to violate citizens' rights. Speaking against "anti-gunners"—select representatives and senators like Charles Schumer (D-New York.), Ted Kennedy (D-Massachusetts), and Dianne Feinstein (D-California)—LaPierre notes, "It doesn't matter to them that the Brady Bill is a failure." Moreover, in language mimicking that examined in chapter 3 as core to militia ideology, LaPierre insists:

It doesn't matter to them that the Brady Law has become one more tool that government agents are using to deny the Constitutional rights of law abiding citizens.

It doesn't matter to them that the semi-auto ban gives jack-booted government thugs more power to take away our Constitutional rights, break in our doors, destroy our property, and even injure or kill us.

"President Clinton's army of anti-gun government agents continues to intimidate and harass law-abiding citizens," LaPierre argues.

In Clinton's administration, if you have a badge, you have the government's go-ahead to harass, intimidate, even murder law-abiding citizens.

Randy Weaver at Ruby Ridge . . . Waco and the Branch Davidians. . . . Not too long ago, it was unthinkable for Federal agents wearing nazi bucket helmets and black storm trooper uniforms to attack law-abiding citizens.

Ultimately, like militia members, LaPierre links the NRA's battle against the "anti-gunners" to the battle for American liberty itself, a new opportunity for the militia to save the nation:

> Most Americans don't realize that our freedoms are slowly slipping away.
>
> They don't understand that politicians and bureaucrats are chipping away at the American way of life.
>
> They're destroying business, destroying our economy, destroying our property rights, destroying our moral foundation, destroying our schools, destroying our culture. . . .
>
> . . . Destroying our Constitution.
>
> And the attack, either through legislation or regulation, on the Second Amendment is only the first in a long campaign to destroy the freedoms at the core of American life.
>
> You can see it in the gun bans, certainly. But you can see it in closed ranges, closed hunting lands, confiscated collectors' firearms, banned magazines and ammunition taxes.
>
> You can see it when jack-booted government thugs, wearing black, armed to the teeth, break down a door, open fire with an automatic weapon, and kill or maim law-abiding citizens.
>
> America's gun owners will only be the first to lose their freedoms.
>
> If we lose the right to keep and bear arms, then the right to free speech, free practice of religion, and every other freedom in the Bill of Rights are sure to follow. . . .
>
> This, the battle we're fighting today, is a battle to retake the most precious, most sacred ground on earth. This is a battle for freedom.[37]

While his analysis of the relationship between guns and freedom mirrored that offered by the militia and examined in chapter 3 and is grounded in the myths and cultural conditions explored in chapters 1 and 2, LaPierre's political strategy was very different from the militia's. LaPierre's plan was for gun-rights activists to overwhelm the political system with petitions that would be so numerous that politically vulnerable incumbents would be afraid to defy the NRA and its supporters by voting for additional gun control legislation. "I need you to sign the enclosed Petitions to the United States Congress," LaPierre says. "Please be sure to sign all five petitions, then fold them and place them in the enclosed, postage-paid envelope addressed to me at NRA headquarters. . . . I want to personally deliver your five petitions, and the petitions of all 3.5 million of your fellow NRA members—17.5 million petitions in all—to Congress." This drive, LaPierre continues, will essentially intimidate members of Congress elected with small margins of victory into compliance with the NRA's gun-rights agenda:

> Your Petitions to Congress also sends another message—a message not spelled out on the Petitions themselves.
> Each Congressman, on average, will receive 8,000 Petitions from NRA members demanding action. 8,000 messages from angry voters sounds an alarm in every Congressman's head.
> You see, most Congressional elections were won or lost by 5,000 votes or less. So, they'll realize that failing to defend the Second Amendment and failing to retake the Constitutional freedoms lost to the anti-gunners, could result in big losses in the next election!

Using such pressure, LaPierre insists, will protect gun rights—and other American freedoms—into the future:

> These petitions are our D-Day.
> Armed with these petitions and our First Amendment rights, we are going to storm Congress, knock out anti-gunner strongholds and recapture every bit of ground we lost since Bill Clinton took office.
> And if we're successful, these petitions will be the turning point in the history of the Constitution. . . . A day when our sacred right to keep and bear arms will be secure for the next generation of law-abiding Americans.[38]

In addition to mobilizing voters, gun-rights groups also threw money at their cause. Groups opposed to increased limits on gun ownership or registration spent $3.7 million in political action committee, individual, and soft-money contributions in just the 1999–2000 election cycle. Such groups gave over $13 million in the 1990s. The National Rifle Association accounted for over 90 percent of these contributions. By contrast, pro-control groups and individuals contributed only $394,000 to political campaigns in the same period. Since 1990, advocates of greater gun control have given only $1.3 million to candidates.[39]

One other arena of combat remained open in the gun control debate: courts. Mirroring the strategy used by organizations like the Southern Poverty Law Center in combating racist groups nationwide, individuals and even cities across the United States began to sue gun manufacturers. These suits held that the manufacturers were liable if a gun was used in a way that promoted crime, violence, or death. Their intent was to end the production of guns by driving the companies that produced weapons out of business.

In 2001, however, the U.S. Supreme Court let stand a lower-court ruling that a city, in this case New Orleans, could be blocked from suing gun manufacturers by state law. Accordingly, while the issue of court actions against weapons producers had not been resolved by December 2002, manufacturers that can persuade state governments to oppose city-sponsored lawsuits will be protected from further actions.

In the end, in addition to manufacturers' success in court, the failure of gun control legislation in the United States since 1994 can be attributed to the core insight of the NRA funding letter: mobilized minority populations that emphasize one or two key issues to the exclusion of nearly every other concern can constitute formidable electoral threats to vulnerable elected officials. Put simply, while majorities of Americans favor various gun control schemes, the issue is not important enough in their political thinking to dominate their behavior. Other concerns, from education through child care, have greater salience for most voters. Accordingly, elected officials are faced with a choice to satisfy the interests of vaguely concerned, relatively unmotivated voters who cannot be expected to unfailingly support the official in a future election, or to satisfy the interests of a highly mobilized constituency engaged enough and numerous enough to prevent the official's reelection if they grow disenchanted. In such a context, mobilized minorities regularly win their way in the U.S. political system, particularly if they are backed up by substantial campaign contributions.

This pattern of mobilized minorities holding disproportionate influence in the political system is exacerbated by the federal structure of American government. As has been noted throughout this book, militia members and their supporters generally live in rural, relatively isolated communities across the United States Elections for every federal office, whether congressional or presidential, are ultimately contests for the plurality of votes in a given region, whether it be a congressional district or a state: the winner of the plurality of votes in the district is automatically elected to Congress, while the winner of the plurality of votes in a given state almost always wins that state's electors in the electoral college in the presidential election. Thus, congressional and presidential elections—not to mention state, county, and local ones—are really contests for sufficient support among localized constituencies to finish at least slightly ahead of everyone else. In such circumstances, highly mobilized constituencies can have a great deal of political influence. And when the ideas of such an active group are also popular, as is the case with anti-gun-control sentiments throughout much of the rural United States, the combination of strong organization and political popularity can become overwhelming. Given that even federal officials are elected in local districts and states, or by an electoral college dominated by states, it is obvious that representatives from predominantly rural areas can be expected to represent the gun-rights lobby in Congress. Aggregate polls that show that 70 percent of Americans favor greater gun control are ultimately irrelevant: the groups that elect large numbers of congressional officials and cause presidential candidates to win a state's electoral votes are important in local areas to a degree that far exceeds their numerical percentage among all Americans.

It is, of course, impossible to prove that the militia movement caused the shift in gun control policies in the United States. Indeed, the attempt to find such a link between an individual group and any policy is usually a fruitless effort. However, it is reasonable to assume that, given a choice between supporting pro- and anti-gun-control candidates in elections, those militia members who chose to vote voted for the gun-rights candidate. Indeed, their role in the districts in which they lived was likely to be influential precisely because they were mobilized and motivated.

Whether or not the militia movement *caused* the end of increased limits on gun ownership that characterized the late 1990s, it is clear that the success of the anticontrol lobby ultimately undermined the relevance of the militia. As was the case with the change in federal government actions toward right-wing groups after Waco, the failure of legislation promoting increased regulation and registration of firearms knocked one of the pillars on which the militia movement's self-described importance rested. It became difficult to argue that the federal government was on a path of removing all guns from Americans' homes when the government itself continually defeated legislation with such an intent. In the end, then, the success of the gun-rights lobby, however related it was to militia activism, made the movement seem unnecessary and promoted its decline.

Co-optation and the Militia

A final reason for the decline of the militia movement in the late 1990s was the co-optation of many of its core issues and ideological perspectives by mainstream political forces, usually Republican elected officials and conservative political commentators. By the end of the 1990s, in contrast with the early years of the decade, antigovernment activists would have a means to influence the federal government through traditional political activities like voting, lobbying, and media-agenda setting. Accordingly, support for alternative action declined.

The logic of co-optation is grounded in the structure of American elections. As was explained in the last section, elections are won by gaining the support of pluralities of voters in particular districts or states. Highly mobilized groups that deliver substantial percentages of votes at crucial times can have a disproportionate influence on a particular campaign. This is especially true in less-populated areas in which a few hundred votes can make a profound difference in the outcome of an election. As groups of voters adopt new political positions that do not easily correspond with the dominant platform of major parties, third parties or counterpolitical movements tend to form. The established parties, then, face a choice: see potential supporters leave their alliance to join a new organization, or shift their platforms to accommodate, to the fullest extent possible, the interests of the newly mobilized voters. Generally, parties shift platforms to protect their positions by co-opting the core ideas of the new movement. If possible, the platform of the established party is adjusted to appeal to groups currently not supporting its positions. This process of co-optation, in turn, leaves supporters and potential allies of the new movement with a choice: support an established institution with a credible chance of electoral success that also generally supports their personal values, or support a new group with declining support and limited prospects for victory. More often than not, the new movement is abandoned, and the recognized party takes the lead in supporting many, if not all, of the movement's goals.

The groundwork for the co-optation of the militia movement was laid by Republicans from western states. Helen Chenoweth (R-Idaho), among others, used her position in Congress to advocate positions favored by the militia. For example, in 1995 she sponsored legislation that would require federal authorities to gain permission from county law enforcement agents, particularly sheriffs, before conducting searches, making arrests, or undertaking any federal law enforcement action even if it was supported by a federal warrant. Chenoweth argued, "They [federal agents] shouldn't be armed unless they are deputized by the local sheriff." This stunning reversal of the Constitution's supremacy clause is strongly favored by common law and militia groups on the grounds that the county level is the highest level in which law enforcement power can be legitimately located. Her bill, which ultimately failed, was cosponsored by numerous, mostly western, Republicans: Steve Stockman (Texas), Roscoe Bartlett (Maryland), Wes Cooley (Oregon), John Doolittle (California), John Hostetter (Indiana), Jack Metcalf (Washington), and Linda Smith (Washington).[40]

Chenoweth's ideas extended beyond reversing Article 6 of the U.S. Constitution. She also linked the federal government to the Shadow Government of militia ideology and, in rhetoric that played on the worst fears of conspiracy theorists, insisted that the U.S. Fish and Wildlife Service was using "armed agency officials and helicopters" to enforce the Endangered Species Act. Additionally, she claimed—in yet another reversal of the constitutional guarantee that it, and not state constitutions, was the law of the land—that legislation like the Endangered Species Act was illegal because it violated the Idaho state constitution. The Militia of Montana sold a tape of one of Chenoweth's speeches—made in 1993 before she was elected to Congress—in which she says, "We are in a day and an age now when we are facing an unlawful government from time to time." Environmentalists, she claimed, were a "Communist threat" to the United States, and endangered-species legislation would cause a "breakdown in state sovereignty and possibly [lead] to One World Government."[41]

Even Chenoweth's reaction to the bombing in Oklahoma City expressed pro-militia thinking. After the Murrah Building was destroyed, Chenoweth noted:

> I don't think violent acts like that can be condoned and must be punished. While we can never condone this, we still must begin to look at the public policies that may be pushing people too far. . . . I'm not opposed to the concept of a militia, because I think people ought to be able to protect themselves, and I think it was a concept embraced by our founding fathers.[42]

In effect, Chenoweth argued that while McVeigh went too far, the underlying logic of the militia movement was correct: the federal government had grown abusive of liberty and needed to be resisted.

There were other pro-militia politicians active in Washington, D.C., in the 1990s. Steve Stockman (R-Texas), one of the cosponsors of Chenoweth's county sheriffs bill, may have had militia members as active supporters of his successful 1994 bid for office. Joe Knollenberg (R-Michigan) campaigned with Michigan Militia members at a rally of anti-gun-control activists.[43] In a letter that might have been dismissed as the delusions of a militia extremist had it not been signed by Senators Larry Craig (R-Idaho) and Lauch Faircloth (R-North Carolina), the two senators asked Attorney General Janet Reno whether rumors that federal military agencies were training law enforcement authorities in military tactics were true.[44] Militia ideology was, at least to some extent, becoming commonly adopted in statements from some Republican Party members.

While Chenoweth's—or Stockman's or Knollenberg's—significance for the militia movement can be overstated, their presence in Washington, D.C., at the center of the government alleged to be engaged in destroying American liberties, was an important step in the co-optation of militia principles by conservative political forces. After the election of 1994, it became possible for the first time for militia members and sympathizers to vote for or otherwise support federal officials who appealed to the militia cause. Unconventional political action could be supplemented with traditional behavior.

The co-optation of militia issues by the Republican Party went further than just electing politicians to office. As was discussed in the prior section, gun control was a central issue for the militia. In the National Rifle Association's fundraising letter the organization is explicit in naming political leaders who favored the NRA's position. The letter lists Senator Phil Gramm (R-Texas), Speaker of the House Newt Gingrich (R-Georgia), and Congressman Bill McCollum (R-Florida), among others, as supporters of the anti-gun-control movement. The letter further requests that members send in a "special contribution" to the NRA so that it could aid its allies and oppose its enemies in the next election. "With your special contribution," LaPierre writes, "I can increase the NRA's public exposure on talk shows, at rallies and shows, in radio and T.V. advertising and through broadcasts like the NRA's Town Meeting that first sounded our alarm in 16 million households, last summer." Finally, the letter discusses an NRA-sponsored plan to "Repeal, Reform, and Investigate": to repeal existing gun limitations, reform laws and institutions, and to investigate government abuses. The NRA's strategy, then, was not just to mobilize angry voters. It was also an attempt to encourage and support those officials who would advance the NRA's anti-gun-control agenda.

As was the case with Helen Chenoweth, the significance of the NRA's activities did not lie in their explicit militia connection or support for the militia movement. Instead, as a result of NRA lobbying, fundraising, and political mobilization, in combination with the activities of other anticontrol forces, the Republican Party adopted strong language in the party's platform opposing further limitation on gun ownership. Moreover, many, if not most, Republican candidates for federal office in the 1990s ran on an anti-gun-control agenda. Indeed, during the 2000 presidential election, an NRA official claimed that if George W. Bush were elected president, the NRA would have a presence in the Oval Office itself. In 2001 President Bush's attorney general, John Ashcroft, issued a statement reversing the federal government's long-standing position that the right to bear arms is a collective, rather than an individual, right. Historically, the federal government has argued that states have the right to regulate gun ownership to protect the interests of the broader community. Most advocates of gun rights have insisted, in contrast, that the right to bear arms is individual, meaning that anyone should be able to own whatever weapons he desires with little or no state regulation. Ashcroft's interpretation of the status of gun rights corresponds closely with the position held by militia members and sympathizers. Accordingly, by 2002, individuals motivated by militia-like values on the question of gun control had an option that they lacked in 1992: they could vote for candidates who supported their values and who might actually win office and do something about it.

The Republican Party further signaled its antigovernment sentiments in the hearings it conducted regarding the government's (mis)deeds in Ruby Ridge and Waco. The House and Senate hearings on these incidents quickly deteriorated into partisan affairs in which Democrats attempted to exonerate President Clinton, Attorney General Janet Reno, and federal law enforcement officials, while Republicans inevitably painted the Weavers and the Branch Davidians as ordinary people victimized by an oppressive government.

Militia members and sympathizers were given a platform to express their ideas. Again, potential militia supporters were presented with an apparently sympathetic alternative to militia membership: the Republican Party.

Conservative talk radio and other media outlets also provided a platform for militia ideas and attitudes in the 1990s. As early as 1994, for example, conservative icon and radio host Rush Limbaugh said, "The second violent American revolution is just about—I got my fingers about a quarter of an inch apart—is just about that far away. Because these people are sick and tired of a bunch of bureaucrats in Washington driving into town and telling them what they can and can't do with their land."[45] Similarly, Watergate figure -turned talk show host G. Gordon Liddy insisted:

> You got a big target there . . . says ATF. Don't shoot at them because they got a vest on underneath that. Head shots. Head shots. . . . Kill the sons of bitches. . . .
>
> You have every right to fear your government. Look at what the brutal thugs of the Bureau of Alcohol, Tobacco, and Firearms do, smashing into homes, shooting as they come in, killing people. When they don't do that, they *trash* the home, *steal* the money from the people who have *never* been accused of a crime, take their possessions, *stomp* the cat to death on the way out, then threaten the wife that if she talks about it, *that they'll be back,* and they're federal agents—they can do *anything they want to.* That's the kind of people we're talking about here, the kind of people that take a pregnant woman and *smash* her against a concrete wall—that's the Bureau of Alcohol, Tobacco and Firearms—so she loses her *baby.* You'd better be afraid of 'em![46]

In and of itself, talk radio may not have had much influence on the militia movement, other than to inflame its members' passions. Indeed, concerns that right-wing broadcasts had stimulated the militia led President Clinton on April 24, 1995, to complain about the "purveyors of hatred" who dominated the nation's talk radio programs. "They spread hate," Clinton insisted, and "they leave the impression that, by their very words, violence is acceptable."[47] This complaint, however, misses the real influence of talk radio on the movement: by signaling—and encouraging—a conservative turn in the electorate, talk radio hosts provided further evidence to Republican Party leaders that it was important to reach out to the hard right to maintain and expand the party's electoral base. Mirroring right-wing radio, for example, then Speaker Newt Gingrich insisted in 1995 that Bill Clinton and his supporters were "the ene-mies of normal Americans." Gingrich argued that the Democratic Party's leadership "despises the values of the American people" while espousing a "multicultural nihilistic hedonism" ultimately motivated by the idea that "the government should control every-thing."[48] Gingrich, of course, was not a fringe candidate isolated from the political mainstream: he used his position as House mi-nority whip to promote an electoral strategy that brought the Re-publican Party to majority control of the House of Representatives in 1994. It also made him Speaker. His rhetoric provided a reason for militia members and sympathizers to support the Republican Party: we believe in your values, Gingrich insisted, thus we are de-serving of your support. Given his position, this claim was credible.

The clearest link between the militia movement and at least some elements of the Republican Party can be seen in the role Larry Pratt played in conservative talk show host Pat Buchanan's cam-paign for the 1996 Republican Party nomination for president of the United States. Buchanan, whose conservative, insurgent cam-paign for the 1992 Republican Party nomination undermined in-cumbent President George H. W. Bush's prospects for reelection by demobilizing conservative support for the party's eventual nomi-nee, named Pratt cochair of his 1996 campaign. Pratt was active among militia and other far-right groups. In addition to having participated in broadcasts that advanced Christian Identity and other racist principles earlier in the 1990s,[49] Pratt also attended the October 1992 meeting in Estes Park, Colorado, that followed the Ruby Ridge incident and set in motion the organization of the mili-tia movement.[50] He was one of the leading supporters of creating militias nationwide.

Pratt was also founder of Gun Owners of America, a group that thought the NRA was "soft" on the issue of gun control.[51] In addi-tion, he advocated the use of armed civilian patrols to maintain law and order in society, arguing that "It is time that the United States return to reliance on an armed people."[52] "There is no acceptable alternative," he continued. Moreover, after Oklahoma City, Pratt claimed that "whoever did that in Oklahoma City had descended to the level of the FBI."[53] He also served as contributing editor to *The Fifty States Constitutionalist*, a magazine advocating common law and militia programs.[54]

In other words, Pratt was a militia activist cochairing a campaign for the nomination of the Republican Party candidate for president of the United States. Underscoring the significance of the hard right in his campaign, when controversy about Pratt's past surfaced during the election, Buchanan defended his pick: "All I know is Larry Pratt of the Gun Owners of America has been a loyal early supporter of mine when no one else did [sic]."[55] Buchanan continued by insisting that Pratt was being "smeared" by "dogs" because he was a "devout Christian."[56]

While Pratt was eventually forced to take a leave of absence from the campaign,[57] his presence in the campaign at all serves as a demonstration of the degree to which at least the conservative wing of the Republican Party had moved to co-opt the militia movement. Militia members and sympathizers were understood to be a potentially powerful bloc of voters on whom a campaign for a nomination could be grounded and through whom the presidency itself might be won. Likewise, militia members and sympathizers could look at the Buchanan candidacy or at his advisers and recognize that they had an electoral alternative through which to express their political values. Traditional political behavior became an appropriate tool to advocate the militia's political platform.

As a result of such co-optation, along with members' extremism, changed government responses to militia activity, and the movement's success in achieving some of its core objectives, the militia movement has declined. Not only is it not growing in membership, but also fewer and fewer people are showing up at militia events, recruiting seminars, and even militia-government confrontations. However, this mathematical decline has not translated into reduced influence: given the presence of militia-related ideas in major political parties and powerful interest groups, the ironic effect of the decline of the movement may be the accomplishment of many of its goals. In the long run, then, the militia may be more successful as a former movement than it was as a current one.

Given that success often breeds momentum, however, it is important to consider whether or not the movement is truly moribund. The prospects that the militia movement, or a related one, may reemerge as a force in American politics needs to be addressed. As will be seen, the movement is not dead, and the cultural and ideological factors that shaped its rise (see chapters 1, 2, and 3) are still broadly accepted in American society. The movement, or a similar one, could easily flare up again if proper fuel is applied to the coals left over from the militia fire. It is to understanding this possibility that the epilogue turns.

Epilogue:
The Movement and
Homeland Security

Taken together, the isolation from the mainstream of most radical militia activists, police actions to prevent militia violence, changed government responses to militia incidents, the failure of gun control legislation, and the co-optation of the less radical parts of the movement by established political organizations like the Republican Party can be seen to have led to the decline of the modern militia movement. This decline, however, does not necessarily mean the movement's end. This epilogue will explore the prospects of a resurgence of the militia movement, or something like it, in the future.

Racism and a New Militia Movement?

There is reason to believe that the movement has not really declined. As was discussed in chapter 3, militia ideology, while asserting its antiracist character, nonetheless has racist principles at its core. For example, the notion of the "sovereign citizen" is an exclusively white concept, and the New World Order manipulating the U.S. government in pursuit of some corrupt agenda is tightly linked with the theory expounded in the fictional text *The Protocols of the Elders of Zion* that a Jewish superelite really controls the world. Accordingly, it is not a substantial stretch of one's militia values to move from a militia to an explicitly hate-oriented group.

It is also the case that many of the leaders present at the 1992 Estes Park, Colorado, meeting in which the modern militia movement was effectively born were hard-core racists who chose race-free language as the best tool through which to advance their cause. In such conditions, it seems likely that rather than just going away, the movement simply found its real, racist roots.

Moreover, there has been a resurgence of explicitly racist groups on the right even as the militia movement has ostensibly declined. While the number of militia and associated groups declined in the late 1990s, the number of white supremacist groups increased. Some movement from militia to racist groups seems to have taken place, at least to a limited degree: while rosters are not available for these groups, in the late 1990s and early 2000s, the number of right-wing hate groups has increased dramatically. By 2000, for example, the Southern Poverty Law Center had identified 602 hate groups in the United States. These ranged in ideology and values from well-established groups like the Ku Klux Klan to more recent, more militia-related groups like the Christian Identity and Neo-Confederate movements.[1] It may be more accurate to say the movement has evolved than to declare its death.

It is also the case that some right-wing hate groups have managed to use the terrorist attacks of September 11, 2001, as motivational and recruitment material. August Kreis, a leader of the Pennsylvania-based Sheriff's Posse Comitatus, wrote, "May the WAR be started. DEATH to His [God's] enemies, may the World Trade Center BURN TO THE GROUND! . . . We can blame no others than ourselves for our problems due to the fact that we allow . . . Satan's children, called jews today, to have dominion over our lives."[2] Former Ku Klux Klan leader and Republican Party candidate David Duke noted that the attacks were a consequence of U.S. support for Israel: "Let me be very, very blunt," Duke said. "The ultimate cause of this terrorism stems directly from our involvement in and support of the criminal behavior of Israel."[3] Michael Hill, leader of the League of the South, insisted that the attacks were caused by American's moral collapse in modern times: "In part, these events sprang from an 'open borders' policy that has for the past four decades encouraged massive Third World immigration and thus cultural destabilization. . . . This is America's wake-up call to forsake its idolatry and to return to its true Christian and Constitutional foundations."[4] Similar language was offered by more mainstream political and religious figures like Jerry Falwell: "I really believe that the pagans, and the abortionists, and the feminists, and the gays and the lesbians. . . . I point the finger in their face and say 'You helped this happen.'"[5] As a final example, Matt Hale, leader of the Illinois-based World Church of the Creator, claimed: "The time is at hand to preach . . . why these attacks: the control of the United States government by International Jewry. . . . We must NOT allow this opportunity to be squandered."[6] Even the horrible crimes of September 11, then, have provided material for the growing hate movement in the United States, suggesting that this reemergent, vigorous group has absorbed the declining militia movement.

While it is impossible to completely discount this explanation of militia decline—neither the militia nor white supremacist groups publish lists of members whose names might be cross-checked—it is not entirely persuasive. As was shown in chapter 7, several existing militia groups splintered on the question of how radical they should be after Oklahoma City. As some elements grew more extreme, often espousing overtly racist values, many individuals who had originally turned to the movement because it appeared free of racism either began to form their own groups or left the movement entirely. Indeed, this process of leaving was eased by the rise of mainstream alternatives to militia action. Ultimately, then, the hard core of the movement either survived or moved into white supremacy, while more-moderate militia members left the movement. If this is the case, the important question that needs to be answered is: Is the decline of the movement permanent, or might it or one of its variants rise to prominence again?

Is the Militia Dead?

There are reasons to suppose the movement is finished for good. For example, the United States recently completed its undeclared war against the Taliban rulers of Afghanistan and remains enmeshed in a worldwide fight against Osama bin Laden's al Qaeda terrorist organization, and terrorism generally. As this chapter is being written, the United States is also apparently on the verge of a second war with Iraq. Popular support for these actions and the federal government generally is high. Accordingly, a movement grounded on the mistrust of government is likely to find little support in an era in which substantial majorities trust and support their government.

Moreover, the tactics that led to the decline of the militia in the late 1990s are still in place in 2002. Indeed, as will be discussed later, the use of informants, investigations, and aggressive use of legal sanctions against right-wing groups have been expanded. Federal, state, and local law enforcement authorities remain careful and patient in their interactions with right-wing groups, thus undermining an ideology that insists that the federal government is engaged in a plot to destroy American freedoms and liberties in support of the New World Order. Mainstream political actors continue to provide alternative venues of conservative political action in the system. The resurgence of the movement in conditions like these seems hard to imagine.

The Foundations of a Potential Militia Renaissance

Yet the idea that the movement, and its variants, is "done" is naïve for at least two reasons. First is the possibility that the current context of pro-government attitudes will change. The other is the nature of American political culture, ideology, and myth.

Political Context and the Renaissance of the Militia

One possible stimulus for a resurgent militia movement might be a change in political circumstances that would once again favor militia paranoia. One such factor could be the antiterrorism bill passed by Congress in the aftermath of September 11 and signed into law by President George W. Bush on October 25, 2001. Its provisions grant the federal government many of the powers that militia members contend it already abuses: the right to hold people in detention for indeterminate, lengthy periods without charges (and thus without attorneys) if they are suspected of involvement in terrorism; monitoring of suspects' conversations with their attorneys; increased authority to wiretap suspects' phones, regardless of location; federal authority to obtain and enforce nationwide search warrants; increased monitoring of e-mail and computer accounts

of suspected terrorists; authorization for intelligence agencies—
e.g., the Central Intelligence Agency—to obtain wiretap orders
from a special intelligence court if it suspects terrorism is an issue,
even inside the United States; and increased regulation of U.S.
banks, particularly in their interactions with overseas banks, to
stop funds transfers for suspected terrorists.[7] While many of these
provisions are aimed at foreign nationals residing in the United
States, many of the powers are so broad as to be applied to anyone
suspected of terrorism—with the government the arbiter of who is
a suspect. Even lawyers' conversations with suspected terrorists
are now monitored routinely. Of course, such powers may be important and useful, and they may be popular in the short run, but
it is easy to imagine a backlash building against the government if
stories of abuse emerge and continue over time. This is particularly the case if the abuses are aimed at "Americans" and not "foreigners": rightly or wrongly, militia ideology is grounded on an
American nativism that elevates the native-born above foreign nationals. (This nativism seems to explain popular support for detention of some U.S. citizens, such as Jose Padilla and John Walker
Lindh. Padilla, a U.S. citizen who converted to Islam in prison, and
Lindh, the so-called American Taliban who fought with the conservative Islamic regime in Afghanistan, have both been detained for
an extended period by the federal government with little public
protest. Their Islamism and apparent loyalty to foreign powers
seems to de-Americanize these people in the public mind, and so
to link them with the "foreigners" with whom the United States is
apparently at war.) For those who share militia values, however,
the abuse of Americans over time may become the foundation of a
resurgent antigovernment movement.

President Bush has also issued an executive order allowing special military courts, rather than civilian ones, to take charge of the
trials of any captured foreign-national, terrorists. Such courts, importantly, do not face the same rules of evidence, procedure, and
disclosure that civilian courts must follow; thus, Bush and Attorney General John Ashcroft have argued, they are better venues for
investigating the crimes committed by terrorist organizations. Yet
this order has been highly controversial, even among conservative
political leaders, many of whom believe that it has resulted in too
much power being concentrated in the hands of the federal government. For example, conservative newspaper columnist William

Safire has called for fellow conservatives to oppose President Bush's order, and former conservative Georgia Republican congressman Bob Barr, a Clinton-impeachment manager who has spoken to racist, militia-oriented groups, called for a congressional investigation into Bush's directive. Even in the midst of a highly popular war, then, the natural instincts of political conservatives are to fear the concentration of political power in the federal government. Under such conditions, backlash can be expected.

The logic of the federal government's post–September 11 actions—that increased government power at the cost of some individual liberties is necessary in order to fight a war against terrorism—found institutional expression in the creation of the Department of Homeland Security in November 2002. This new department combines dozens of law enforcement, intelligence-gathering, and emergency service agencies (or parts of agencies) into a sophisticated, highly cooperative organization capable of detecting, undermining, and responding to terrorist actions against Americans both in the United States and overseas. As a consequence, one federal agency will, for the first time, combine the power to spy on U.S. citizens as well as foreign nationals with the power to arrest, detain, and enforce the law. Moreover, the agency's employees will lack traditional civil service and union protections available to most federal employees, meaning they may be subject to pressure from political leaders to pursue partisan goals. In other words, at least from the perspective of those sympathetic to militia ideology, the federal government has created an agency with remarkable, centralized power to enforce the will of the political elite. This agency's actions may, over time, stimulate a resurgence of militia-like antigovernment activism.

More broadly, the changes to American society associated with the terrorist attacks of September 11 may also induce a backlash over time. After all, Americans have become used to relative freedom, whether it is at airports, on the roads, or in Internet use. Other examples can be listed easily. Long lines waiting to get airline tickets, random and thorough searches of bags and cars, or increased monitoring of electronic communications generally perceived to be private (like e-mail) may provide a context in which antigovernment sentiments make sense to large numbers of Americans, particularly if real stories of government abuse of power reemerge. Before the outbreak of the Afghan war, for example, there was substantial and vigorous public discussion of a recently developed FBI e-mail monitoring and tracking program known as Carnivore; most conservatives considered it a dangerous invasion of individual rights and a serious concentration of power in the federal government's hands. Similarly, a proposal to allow the FBI to gather intelligence by placing a device in a suspect's computer keyboard that would allow investigators to monitor every keystroke was highly controversial. Thus, the potential is high for new stories of government abuse of individual rights—even the rights of "ordinary" Americans—to emerge. Just as a short-term cause—the terrorist attacks—led to increased levels of support for the government, it is likely that repeated government actions that many Americans decide violate their rights and liberties may restore antigovernment sentiments to prominence in contemporary politics.

In addition, in the months following the attacks of September 11, the federal government announced that it had been using a satellite facility to back up its operations. This complex is built into caves and bunkers somewhere—its exact location is, of course, secret. It has the capacity to process the daily work of government (Social Security checks, regulatory oversight, defense and national security direction, and the like) from a secure location. Evocatively, and from the perspective of the militia movement's adherents, tellingly, this secondary facility is known as the "Shadow Government." In other words, the government's own term for a secret facility capable of using the increasingly far-reaching powers of the federal government for whatever purposes it has in mind is the same as the term movement members use to describe the corrupt system it believes dominates government today. This is tailor-made for a potential reemergence of the movement, particularly if this Shadow Government is perceived to be directing or using the newly asserted power of the federal government for purposes that militia-leaning members of the population consider wrong, evil, or corrupt.

Such a backlash seems particularly likely since the terrorist attacks of September 11 led to a dramatic rise in gun sales in the United States. While sales of handguns had been declining in the United States in the late 1990s, the sales of personal firearms jumped dramatically in the weeks and months after the September bombings. Thus, instinctively, Americans returned to the logic of the gun myth described in chapter 2 and insisted on their personal rights to self-defense. If, as a result of the antiterrorism legislation recently passed by Congress and signed by President Bush, Americans perceive their fundamental liberties to be under assault, armed resistance can be expected again.

Culture, Ideology, Myth, and a Resurgent Militia Movement

Americans' rush to guns after September 11 suggests the second, deeper, reason to suppose that the militia movement or a variant may reemerge in the United States: the movement's cultural, ideological, and mythical foundations. As was examined in chapters 1 and 2, the modern militia movement was built on values and myths that are central to American political culture. The link that members built between guns and liberty is grounded on the militia myth of the American Revolution. The ideology the movement espouses is tied to ideas, values, and principles that are deeply embedded in American political life. Culture provides the context in which militia ideology finds meaning.

Culture, myth, and ideology endure. Changes, when they occur, are usually incremental and slow. Thus there is no reason to suppose that the terrorist attacks of September 11 caused a permanent values shift in the United States, turning a nation filled with individuals significantly skeptical of national political authority into a community of pro-government activists. In the aftermath of September 11, then, many Americans perceive that the government has to play an important role in protecting their safety. Once the perceived danger has passed, however, or even if Americans simply come to accept terrorism as a part of the cost of life in the world's only remaining superpower, the desire to be left largely alone by government can be expected to reassert itself in American political discourse. Short-term events like government abuses of its newly granted antiterrorism powers may encourage the resurgence of antigovernment attitudes more quickly than would otherwise be the case, but such attitudes are far more deeply rooted and common in American political culture than are pro-government ones. In such circumstances, the only question is when such attitudes will return to prominence, not whether this return will occur.

Two events that occurred after September 11 illustrate the permanent hold the militia and its associated movements have on the American mind. Shortly after the September attacks, a wave of letters containing lethal concentrations of anthrax was sent to both public figures and ordinary citizens. Several people died from exposure to the virus, several U.S. congressional buildings had to be decontaminated as a result of letters being mailed to members' offices, many post offices required inspection and decontamination, and a general fear struck millions of Americans. Postal service was disrupted to many homes and businesses, and demand for vaccination against anthrax far outstripped the vaccine supply. Two groups were immediately suspected: Osama bin Laden's al Qaeda organization and militia groups. Indeed, some conspiracists had the two groups working together in a joint campaign to destroy their mutual enemy, the U.S. government. While the case has yet to be solved, experts increasingly agree that the level of concentration of the anthrax was so high that it could have come only from a U.S. government–owned, military-related laboratory. The sense that a right-wing group of antigovernment activists could have undertaken this attack lingers, however.

Similarly, in spring 2002 a series of attacks occurred throughout the American Midwest and Southwest in which pipe bombs were used to destroy mailboxes. Six people were injured in the ensuing explosions. In addition, mail service was disrupted in many areas. Both postal carriers and citizens often refused to deliver or check mail. As was the case with the anthrax letters, speculation was widespread that it must be a militia terror campaign initiated in response to the increased authority of the federal government. (Notably, there was little suggestion that a foreign terror organization was responsible for these attacks.) A suspect, a young, confused, anarchistic man, was eventually caught and confessed. However, the instinctive, intuitive jump from bomb to militia illustrates the lingering sense that many Americans have that some other Americans perceive the federal government to be abusive and dangerous and worth fighting at all costs.

In the end, then, the militia and its variants are likely to be a permanent fixture of American political life because they grow out of the dynamics of American political culture. Militias are not dinosaurs in a zoo—oddities to be gawked at and scarcely believed. They are a manifestation of American individualism taken to its extreme and validated by a myth of ideal American identity. Only in recognizing that the militia are, in fact, as "American as apple pie" can we understand where the movement comes from, why it took the shape it did, and whether it, or another version of it, can be expected to reemerge in the United States. More importantly, it is only in understanding that the militia reflect the ideal of American politics in a twisted and warped way that we can hope as a society to establish the kinds of plans and programs that will help us build the just, free, and democratic future that is at the heart of the American experiment.

Notes

Introduction

1. William Gamson and William Meyer, *Comparative Perspectives on Social Movements: Political Opportunities, Mobilizing Structures, and Cultural Framings* (New York: Cambridge University Press, 1996), 283.

2. Donatella della Porta and Mario Diani, *Social Movements: An Introduction* (Malden, Mass.: Blackwell Publishers, 1999), 66.

3. C. Mueller, "Building Social Movement Theory," in *Frontiers in Social Movement Theory,* ed. A. Morris and C. Mueller (New Haven: Yale University Press, 1992), 7.

4. Doug McAdam, *Political Process and the Development of Black Insurgency, 1930–1970* (Chicago: University of Chicago Press, 1982); R. Turner and L. Killian, "The Field of Collective Behavior," in *Collective Behavior and Social Movements.* ed. R. Curtis Jr. and E. Aguirre (Boston: Allyn & Bacon, 1993).

5. M. Zald and R. Ash, "Social Movement Organizations: Growth, Decay and Change," *Social Forces* 44 (March 1966): 3–4.

6. Joel Dyer, *Harvest of Rage: Why Oklahoma City Is Only the Beginning* (Boulder, Colo.: Westview, 1998).

7. As discussed in Ronald Inglehart, *Modernization and Postmodernization: Cultural, Economic, and Political Change in Forty-three Societies* (Princeton, N.J.: Princeton University Press, 1997).

8. Dyer, *Harvest.*

9. For a fuller discussion of these points, see Richard Abanes, *American Militias: Rebellion, Racism, and Religion* (Downer's Grove, Ill.: Intervarsity Press, 1996); Morris Dees, *Gathering Storm: America's Militia Threat* (New York: HarperCollins, 1996); Neil Hamilton, *Militias in America* (Denver: ABC-CLIO, 1996); David Niewert, *In God's Country: The Patriot Movement and the Pacific Northwest* (Pullman: Washington State University Press, 1999); Robert Snow, *The Militia Threat: Terrorists Among Us* (New York: Plenum Trade, 1999); and Kenneth Stern, *A Force upon*

the Plain: The American Militia Movement and the Politics of Hate (New York: Simon & Schuster, 1996).

10. Doug McAdam, "Culture and Social Movements," in *New Social Movements: From Ideology to Identity,* ed. Enrique Laraña, Hank Johnston, and Joseph Gusfield (Philadelphia: Temple University Press, 1994).

11. della Porta and Diani, *Social Movements.*

12. Abanes, *American Militias;* Dees, *Gathering Storm;* Hamilton, *Militias in America;* Niewert, *God's Country;* Snow, *Militia Threat;* Stern, *Force upon the Plain.*

13. D. Snow et al., "Frame Alignment Processes, Micromobilization, and Movement Participation," *American Sociological Review* 51 (1986): 464–81.

14. McAdam, "Culture and Social Movements."

15. Michael Burawoy et al., *Ethnography Unbound* (Berkeley and Los Angeles: University of California Press, 1991); Margot Ely et al., *Doing Qualitative Research* (New York: Falmer Press, 1991); Robert C. Euler, *Ethnographic Methodology* (Carbondale: Southern Illinois University Press, 1967); Robert C. Prus, *Subcultural Mosaics and Intersubjective Realities* (Albany: State University of New York Press, 1997).

Chapter 1

1. Mary Douglas, *Natural Symbols: Explorations in Cosmology* (London: Barrie & Rockliff, 1970); Michael Thompson, Richard Ellis, and Aaron Wildavsky, *Cultural Theory* (Boulder, Colo.: Westview Press, 1990); Mary Douglas, *In the Active Voice.* (London: Routledge & Kegan Paul, 1982).

2. Lyman Tower Sargent, *Contemporary Political Ideologies: A Comparative Analysis,* 11th ed. (New York: Harcourt Brace College Publishers, 1999), 3.

3. Terrell Carver, "Ideology: The Career of a Concept," in *Ideals and Ideologies: A Reader,* ed. T. Ball and R. Dagger (New York: Longman, 1998), 9.

4. Paul Ricoeur, *Lecture on Ideology and Utopia,* ed. G. Taylor (New York: Columbia University Press, 1986). See also Manfred B. Steger, *Globalism: The New Market Ideology* (Lanham, Md.: Rowman & Littlefield, 2002), as an excellent example of such analysis.

5. Ricoeur, *Lecture.*

6. Ricoeur, *Lecture.*

7. Ricoeur, *Lecture.*

8. Henry Tudor, *Political Myths* (New York: Praeger, 1972), 16–17.

9. Tudor, *Political Myths,* 137–39.

10. Joseph Campbell, with Bill Moyers, "The Hero's Adventure," in *The Power of Myth* (New York: Doubleday, 1988), 123–63.

11. Richard J Ellis, *American Political Cultures* (New York: Oxford University Press, 1993); William A. Galston, *Liberal Purposes: Goods, Virtues, and Diversity in the Liberal State* (New York: Cambridge University Press, 1991); Stephen Macedo, *Liberal Virtues: Citizenship, Virtue, and Community in Liberal Constitutionalism* (Oxford:

Clarendon, 1990); Alasdair Macintyre, *After Virtue: A Study in Moral Theory* (Notre Dame, Ind.: University of Notre Dame Press, 1984).

12. Robert N. Bellah et al., *Habits of the Heart: Individualism and Commitment in American Life* (New York: Harper & Row, 1985); Ellis, *American Political Cultures;* Lawrence H. Fuchs, *The American Kaleidoscope: Race, Ethnicity, and the Civic Culture* (Hanover, N.H.: University Press of New England, 1990); Philip Gleason, "American Identity and Americanization," in *Concepts of Ethnicity,* ed. William Petersen, Michael Novak, and Philip Gleason (Cambridge: Harvard University Press, 1980); Kenneth L. Karst, *Belonging to America: Equal Citizenship and the Constitution* (New Haven: Yale University Press, 1989); Anne Norton, *Alternative Americas: A Reading of Antebellum Political Culture* (Chicago: University of Chicago Press, 1986); Rogers Smith, "Beyond Tocqueville, Myrdal, and Hartz: The Multiple Traditions in America," *American Political Science Review* 87: 549–66.

13. Marc Howard Ross, "Culture and Identity in Comparative Political Analysis," in *Comparative Politics: Rationality, Culture, and Structure,* ed. Mark Lichbach and A. S. Zuckerman (New York: Cambridge University Press, 1997), 42–80.

14. This is not to insist that public culture can ever be fully understood or all its dimensions addressed. Instead, it is to assert that public culture provides an accessible foundation for culturalist interpretations of political life, one with shareable texts and arguments that can be seen as more or less persuasive—better—in specific analyses.

15. See also Lane Crothers, "American Culture, Franklin Roosevelt, and the Winning of the NRA," *Journal of Contemporary Thought* 6 (1996): 107–30; Daniel Devine, *The Political Culture of the United States* (Boston: Little, Brown, 1972); Daniel Elazar, *American Federalism* (New York:, Harper & Row, 1988); Daniel Elazar, *The American Mosaic* (Boulder, Colo.: Westview, 1994).

16. I am indebted to Manfred Steger of Illinois State University for his insight on this point.

17. Obviously, this is only a brief sketch. For fuller discussions of each of these points, see Daniel Boorstin, *The Genius of American Politics* (Chicago: University of Chicago Press, 1953); Louis Hartz, *The Liberal Tradition in America* (New York: Harcourt, Brace, 1955); Frederick Jackson Turner, *The Frontier in American History* (New York: Holt, 1962); Richard Hofstadter, *The American Political Tradition* (New York: Vintage, 1973); Samuel Huntington, *American Politics: The Promise of Disharmony* (Cambridge: Harvard University Press, Belknap Press, 1981); David H. Fischer, *Albion's Seed: Four British Folkways in America* (New York: Oxford University Press, 1989); James Davison Hunter, *Culture Wars: The Struggle to Define America* (New York: Basic Books, 1991); Ellis, *American Political Cultures;* Elazar, *American Mosaic;* Richard Payne, *The Clash with Distant Cultures: Values, Interests, and Force in American Foreign Policy* (Albany: State University of New York Press, 1995).

Chapter 2

1. See also Henry Tudor, *Political Myths* (New York: Praeger, 1972).

2. Don Higginbotham, *The War of American Independence: Military Attitudes, Policies, and Practice, 1763–1789* (New York: MacMillan, 1971), 106–31; James K. Martin and Mark E. Lender, *A Respectable Army: The Military Origins of the Republic, 1763–1789* (Arlington Heights, Ill.: Harlan Davidson, 1982), 1–64; Garry Wills, *A Necessary Evil: A History of Distrust of Government* (New York: Simon & Schuster, 1999), 23–41.

3. Martin and Lender, *Respectable Army*, 19, 36; Wills, *Necessary Evil*, 29–30.

4. Martin and Lender, *Respectable Army*, 65–179; Wills, *Necessary Evil*; Herbert Aptheker, *The American Revolution, 1763–1783; A History of the American People: An Interpretation* (New York: International Publishers, 1969); Higginbotham, *American Independence*.

5. Wills, *Necessary Evil*, 36; John Shy, *A People Numerous and Armed: Reflections on the Military Struggle for American Independence*, rev. ed. (Ann Arbor: University of Michigan Press, 1990), 236–44; Martin and Lender, *Respectable Army*, 17; Don Higginbotham, *War and Society in Revolutionary America* (Columbia: University of South Carolina Press, 1988), 113–23.

6. Wills, *Necessary Evil*, 37.

7. Martin and Lender, *Respectable Army*, 6–9, 13–15, 20–25; Higginbotham, *American Independence*, 174–78.

8. Martin and Lender, *Respectable Army*, 9, 20, 30–34; Higginbotham, *American Independence*, 22, 36; Jan E. Dizard, Robert M. Muth, and Stephen P. Andrews, eds., *Guns in America: A Reader* (New York: New York University Press, 1999), 4; Bernard Bailyn, *The Ideological Origins of the American Revolution* (Cambridge: Harvard University Press, Belknap Press, 1967).

9. Alexander Hamilton, James Madison, and John Jay, *The Federalist Papers*, ed. Clinton J. Rossiter (New York: Penguin, 1961), no. 28, 180–81.

10. Hamilton, Madison, and Jay, *The Federalist Papers*, ed. Clinton J. Rossiter (New York: Penguin, 1961), no. 46, 299.

11. Michael Kammen, "The American Revolution and the Historical Imagination," in *Legacies of the American Revolution*, ed. Larry Gerlach, James A. Dolph, and Michael L. Nicholls (Logan: Utah State University Press, 1978), 17–42.

12. Kammen, "American Revolution," 21.

13. Kammen, "American Revolution," 24.

14. Kammen, "American Revolution," 26.

15. Kammen, "American Revolution," 23.

16. William Hosley, "Guns, Gun Culture, and the Peddling of Dreams," in *Colt: The Making of an American Legend* (Amherst: University of Massachusetts Press, 1996). Reprinted in Dizard, Muth, and Andrews, *Guns in America*, 47–85.

17. Osha G. Davis, *Under Fire: The NRA and the Battle for Gun Control*, expanded ed. (Iowa City: University of Iowa Press, 1998), 21.

18. Davis, *Under Fire*, 20–29.

19. Davis, *Under Fire*, 30–81; Jack Anderson, *Inside the NRA: Armed and Dangerous* (Beverly Hills, Calif.: Dove Books, 1996), 12–46.

20. Charlton Heston, "The Second Amendment: America's First Freedom," speech to the National Press Club, Washington, D.C., September 11, 1997. Reprinted in Dizard, Muth, and Andrews, *Guns in America*, 202.

21. Heston, "Second Amendment," 203–4.

Chapter 3

1. Sara Diamond, *Roads to Dominion: Right-Wing Movements and Political Power in the United States* (New York: Guilford Press, 1995), 9.

2. Chip Berlet and Matthew N. Lyons, *Right-Wing Populism in America: Too Close for Comfort* (New York: Guilford Press, 2000), 6–13.

3. Margaret Canovan, *Populism* (New York: Harcourt Brace Jovanovich, 1981), 293–94.

4. Berlet and Lyons, *Right-Wing Populism*, 54–61.

5. Berlet and Lyons, *Right-Wing Populism*, 61–69.

6. Joseph Gusfield, *Symbolic Crusade*, 2d ed.. (Urbana: University of Illinois Press, 1986).

7. Berlet and Lyons, *Right-Wing Populism*, 70–84.

8. Berlet and Lyons, *Right-Wing Populism*, 85–103.

9. Terry Anderson, *The Movement and the Sixties: Protest in America from Greensboro to Wounded Knee* (New York: Oxford University Press, 1995), 43–86. See also Diamond, *Roads to Dominion*, 66–91.

10. Berlet and Lyons, *Right-Wing Populism*, 85–103.

11. Berlet and Lyons, *Right-Wing Populism*, 104–20.

12. Berlet and Lyons, *Right-Wing Populism*, 121–49.

13. Berlet and Lyons, *Right-Wing Populism*, 150–98; Diamond, *Roads to Dominion*, 92–106.

14. Berlet and Lyons, *Right-Wing Populism*, 199–227; Diamond, *Roads to Dominion*, 228–56.

15. Berlet and Lyons, *Right-Wing Populism*, 247–64.

16. Cf. Diamond, *Roads to Dominion*,

17. Berlet and Lyons, *Right-Wing Populism*, 265–86; Diamond, *Roads to Dominion*, 257–73.

18. Paul Ricoeur, *Lecture on Ideology and Utopia*, ed. G. Taylor (New York: Columbia University Press, 1986).

19. Ricoeur, *Lecture*.

20. www.constitution.org/comperil.htm [accessed May 1, 1998].

21. The scope of this conspiracy is seen as so vast, and the belief in it expresses itself in so many dimensions of militia thought, that there is no way to present every argument militia groups make in relation to it. In addition to the sites discussed in the text, the following sites are very useful for understanding the dimensions of the

conspiracy as alleged by the militia: www.the-oil-patch.com/archive/
wakefield.html [accessed June 19, 2001]; "A Fairy Tale of Taxation," www.civil
-liberties.com, [accessed June 20, 2001]; "Is the Income Tax legally enforced?" www.
civil-liberties.com [accessed June 20, 2001]; "For What Purposes Can the Federal
Government Tax the People?" www.civil-liberties.com [accessed June 20, 2001];
"How and Why the Federal Government Legislates Outside the Constitutional
Limitation," www.civil-liberties.com [accessed June 20, 2001]; www.constitution
.org/col/intent_14th.txt [accessed June 20, 2001]; www.the-oil-patch.com/
archive/unfraud.html [accessed June 19, 2001]; www.the-oil-patch.com/
archive/milleniumsummit.html [accessed June 19, 2001]; www.jbs.org/un/
un12.htm [accessed June 20, 2001]; www.the-oil-patch.com/archive/federal-
reserve.html [accessed June 19, 2001]; www.the-oil-patch.com/links-fed-res.html
[accessed June 19, 2001]; "A Time Line of the National Bank," www.civil-liberties
.com [accessed June 20, 2001]; www.ptialaska.net/~swampy/banks/federal_
reserve.txt [accessed June 20, 2001]; www.the-oil-patch.com/archive/power.html
[accessed June 19, 2001]; www.amendment_13.org [accessed June 19, 2001]; "The
Missing Thirteenth Amendment: Old Conspiracy or New Conspiracy?" www
.civil-liberties.com [accessed June 20, 2001]; indianamilitia.homestead.com/
declaration2001.html [accessed June 20, 2001]; www.ifas.org/library/militia/1-4
.html [accessed June 20, 2001]; www.sonic.net/sentinel/gvcon6.html [accessed
June 20, 2001]; www.the-oil-patch.com/archive/10thAmendment.html [accessed
June 19, 2001]; www.PetitionOnline.com/usdeclar/petition.html [accessed June 20,
2001].

22. www.constitution.org/grievered.htm [accessed May 1, 1998].

23. www.constitution.org/grievered.htm [accessed May 1, 1998].

24. www.the-oil-patch.com/aarchive/reclaimus.html [accessed June 19, 2001].

25. www.ifas.org/library/militia/1-3.html [accessed June 20, 2001]. See also
www.constitution.org/leglrkba.htm [accessed May 1, 1998].

26. www.ifas.org/library/militia/1-3.html [accessed June 20, 2001]. See also
www.ptialaska.net/~swampy/interest/firearms_1.html [accessed June 20, 2001];
www.guntruths.com [accessed June 20, 2001]; www.jpfo.org/GCA_68.htm [ac-
cessed June 20, 2001]; www.jpfo.org/genocide.htm [accessed June 20, 2001];
www.gunssavelife.com [accessed June 20, 2001] for similar discussions of the significance of gun ownership.

27. www.barefootsworld.net/1stmillionmom.html [accessed June 19, 2001].

28. www.barefootsworld.net/1stmillionmom.html [accessed June 19, 2001].

29. Cf. www.barefootsworld.net/1stmillionmom.html [accessed June 19,
2001].

30. www.frii.com/~gosplow/liberty.html [accessed June 20, 2001].

31. www.barefootsworld.net/1stmillionmom.html [accessed June 19, 2001].

32. www.frii.com/~gosplow/liberty.html [accessed June 20, 2001], emphasis
in original.

33. www.constitution.org/shad4816.htm [accessed May 1, 1998]; www.consti-
tution.org/grievered.htm [accessed May 1, 1998].

34. www.the-oil-patch.com/archive/naziamerica.html [accessed June 19, 2001]; emphasis in original.

35. www.the-oil-patch.com/archive/reclaimus.html [accessed June 19, 2001].

36. www.constitution.org/shad4816.htm [accessed May 1, 1998].

37. www.constitution.org/shad4816.htm [accessed May 1, 1998].

38. www.constitution.org/shad4816.htm [accessed May 1, 1998].

39. www.the-oil-patch.com/archive/10thAmendment.html [accessed June 19, 2001].

40. www.constitution.org/powright.htm [accessed May 1, 1998].

41. www.the-oil-patch.com/archive/10thAmendment.html [accessed June 19, 2001].

42. www.PetitionOnline.com/usdeclar/petition.html [accessed June 20, 2001].

43. www.civil-liberties.com/pages/usax3.html [accessed June 20, 2001].

44. www.ptialaska.net/~swampy/amend_14/Citizen_v_citizen.txt [accessed June 20, 2001].

45. www.ptialaska.net/~swampy/amend_14/Citizen_v_citizen.txt [accessed June 20, 2001].

46. Cf. www.lawresearch-registry.org/two_us.htm [accessed June 19, 2001]; www.civil-liberties.com/pages/usax3.html [accessed June 20, 2001]; www.ptialaska.net/~swampy/amend_14/usa.html [accessed June 20, 2001].

47. www.frii.com/gosplow/liberty.html [accessed June 20, 2001].

48. www.mainemilitia.homestead.com/files/MILITIAMANUAL1.htm [accessed June 20, 2001].

49. www.mainemilitia.homestead.com/files/MILITIAMANUAL1.htm [accessed June 20, 2001].

50. www.ifas.org/library/militia/2-1html [accessed June 20, 2001].

51. www.ifas.org/library/militia/2-1html [accessed June 20, 2001].

52. www.ifas.org/library/militia/2-1html [accessed June 20, 2001].

53. www.ifas.org/library/militia/2-1html [accessed June 20, 2001].

54. www.ifas.org/library/militia/2-1html [accessed June 20, 2001].

55. www.theofficenet.com/~redorman/pagepm.htm [accessed June 20, 2001].

56. www.frii.com/~gosplow/liberty.html [accessed June 20, 2001].

57. www.constitution.org/leglrkba.txt [accessed June 20, 2001].

58. www.ifas.org/library/militia/1-3.html [accessed June 20, 2001].

59. www4.law.cornell.edu/uscode/unframed/10/311.html [accessed June 20, 2001].

60. www.netpath.net/~jeffr/milorg.htm [accessed June 20, 2001]. For similar discussions, see www.mainemilitia.homestead.com/files/MILITIAMANUAL1 .htm [accessed June 20, 2001]; and www.mo51st.org/bylaws1.htm [accessed June 20, 2001], among others.

61. www.netpath.net/~jeffr/nccm.htm [accessed June 20, 2001].

62. indianamilitia.homestead.com/declaration2001.html [accessed June 20, 2001].

63. www.ifas.org/library/militia/2-1.html [accessed June 20, 2001].

64. www.netpath.net/~jeffr/milorg.htm [accessed June 20, 2001].

65. www.mainemilitia.homestead.com/files/MILITIAMANUAL1.htm [accessed June 20, 2001]. Similar statements can be found at www.mo51st.org/bylaws1.htm [accessed June 20, 2001]; and www15.brinkster.com/ivcm/goal.hrm [accessed June 20, 2001].

66. www.PetitionOnline.com/usdeclar/petition.html [accessed June 20, 2001]. Interestingly, this document, presented in a form of a petition to all Americans and their government, had 5,961 electronic signatures as of June 20, 2001. Many of these signatures include comments from the signatories. Comments like "The breakup of the former U.S.S.R. is a Sunday school picnic in comparison the the [*sic*] bloody breakup this country is presently headed toward, unless things do a 180 turnaround soon"; "WITHOUT OUR RIGHTS WE HAVE NO LIFE. I WILL NOT BE A SLAVE TO NO MAN OR GOVERNMENT. I HAVE FOUGHT FOR THIS COUNTRY BEFORE. I WILL FIGHT AGAIN. BEWARE TYRANTS OR SUFFER THE FATE OF ALL TYRANTS"; and "Every level of government violates the Constitution, including your local government. All violations, regardless of level, must be halted" are common.

67. geocities.com/CapitolHill/Congress/2608/whoarewe.htm [accessed June 20, 2001].

68. geocities.com/CapitolHill/Congress/2608/why.htm [accessed June 20, 2001].

69. indianamilitia.homestead.com/declar2001.html [accessed June 20, 2001].

70. Berlet and Lyons, *Right-Wing Populism*.

71. www.mo51st.org/bylaws1.htm [accessed June 20, 2001].

Chapter 4

1. Jess Walter, *Every Knee Shall Bow: The Truth and Tragedy of Ruby Ridge and the Randy Weaver Family* (New York: Regan Books, 1995), 14–21.

2. Walter, *Every Knee*, 22–45.

3. Walter, *Every Knee*, 30–33.

4. Hal Lindsey, with C. C. Carlson, *The Late Great Planet Earth* (Grand Rapids, Mich.: Zondervan, 1970).

5. Walter, *Every Knee*, 30–46.

6. Walter, *Every Knee*, 48–55.

7. Walter, *Every Knee*, 56–72.

8. Walter, *Every Knee*, 95–96.

9. Walter, *Every Knee*, 61–63.

10. Walter, *Every Knee*, 90–96.

11. Walter, *Every Knee*, 96–101.

12. Walter, *Every Knee*, 107–13.

13. Walter, *Every Knee*, 91.

14. Walter, *Every Knee*, 114.

15. Walter, *Every Knee*, 120–22. See also Alan Bock, *Ambush at Ruby Ridge: How*

Government Agents Set Randy Weaver Up and Took His Family Down (Irvine, Calif.: Dickens Press, 1995), 49–50.

16. Walter, *Every Knee*, 123–24; Bock, *Ambush*, 50.

17. Walter, *Every Knee*, 138–44; Bock, *Ambush*, 50–52.

18. Walter, *Every Knee*, 145–52.

19. Walter, *Every Knee*, 164.

20. Walter, *Every Knee*, 166–71.

21. Walter, *Every Knee*, 171–74.

22. Walter, *Every Knee*, 177–89.

23. Walter, *Every Knee*, 191–95.

24. Walter, *Every Knee*, 200–201.

25. Walter, *Every Knee*, 206.

26. Walter, *Every Knee*, 212.

27. Walter, *Every Knee*, 207–08.

28. Walter, *Every Knee*, 228–31.

29. Walter, *Every Knee*, 231–33.

30. Walter, *Every Knee*, 233–36.

31. Walter, *Every Knee*, 237.

32. Walter, *Every Knee*, 239–43.

33. Walter, *Every Knee*, 248.

34. Walter, *Every Knee*, 275–312; see also Bock, *Ambush*, 135–80, and Gerry Spence, *From Freedom to Slavery: The Rebirth of Tyranny in America* (New York: St. Martin's Griffin, 1993), 13–48.

35. Spence, *From Freedom*, 13–48; Walter, *Every Knee*, 320–44; Bock, *Ambush*, 135–98.

36. Walter, *Every Knee*, 357.

37. "Judge: Kevin Harris Can't Be Tried Again," *Idaho Statesman*, October 3, 1997, A1.

38. Walter, *Every Knee*, 357–66.

39. Walter, *Every Knee*, 368.

40. Walter, *Every Knee*, 371–72.

41. Walter, *Every Knee*, 371; Bock, *Ambush*, 220–39.

42. Henry Weinstein, "Court Blasts FBI Actions at Ruby Ridge," *Los Angeles Times*, September 26, 1997, 1.

43. Cf. Spence, *From Freedom*, 13–48.

44. *Pantagraph*, June 15, 2001, A11.

45. Walter, *Every Knee*, 250.

46. www.splcenter.org/intelligenceproject/ip_4m1.html [accessed May 9, 2000].

47. www.splcenter.org/intelligenceproject/ip_4m1.html [accessed May 9, 2000]. See also Kenneth Stern, *A Force upon the Plain* (New York: Simon & Schuster, 1996), 35–37.

48. Morris Dees, *Gathering Storm: America's Militia Threat* (New York: Harper-Collins, 1996), 1.

49. Dees, *Gathering Storm*, 2.

50. Dees, *Gathering Storm*, 54–55; Stern, *Force*, 36.

51. Stern, *Force*, 36.

52. Timothy Egan, "Fugitive in Idaho Cabin Plays Role of Folk Hero," *New York Times*, August 25, 1992, A14.

53. Ashley Dunn, "Mountain Standoff Rallies Idaho Cradle of the Fringe: Holdout in a Rugged Land That Harbors Religious Zealots, Racists, and Outlaws, Randy Weaver Is a Hero," *Los Angeles Times*, August 28, 1992, A1.

54. Dunn, "Mountain Standoff," A1.

55. Dunn, "Mountain Standoff," A1.

56. Egan, "Fugitive in Idaho," A14.

57. Egan, "Fugitive in Idaho," A14.

58. Timothy Egan, "The Nation: Hate Groups Hanging On in Idaho Haven," *New York Times*, August 30, 1992, D3.

59. Egan, "Fugitive in Idaho," A14.

60. Egan, "Fugitive in Idaho," A14.

61. *Congressional Record*, March 6, 1996.

62. *Congressional Record*, September 27, 1994.

Chapter 5

1. James D. Tabor and Eugene V. Gallagher, *Why Waco? Cults and the Battle for Religious Freedom in America* (Berkeley and Los Angeles: University of California Press, 1995), 33–41.

2. Tabor and Gallagher, *Why Waco?* 44–49.

3. Tabor and Gallagher, *Why Waco?* 33–35.

4. Tabor and Gallagher, *Why Waco?* 38.

5. Tabor and Gallagher, *Why Waco?* 38–41.

6. Tabor and Gallagher, *Why Waco?* 41.

7. Tabor and Gallagher, *Why Waco?* 41.

8. Tabor and Gallagher, *Why Waco?* 41–42.

9. Tabor and Gallagher, *Why Waco?* 42.

10. Tabor and Gallagher, *Why Waco?* 42–43.

11. Tabor and Gallagher, *Why Waco?* 43.

12. Tabor and Gallagher, *Why Waco?* 58.

13. Tabor and Gallagher, *Why Waco?* 49–56.

14. Tabor and Gallagher, *Why Waco?* 23–24.

15. Tabor and Gallagher, *Why Waco?* 84–85.

16. Tabor and Gallagher, *Why Waco?* 100–101.

17. David B. Kopel and Paul H. Blackman, *No More Wacos: What's Wrong with Federal Law Enforcement and How to Fix It* (Amherst, N.Y.: Prometheus Books, 1997), 48–64.

18. Tabor and Gallagher, *Why Waco?* 101.

19. Kopel and Blackman, *No More Wacos*, 99.

20. Kopel and Blackman, *No More* Wacos, 96.
21. Kopel and Blackman, *No More Wacos,* 98–99.
22. Kopel and Blackman, *No More Wacos,* 96–100.
23. Kopel and Blackman, *No More Wacos,* 96–100.
24. Tabor and Gallagher, *Why Waco?* 2–3.
25. Tabor and Gallagher, *Why Waco?* 3–6.
26. Kopel and Blackman, *No More Wacos,* 133–48.
27. Kopel and Blackman, *No More Wacos,* 133.
28. Kopel and Blackman, *No More Wacos,* 133.
29. Kopel and Blackman, *No More Wacos,* 133–34.
30. Kopel and Blackman, *No More Wacos,* 133–34.
31. Kopel and Blackman, *No More Wacos,* 134–37.
32. Tabor and Gallagher, *Why Waco?* 13–14; Department of Justice, *Report to the Deputy Attorney General on the Events at Waco, Texas, February 28 to April 19, 1993,* redacted version (Washington, D.C.: Department of Justice, 1993), 158–202.
33. Kopel and Blackman, *No More Wacos,* 137.
34. Kopel and Blackman, *No More Wacos,* 140.
35. Kopel and Blackman, *No More Wacos,* 148–52.
36. Kopel and Blackman, *No More Wacos,* 154–57.
37. Kopel and Blackman, *No More Wacos,* 154–57.
38. Kopel and Blackman, *No More Wacos,* 161.
39. Kopel and Blackman, *No More Wacos,* 161–62.
40. Kopel and Blackman, *No More Wacos,* 161–91.
41. Kopel and Blackman, *No More Wacos,* 198.
42. Kopel and Blackman, *No More Wacos,* 186–91.
43. Kopel and Blackman, *No More Wacos,* 198.
44. Kopel and Blackman, *No More Wacos,* 203.
45. Dirk Johnson, "Last Hours in Waco," *New York Times,* April 26, 1993, A1.
46. Dick J. Reavis, *The Ashes of Waco: An Investigation* (Syracuse, N.Y.: Syracuse University Press, 1995), 281–300.
47. Reavis, *Ashes,* 281–300.
48. Reavis, *Ashes,* 282–83.
49. Reavis, *Ashes,* 296–97.
50. Reavis, *Ashes,* 298–99.
51. Kopel and Blackman, *No More Wacos,* 246–48.
52. Kopel and Blackman, *No More Wacos,* 268–69.
53. Kopel and Blackman, *No More Wacos,* 232–36.
54. Kopel and Blackman, *No More Wacos,* 250–64.
55. Kopel and Blackman, *No More Wacos,* 236.
56. John C. Danforth, *Interim Report to the Deputy Attorney General Concerning the 1993 Confrontation at the Mt. Carmel Complex, Waco, Texas,* July 21, 2000, www.cesnur.org/testi/DanforthRpt.pdf [accessed Jan. 9, 2003].
57. Kenneth Stern, *A Force upon the Plain* (New York: Simon & Schuster, 1996), 61.
58. Stern, *Force,* 61.

59. Stern, *Force*, 61–63.

60. *Waco: The Rules of Engagement,* video produced by William Gazecki, Dan Gifford, and Michael McNulty, 1997.

61. Kopel and Blackman, *No More Wacos,* 225–91.

62. Stern, *Force,* 68.

63. Stern, *Force,* 77–78.

64. Stern, *Force,* 68–70

65. Stern, *Force,* 71.

66. Stern, *Force,* 67.

67. Stern, *Force,* 80–81.

68. Stern, *Force,* 96.

69. Stern, *Force,* 83.

70. Stern, *Force,* 98.

71. Stern, *Force,* 97.

72. Stern, *Force,* 122–23.

73. Stern, *Force,* 133–34.

74. Stern, *Force,* 135.

75. Stern, *Force,* 135.

76. Stern, *Force,* 135.

77. Stern, *Force,* 135.

Chapter 6

1. See also Brandon M. Stickney, *"All-American Monster": The Unauthorized Biography of Timothy McVeigh* (Amherst, N.Y.: Prometheus Books, 1996); Mark S. Hamm, *Apocalypse in Oklahoma: Waco and Ruby Ridge Revenged* (Boston: Northeastern University Press, 1997).

2. Stickney, *All-American Monster,* 51–74.

3. Stickney, *All-American Monster,* 65–81.

4. Stickney, *All-American Monster,* 89–97.

5. Stickney, *All-American Monster,* 94–107.

6. Stickney, *All-American Monster,* 102–7.

7. Stickney, *All-American Monster,* 90–101.

8. Stickney, *All-American Monster,* 90–95.

9. Andrew MacDonald, *The Turner Diaries* (Arlington, Va.: National Vanguard Books, 1978).

10. Stickney, *All-American Monster,* 159.

11. Stickney, *All-American Monster,* 101–2.

12. Stickney, *All-American Monster,* 108.

13. Stickney, *All-American Monster,* 108–20.

14. Stickney, *All-American Monster,* 110–13.

15. Stickney, *All-American Monster,* 120–42.

16. Stickney, *All-American Monster,* 144.

17. Stickney, *All-American Monster*, 145–49.
18. Stickney, *All-American Monster*, 150–53.
19. Stickney, *All-American Monster*, 155.
20. Stickney, *All-American Monster*, 151.
21. Stickney, *All-American Monster*, 160–68.
22. Stickney, *All-American Monster*, 167.
23. Stickney, *All-American Monster*, 31.
24. Stickney, *All-American Monster*, 31.
25. Hamm, *Apocalypse in Oklahoma*, 42.
26. Stickney, *All-American Monster*, 171–73.
27. Stickney, *All-American Monster*, 184–85.
28. Stickney, *All-American Monster*, 36.
29. Stickney, *All-American Monster*, 50, 64.
30. Stickney, *All-American Monster*, 26.
31. Stickney, *All-American Monster*, 25.
32. Hamm, *Apocalypse in Oklahoma*, 56–69.
33. Stickney, *All-American Monster*, 175–77.
34. Stickney, *All-American Monster*, 177.
35. Stickney, *All-American Monster*, 177.
36. Stickney, *All-American Monster*, 221–72.
37. Richard A. Serrano, *One of Ours: Timothy McVeigh and the Oklahoma City Bombing* (New York: Norton, 1998), 273–92.
38. abcnews.go.com/sections/us/DailyNews/MCVEIGH_setup.html, [accessed October 9, 2001].
39. Stickney, *All-American Monster*, 273–92.
40. Stickney, *All-American Monster*, 265.
41. Stickney, *All-American Monster*, 266.
42. "Sentence Overturned in Oklahoma City Bombing," *New York Times*, July 1, 1999, A14.
43. Jo Thomas, "Nichols's Lawyers Try to Show McVeigh Was an Extremist," *New York Times*, December 6, 1997, A13.
44. Richard A. Serrano, "Nichols' Lawyers Point to Another Suspect," *Los Angeles Times*, December 6, 1997, A21.
45. Jo Thomas, "The Bombing Verdict: The Overview; Nichols Convicted of Plot and Manslaughter Counts but Not of Actual Bombing," *New York Times*, December 24, 1997, A1.
46. "Nichols Offer to Waive Appeals in Oklahoma City Bombing," *New York Times*, September 5, 2001.
47. Kenneth Stern, *A Force Upon the Plain* (New York: Simon & Schuster, 1996), 203–4.
48. Stern, *Force*, 203–4.
49. Stern, *Force*, 203–4.
50. Stern, *Force*, 206.
51. Stern, *Force*, 204.
52. Stern, *Force*, 206.

53. Richard Gage, "The Record Since Oklahoma City," *U.S. News and World Report*, December 29, 1997/January 5, 1998, 24.

54. David E. Kaplan and Mike Tharp, "Terrorism Threats at Home," *U.S. News and World Report*, December 29, 1997/January 5, 1998, 23–27.

55. "The Militia Threat," *New York Times*, June 14, 1997, A20.

56. Philip Shenon, "Militias Aim to Lure Elite Army Troops, U.S. Generals Fear," *New York Times*, March 22, 1996, A1, A22.

57. Mike Tharp and William J. Holstein, "Mainstreaming the Militia," *U.S. News and World Report*, April 21, 1997, 24–37.

58. Southern Poverty Law Center, "The Patriot Movement: Fewer, but Harder, Patriot Groups in 1997," *Intelligence Report*, Spring 1998. www.splcenter.org/intelligenceproject/ip-4fl.html [accessed, May 9, 2000].

59. Joel Dyer, *Harvest of Rage: Why Oklahoma City Is Only the Beginning* (Boulder, Colo.: Westview, 1998), 279–80.

60. Stern, *Force*, 209.

61. Southern Poverty Law Center, *Intelligence Project*, "Active 'Patriot' Groups in the U.S. in 2000," www.splcenter.org/intelligenceproject/ip-index.html [accessed October 12, 2001]; and Southern Poverty Law Center, *Intelligence Project*, www.splcenter.org/intelligenceproject/ip-index.html [accessed October 12, 2001].

62. Stickney, *All-American Monster*, 234.

Chapter 7

1. Doug McAdam, "The Decline of the Civil Rights Movement," in *Waves of Protest: Social Movements since the Sixties*, ed. Jo Freeman and Victoria Johnson (New York: Rowman & Littlefield, 1999), 325–48.

2. McAdam, "Decline of the Movement," 325–48.

3. McAdam, "Decline of the Movement," 325–48.

4. McAdam, "Decline of the Movement," 325–48.

5. Carol W. Lewis, "The Terror That Failed: Public Opinion in the Aftermath of the Bombing in Oklahoma City," *Public Administration Review* 60 (May/June 2000): 206.

6. Lewis, "Terror That Failed," 205.

7. Lewis, "Terror That Failed," 205.

8. Lynn M. Kuzma, "The Polls—Trends: Terrorism in the United States," *Public Opinion Quarterly* 64: 101.

9. Kuzma, "The Polls," 102.

10. Kuzma, "The Polls," 102.

11. Patricia King, "'Vipers' in the 'Burbs," *Newsweek*, July 15, 1996, 20–23.

12. Thomas J. Watts, "Militias Growing, but There Are Changes," *San Diego Union Tribune*, December 20, 1996, A30.

13. "Militia Extremists Challenge Leadership," *Detroit News,* March 4, 1998, detnews.com/1998/metro/9803/04/03040142.htm [accessed Feb. 3, 1999].

14. Michael D'Antonio, "Up from Hatred," *Los Angeles Times Magazine,* August 10, 1997, 18.

15. Daniel Klaidman and Michael Isikoff, "The Feds' Quiet War," *Newsweek,* April 22, 1996, 47.

16. Richard Lacayo, "State of Siege," *Time,* April 8, 1996, 24–27.

17. Lacayo, "State of Siege," 24–27.

18. Mike Tharp and Gordon Witkin, "A Showdown in Montana," *U.S. News and World Report,* April 8, 1996, 28–29.

19. Mike Tharp, "FBI Patience Outlasts Freemen's Endurance," *U.S. News and World Report,* June 24, 1996, 14; Mike Tharp, "In the Shadow of Ruby Ridge," *U.S. News and World Report,* December 4, 1995, 59–60.

20. Tharp and Witkin, "Showdown," 28–29.

21. Louis Sahagun and Richard A. Serrano, "FBI Found Rightists Key to Ending Montana Standoff," *Los Angeles Times,* June 15, 1996, A1.

22. Sahagun and Serrano, "FBI Found Rightists Key," A1; James L. Pate, "Big Sky Surrender," *Soldier of Fortune,* September 1996, 54–57, 70–71.

23. Melissa Healy, "Government, Militia Urge Calm in Standoff," *Los Angeles Times,* April 1, 1996, A1.

24. "The Alamo, Again," *Economist,* May 3, 1997, 25.

25. "The Alamo," 25.

26. "The Alamo," 25.

27. "The Alamo," 25; Susana Hayward, "One Death Only Blot on Siege's Aftermath," *San Antonio Express,* May 6, 1997, A1; Allan Turner, "Authorities Urge Waiting in West Texas Standoff," *Denver Rocky Mountain News,* April 30, 1997, A2.

28. "The Alamo," 25.

29. Hayward, "One Death," A1.

30. Joe Mahr, "Standoff Continues in Roby," Copley News Service, September 26, 1997.

31. Christopher Smith, "Ruby Ridge, Utah?" *Salt Lake Tribune,* September 14, 1997, A1.

32. Ben Winslow, "No Waco as St. George Police Wait Out, Arrest Bangerter," *Salt Lake Tribune,* May 21, 1998, D6.

33. "Plans Dropped to Break Up Logging Protest on Orders from White House," Associated Press, October 13, 1999, proxy.lib.ilstu.edu:2096/.

34. "Militia Member Vetoed Violence," *Detroit News,* November 11, 1998.

35. "Aryan Nations," www.gospelcom.net/apologeticsindex/a83.html [accessed October 16, 2001].

36. BBC News Online, "US Politics and Gun Control," news.bbc.co.uk/low/English/world/Americas/newsid_407000/407576.stm [accessed October 16, 2001]; ABC News, "Gun Control Support Nothing New," abcnews.go.com/sections/politics/DailyNews/gun_polls.html [accessed October 16, 2001]; ABC News, "Politicians Set Sights on Gun Control Issue," abcnews.go.com/sections/politics/DailyNews/guns000420.html [accessed October 16, 2001].

37. "Letter from the National Rifle Association," *Congressional Record,* Senate, April 27, 1995, thomas.loc.gov/cgi-bin/query/D?r104:16/temp/~r104nFucf9:e0: [accessed July 7, 2001].

38. "Letter from the National Rifle Association."

39. "Gun Control vs. Gun Rights," www.opensecret.org/news/guns [accessed October 16, 2001].

40. Kenneth Stern, *A Force upon the Plain* (New York: Simon & Schuster, 1996), 213.

41. Stern, *Force,* 213–24.

42. Stern, *Force,* 214.

43. Howard Fineman, "Friendly Fire," *Newsweek,* May 8, 1995, 36–38.

44. Joseph P. Shapiro, "An Epidemic of Fear and Loathing," *U.S. News and World Report,* May 8, 1995, 37–45.

45. Stern, *Force,* 222.

46. Stern, *Force,* 222 (emphasis in original).

47. "The Politics of Blame," *Economist,* April 29, 1995, 27.

48. TRB, "Did Newt Do It? " *New Republic,* May 15, 1995, 44.

49. "Who Is Larry Pratt?" *New Republic,* March 11, 1996, 9.

50. Morris Dees, *Gathering Storm* (New York: HarperCollins, 1996), 49.

51. Dees, *Gathering Storm,* 49, 52–56.

52. "Who Is Larry Pratt?" 9.

53. "Who Is Larry Pratt?" 9.

54. James Ridgeway, "Pratt Poison," *Village Voice,* March 5, 1996, 23.

55. "Who Is Larry Pratt?" 9.

56. "Who Is Larry Pratt?" 9.

57. "Who Is Larry Pratt?" 9.

Epilogue

1. Southern Poverty Law Center, *Intelligence Project,* "Active Hate Groups in the U.S. in 2000," www.splcenter.org/intelligenceproject/ip-index.html [accessed October 12, 2001].

2. Jim Nesbitt, "Assault on America," Newhouse News Service, www.new-housenews.com/archive/story1a092601.html [accessed November 26, 2001].

3. Nesbitt, "Assault on America."

4. Nesbitt, "Assault on America."

5. Nesbitt, "Assault on America."

6. Nesbitt, "Assault on America."

7. "Provisions of the Antiterrorism Bill," *New York Times,* October 26, 2001, www.nytimes.com/2001/10/26/national/26CBox.html [accessed October 27, 2001].

Index

About the Author

Lane Crothers is associate professor of politics and government at Illinois State University. He is the author or coauthor of four books on culture, leadership, and the presidency, as well as numerous articles and book chapters on these topics.